French Glossary of Accountancy and Management Terms

French-English
English-French

EuroLexus series

i impact books

First published in Great Britain in 1993 by
Impact Books
151 Dulwich Road, London SE24 0NG

© Lexus Ltd 1993

ISBN 1 874687 26 9

Printed and bound by The Guernsey Press, Guernsey

ont contribué/contributors

Catherine Stringer   Jane Goldie
Claudine Rebersat   Patricia Clarke

TABLE DES MATIERES
CONTENTS

PRÉFACE
PREFACE

Ce lexique contient une grande variété de termes susceptibles d'être utilisés ou rencontrés par ceux qui s'intéressent à la comptabilité ou à la gestion financière. Il en couvre divers aspects particuliers tels que la tenue des livres, les comptes annuels, les bilans comptables, les comptes de pertes et profits, la facturation, etc. Il comporte également des termes se rapportant aux domaines bancaire et boursier, de même qu'une série de mots et expressions relatifs au monde des affaires en général, très utiles à tous ceux qui s'occupent de gestion d'entreprise. Avec des annexes offrant des exemples de documents financiers (une note de crédit, une facture, un bon de commande et, particulièrement important, un bilan et un compte de résultat français ainsi qu'un bilan et un compte de résultat anglais), ce manuel se révèle un ouvrage de référence très pratique.

This glossary covers a wide range of vocabulary that is likely to be used or encountered by those involved in accounting or in financial management. It provides vocabulary for specific areas such as book-keeping, annual accounts, balance sheets, profit and loss accounts, invoicing etc. It also gives some terms from the fields of banking and the Stock Exchange. In addition to this there is a range of general business vocabulary that will be of use to those in business management. With appendices giving examples of financial documents such as a credit note, an invoice, a purchase order and, importantly, of a typical British and a typical French balance sheet and profit and loss statement, this is a highly practical reference book.

*abréviations/*abbreviations

adj	*adjectif/*adjective
Am	American English/*anglais américain*
Br	British English/*anglais britannique*
f	*féminin/*feminine
qch	*quelque chose/*something
qn	*quelqu'un/*somebody
m	*masculin/*masculine
pl	*pluriel/*plural
sb	somebody/*quelqu'un*
sth	something/*quelque chose*
vi	*verbe intransitif/*intransitive verb
vt	*verbe transitif/*transitive verb

abaisser [*prix, etc.*] to lower
abattement *m* tax allowance, tax reduction
absence rémunérée *f* paid leave
absence non rémunérée *f* unpaid leave
absentéisme *m* absenteeism
absorption *f* takeover
abus *m* abuse
abus de confiance *m* breach of trust
abus de droits *m* violation of rights
abus de droits sociaux *m* misappropriation of corporate funds
acceptation *f* acceptance
accessoire [*frais*] incidental
accident du travail *m* industrial accident
accommodement *m* agreement, arrangement; [*avec créditeurs*] composition
accord *m* agreement; *être d'accord avec* to agree with; *se mettre d'accord sur* to come to an agreement on; *tomber d'accord sur* to come to an agreement on
accord commercial *m* trade agreement
Accord général sur les tarifs douaniers et le commerce *m* General Agreement on Tariffs and Trade
accord de clearing *m* clearing agreement

accord de partenariat *m* partnership agreement
accorder to grant
accorder un escompte to give a discount
accrédité *m* beneficiary, payee
accrédité authorized
accréditif *m* credential; [*lettre de crédit*] letter of credit
accroissement *m* increase
accroître to increase
accumulation *f* accumulation; [*en magasin*] stockpiling
accumuler to accumulate; [*en magasin*] to stockpile
accusé de réception *m* acknowledgement (of receipt)
accuser réception de to acknowledge receipt of
achalandage *m* [*clients*] clientele; [*fonds de commerce*] goodwill
achat *m* purchase
achat à crédit *m* purchase on credit, credit purchase
achat à terme *m* forward purchase
achat au comptant *m* cash purchase
achat contre espèces *m* cash purchase
acheter to buy, to purchase
acheter à crédit to buy on credit
acheter à tempérament to buy by instalments
acheter à terme to buy forward
acheter au comptant to buy for cash

acheteur *m* buyer, purchaser

achèvement *m* completion

achever to complete

acompte *m* down payment, payment on account; [*versement*] instalment; ***donner un acompte*** to make a down payment, to make a payment on account

acompte mensuel *m* monthly instalment, monthly payment

acquéreur *m* purchaser

acquisition *f* acquisition

acquit *m* receipt; ***pour acquit*** payment received, received with thanks

acquit de paiement *m* receipt

acquitté [*facture*] paid

acquittement *m* [*de facture*] payment

acquitter [*facture*] to pay; ***considérer pour acquit*** to receipt

acte *m* deed

acte notarié *m* notarized deed

acte récognitif *m* deed of acknowledgment

acte d'association *m* partnership deed

acte de cession *m* deed of transfer, certificate of transfer

acte de propriété *m* title deed

acte de vente *m* deed of sale

actif *m* [*bancaire*] credit balance; [*de société*] asset; assets

actif circulant *m* circulating assets, floating assets, current assets

actif corporel *m* tangible asset

actif fictif *m* fictitious asset

actif immobilisé *m* fixed asset

actif incorporel *m* intangible asset

actif net *m* net assets, net worth

actif soustractif *m* depreciated credit balance

actif stable *m* fixed asset, long-term asset

action *f* share; [*juridique*] action, legal action

action nominative *f* registered share

action ordinaire *f* ordinary share

action privilégiée *f* preference share, preferred share *Am*

action au porteur *f* bearer share

action de jouissance *f* dividend share

actionnaire *mf* shareholder

actionnariat *m* share ownership

actions *fpl* shares, stock *Am*; ***avoir des actions dans*** to have a shareholding in; ***détenir des actions d'une société*** to have shares in a company

activité *f* business; [*d'entreprise*] activity

activité annexe *f* related activity

actuaire *mf* actuary

actualisation *f* [*mise à jour*] update

actualiser [*mettre à jour*] to update

actuariel actuarial

actuel current

adapter to adapt

s'adapter à to adjust to

addition *f* addition

additionner to add

adjoint *m* deputy

adjoint [*directeur, etc.*] associate

administrateur *m* director; ***avoir des talents d'administrateur*** to be a good administrator

administrateur délégué *m* managing director

administrateur judiciaire *m* official receiver

administratif administrative

administration *f* administration

administration fiscale *f* tax authorities

administration du personnel *f* personnel management

adresse de facturation *f* invoicing

address, address for invoicing

affacturage *m* factoring

affaire *f* matter; [*marché*] deal;
[*entreprise*] business; *avoir affaire
à* [*à qn*] to deal with

affaires *fpl* business

affectation *f* [*de personnel*]
assignment; [*d'une ressource*]
allocation

affecter [*personnel*] to assign;
[*ressources*] to allocate

affecter des fonds à to allocate funds
to

affilié *m* affiliated member

affilié affiliated

*s'***affilier à** to join

affirmation *f* statement

affirmation de créance *f* statement
of claim

affirmation sous serment *f* affidavit

affirmer to state

afflux de capitaux *m* inflow of
capital, influx of capital

AG (=Assemblée générale) *f* AGM

agence *f* agency; [*d'une banque*]
branch

Agence nationale pour l'emploi *f*
Jobcentre®

agence de placement *f* employment
agency

agenda *m* [*calendrier*] diary;
[*organisateur*] personal organizer;
[*de bureau*] desk diary

agent *m* agent

agent commercial *m* sales
representative

agent exclusif *m* sole agent

agent mandataire *m* authorized
representative

agent technico-commercial *m* sales
technician

agent de change *m* stockbroker

agent de contact *m* contact

**AGETAC (=Accord général sur les
tarifs douaniers et le commerce)**
m GATT

agio *m* charge

agréé approved, recognized

agréer to approve

agrément *m* approval

aide-comptable *mf* assistant
accountant, accounts clerk

aide fiscale *f* tax credit

aide sociale *f* social security

ajournement *m* postponement

ajourner to postpone ·

ajouter to add

ajustement *m* adjustment

ajuster to adjust

aliénation *f* disposal

alimenter un compte to pay money
into an account

allègement des impôts *m* reduction
of taxes

alléger to reduce

allocataire *mf* recipient, beneficiary

allocation *f* benefit; [*bourse*] grant

allocation de maternité *f* maternity
allowance

allocations de chômage *fpl*
unemployment benefit

allocution *f* speech

allouer to allocate

aménagement *m* [*disposition*]
layout; [*équipement*] fitting out

amende *f* fine

amendement *m* amendment;
[*clause*] additional clause

amiable: à l'amiable out of court

amorti [*bien*] depreciated; [*capital*]
amortized

amortir [*frais, coût*] to amortize, to
write off

amortir une dette [*emprunteur*] to
pay off a debt, to amortize a debt;
[*prêteur*] to write off a debt

amortissement *m* [*de dette*] paying
off, amortization; [*par prêteur*]
writing off; [*dépréciation*]
depreciation

amortissement dégressif *m*
accelerated depreciation

amortissement-dépenses *m*
amortization of expenditure, write-
off of expenditure

amortissement dérogatoire *m*
excess tax depreciation over
normal depreciation

amortissement linéaire *m*
straightline depreciation

amortissements cumulés *mpl*
cumulative depreciation

amortissements différés *mpl*
deferred depreciation

an *m* year; *par an* annually, per year

analyse *f* analysis

analyse des ventes *f* sales analysis

analyser to analyse

analyste *mf* analyst

ancienneté *f* seniority

animation des ventes *f* sales
promotion

année *f* year

année budgétaire *f* financial
year, fiscal year *Am*

année civile *f* calendar year

année comptable *f* accounting year,
financial year, fiscal year *Am*

année fiscale *f* financial year, fiscal
year *Am*

annexe *f* appendix

annexe related

annexé à attached to

annexes *fpl* [*comptabilité*] notes to
the accounts

annuel annual

annuité *f* [*rente*] annuity

annuité constante *f* [*de
remboursement*] fixed annual

payment

annuité d'amortissement *f* annual
depreciation, annual writedown

annulation *f* cancellation

annulation rétroactive *f* retroactive
cancellation

annuler to cancel

**ANPE (=Agence nationale pour
l'emploi)** *f* Jobcentre®

antenne *f* [*de société*] branch

antérieur prior

anticipé [*remboursement de dette*]
early

anticiper un paiement to pay in
advance

antidater to backdate; [*contrat*] to
antedate

APE (=activité principale exercée)
main line of business

**APEC (=Association pour l'emploi
des cadres)** *f* executive
recruitment agency

appareil commercial *m* commercial
structure

appauvrissement *m* [*d'une
entreprise*] decline in the financial
position

appel d'offres *m* call for tenders

appel de fonds *m* [*de société*] call
for capital

appliquer to apply

appointements *mpl* salary

apport de capitaux *m* capital
contribution

apport en capital *m* capital
contribution

apport en nature *m* contribution in
kind

apport en numéraire *m* cash
contribution

apports libérés *mpl* fully paid-up
capital

apposer sa signature à to put one's

signature to
apprentissage *m [formation]* training
approbation *f* approval
approbation des comptes *f* approval
of the accounts
approvisionnement *m* supply
approvisionner to supply
approvisionner qn en qch to supply
sb with sth
approvisionner un compte to pay
money into an account
après imposition after tax
après impôt after tax
apurement *m [de comptes]* auditing
apurer *[comptes]* to audit
apurer une dette to discharge a debt
arbitrage *m* arbitration
arbitrer to arbitrate
argent *m* money
argent comptant *m* cash
argent liquide *m* cash
argent en caisse *m* cash in hand;
[recettes] takings
argumentation *f* argument
arrangement *m* arrangement
arrangement à l'amiable *m* out of
court settlement
arrérages *mpl* arrears
arrêt de paiement *m* stoppage of
payment(s)
arrêt de travail *m* stoppage
arrêt des comptes *m* closing (off)
the accounts
arrêté *m* decree
arrêter un compte to close (off) an
account
arrêter un marché to close a deal
arrhes *fpl* deposit
arriéré *m* arrears
arriéré in arrears
arriver à échéance to fall due; *[bail]*
to expire; *[prêt]* to mature
arrondir to round off

article *m [clause]* article; *[de
compte]* entry
**ASSEDIC (=Association pour
l'emploi dans l'industrie et le
commerce)** *f* French
unemployment benefits department
assemblée *f* meeting
assemblée annuelle *f* annual
(general) meeting
assemblée générale *f* annual general
meeting
assemblée générale extraordinaire *f*
extraordinary general meeting
assemblée générale ordinaire *f*
annual general meeting
assemblée des actionnaires *f*
shareholders' meeting
*s'***assembler** to meet
assiette d'impôts *f* taxable income
assister à une assemblée to attend a
meeting
association *f* society, association;
[forme d'entreprise] partnership
association d'utilité publique *f*
public utility
**association pour l'emploi des
cadres** *f* executive recruitment
agency
associé *m* partner; *[collègue]*
associate, business associate
*s'***associer avec/à** to enter into
partnership with
assujetti *m* person liable for tax
assumer les frais to bear the costs
assumer un risque to take a risk
assurance *f* insurance
assurance chômage *f* unemployment
insurance
assurance crédit *f* credit insurance,
loan insurance
assurance maladie *f* health insurance
assurance multirisque *f*
comprehensive insurance

assurance responsabilité civile *f*
public liability insurance

assurance tous risques *f*
comprehensive insurance

assurance-vie *f* life insurance, life
assurance *Br*

**assurance contre les accidents du
travail** *f* industrial accident
insurance

assurances *fpl* insurances

assuré *m* insured (party)

*s'***assurer** to take out insurance

assureur *m* insurer

attaquer en justice to take legal
action against

attestation *f* certificate

attestation de rejet *f* [*de chèque*]
notification of returned cheque

attester [*sortie d'argent*] to confirm

attitré appointed

attribuer [*actions*] to allot

attribution *f* [*d'actions*] allotment

audit *m* audit

audit d'entreprise *m* company
search

augmentation *f* increase

augmentation de capital *f* increase
in capital

augmentation de prix *f* price
increase

augmentation de salaire *f* pay rise,
raise *Am*

augmenter to increase

authenticité *f* authenticity

authentifier to authenticate

authentique [*copie*] certified

autofinancé financed from cashflow

autofinancement *m* financing from
cashflow, cashflow

autorisé authorized

autoriser to authorize

aval: pour aval guaranteed by

aval bancaire *m* bank guarantee,
aval

avaliser to avalize

avance (de fonds) *f* advance

avancement *m* [*d'employé*]
promotion

avant imposition before tax

avant impôt before tax

avantage fiscal *m* tax benefit

avantage en nature *m* benefit in
kind

avantages sociaux *mpl* fringe
benefits

avenant *m* rider; [*de police*]
endorsement to a policy

avis *m* notification; [*document*]
advice, notice, note

avis d'imposition *m* tax assessment

avis de crédit *m* credit advice

avis de débit *m* debit advice

avis de paiement *m* payment advice

avis de prélèvement *m* direct debit
advice

avis de rejet *m* [*de chèque*] notice of
returned cheque

avis de virement *m* (bank) transfer
advice

avis de la banque *m* bank
notification, bank advice

aviser to inform, to advise

avocat *m* lawyer, attorney *Am*

avoir *m* [*de société*] assets; [*biens*]
possessions; [*capital*] capital; [*sur
compte*] credit; [*note de crédit*]
credit note

avoir-client *m* customer credit

avoir fiscal *m* tax credit

avoir-fournisseur *m* supplier credit

avoir de compte *m* account credit

avoir en banque *m* bank credit

avoir en devises *m* foreign currency
holding

ayant-compte *m* account holder

B

bail *m* lease
bail emphytéotique *m* long lease
bailleur *m* lessor
bailleur de fonds *m* backer
baisse des prix *f* drop in prices
baisser to drop
balance *f* balance
balance avant inventaire *f* pre-inventory balance
balance d'inventaire *f* inventory balance
balance de vérification *f* trial balance
bancaire banking, bank
banque *f* bank
banque centrale *f* central bank
banque commerciale *f* commercial bank
banque compensatrice *f* clearing bank
banque confirmatrice *f* confirming bank
Banque européenne d'investissement *f* European Investment Bank
banque notificatrice *f* advising bank
banque d'affaires *f* merchant bank
banque de crédit *f* credit bank
banque de dépôt *f* deposit bank
banqueroute *f* bankruptcy
banquier *m* banker
barème des prix *m* price scale
barème des salaires *m* salary scale
barrer to cross out

barrer un chèque to cross a cheque
base *f* basis
base amortissable *f* basis for depreciation
base de calcul *f* basis of calculations
base hors taxe *f* [*de TVA*] amount exclusive of VAT
BEI (=Banque européenne d'investissement) *f* EIB
bénéfice *m* profit
bénéfice imposable *m* taxable profit
bénéfice net *m* net profit
bénéfice transféré *m* profit transferred
bénéfice d'exploitation *m* operating profit
bénéficiaire *mf* beneficiary, payee
besoin en fonds de roulement *m* working capital requirements, increase in working capital
bien-fondé *m* validity
biens sociaux *mpl* corporate assets, corporate funds
biens d'équipement *mpl* capital equipment
biens et services *mpl* goods and services
bilan *m* balance sheet
bilan comptable *m* balance sheet
bilan condensé *m* summary balance sheet
bilan financier *m* financial statement
bilan intérimaire *m* interim statement

bilan prévisionnel *m* forecast balance sheet

bilan social *m* social report

bilan d'ouverture *m* opening balance sheet

billet à ordre *m* promissory note

billet de banque *m* banknote, bill *Am*

blocage *m* [*de prix, salaires*] freeze

bloquer [*fonds*] to block

bon *m* voucher, slip, coupon

bon de caisse *m* interest-bearing note; [*justifiant sortie de fonds*] cash voucher

bon de commande *m* purchase order

bon de livraison *m* delivery note

bon pour aval guaranteed by

boni *m* [*supplément*] bonus; [*excédent*] profit, gain

bonification *f* rebate; [*supplément*] bonus

bonus *m* bonus

bordereau *m* [*formulaire*] form; [*liste*] list

bordereau d'escompte *m* list of bills for discount

bordereau d'imputation *m* accounting entry sheet/form

bordereau de caisse *m* cash statement

bordereau de codification *m* accounts coding sheet/form

bordereau de compte *m* statement of account

bordereau de crédit *m* credit note

bordereau de remise (d'espèces) *m* pay-in slip

bordereau de saisie *m* accounting input sheet/form, record form

bordereau de salaires *m* wages sheet

bordereau de versement (d'espèces) *m* paying-in slip

Bourse *f* Stock Exchange

bourse coulisse *f* unlisted market

Bourse des valeurs *f* Stock Exchange

boursier stock market

BPF (=bon pour francs) good for ... francs

branche *f* line of business

branche d'activité *f* area of operations

brevet (d'invention) *m* patent

breveter to patent

briefer to brief

briefing *m* briefing

briseur de grève *m* strike breaker

brouillard *m* day book, cash book

brouillard de caisse *m* cash book

brut gross

budget *m* budget

budget de production *m* production budget

budget de trésorerie *m* cashflow, cash budget

budget des approvisionnements *m* purchase budget

budget des charges *m* overhead budget, cost budget

budget des investissements *m* capital budget

budget des ventes *m* sales budget

budgétaire budget

budgétisation *f* budgeting

bulletin *m* bulletin; [*revue*] report

bulletin de commande *m* order form

bulletin de paie *m* payslip

bulletin de salaire *m* payslip

bulletin de souscription d'actions *m* share subscription form

bulletin de versement *m* paying-in slip, paying-in form

bureau-satellite *m* branch office

bureau d'études *m* design department; [*de recherche*] R&D department

bureau d'ordonnancement *m* scheduling and planning department
bureau de publicité *m* advertising agency
bureau des méthodes *m* O&M (organization and methods) department

C

CA (=chiffre d'affaires) sales, turnover
cabinet conseil *m* consultancy
cabinet juridique *m* law firm
cabinet d'audit *m* firm of auditors
cabinet d'expertise comptable *m* accounting firm
cachet *m* seal
cadre *m* executive
cadre moyen *m* middle manager
cadre supérieur *m* senior executive
cadres moyens *mpl* middle management
cadres supérieurs *mpl* senior management
caisse *f* [*liquide*] cash
caisse d'amortissement *f* sinking fund
caisse de garantie *f* credit guarantee institution
caisse de grève *f* strike fund
caisse de maladie *f* health insurance scheme
caisse de retraite *f* pension fund
calcul *m* calculation

calculer to calculate
calculs en cascade *mpl* tax deficiency deduction calculation
cambiste *mf* foreign exchange broker
camembert *m* pie chart
camoufler un bilan to window-dress the accounts
campagne publicitaire *f* advertising campaign
campagne de promotion *f* promotional campaign
campagne de publicité *f* advertising campaign
campagne de vente *f* sales campaign
candidat *m* applicant
candidature *f* [*pour poste*] application; *poser sa candidature pour un poste* to apply for a job
capacité à emprunter *f* borrowing capacity
capacité d'achat *f* purchasing power
capacité d'endettement *f* borrowing capacity
capital *m* capital
capital appelé *m* called-up capital

capital engagé *m* capital employed

capital fixe *m* fixed capital

capital flottant *m* floating capital

capital improductif *m* idle capital, unproductive capital

capital initial *m* start-up capital

capital nominal *m* nominal capital

capital-risque *m* venture capital

capital roulant *m* working capital

capital social *m* share capital, issued (share) capital

capital souscrit *m* subscribed capital

capital souscrit et appelé *m* called-up subscribed capital

capital souscrit et appelé, non versé *m* subscribed capital called and unpaid

capital souscrit non appelé *m* uncalled subscribed capital

capital de départ *m* start-up capital

capital de réserve *m* reserve capital

capital de roulement *m* working capital

capital non appelé *m* uncalled capital

capitalisation *f* capitalization

capitaliser to capitalize

capitaux disponibles *mpl* available capital

capitaux fébriles *mpl* hot money

capitaux permanents *mpl* long-term capital

capitaux propres *mpl* equity, shareholders' equity, shareholders' funds

carnet de commandes *m* order book

carte accréditive *f* credit card; [*de magasin*] charge card

carte de crédit *f* credit card

carte de paiement *f* payment card

carte de visite *f* business card, card

cas de force majeure *m* act of God

caution *f* guarantee, surety, security

caution de banque *f* bank guarantee

caution de restitution d'acomptes *f* guarantee to refund down payments

cautionnement *m* guarantee

cautionner to stand surety for

C/C (=compte (de) chèque) *m* C/A

CCB (=compte de chèque bancaire) *m* C/A

CCI (=Chambre de commerce et de l'industrie) *f* Chamber of Commerce and Industry

CDI (=Centre des impôts) *m* tax centre, tax office

céder [*actions*] to transfer

CEE (=Communauté économique européenne) *f* EC, EEC; *de la CEE* EC, EEC

centrale syndicale *f* group of affiliated trade unions

centrale d'achat *f* central purchasing group, central buying group

centralisation *f* centralization

centraliser to centralize

centre d'analyse *m* cost centre

centre (d'analyse) auxiliaire *m* secondary cost centre

centre d'analyse opérationnel *m* operational cost centre

centre (d'analyse) principal *m* main cost centre

centre d'analyse de structure *m* fixed cost centre

centre des impôts *m* tax centre, tax office

certificat d'assurance *m* insurance certificate

certificat de dépôt *m* certificate of deposit

certificat de non-paiement *m* [*de chèque*] notification of unpaid cheque; [*de lettre de change*] certificate of dishonour

certificat de titres *m* share certificate
certificat de travail *m* reference
certification *f* certification
certifier to certify
cessation d'entreprise *f* ceasing of trading
cessation de paiement *f* suspension of payments
cesser to stop
cessible transferable
cession *f* [*d'actions*] transfer
cessionnaire *mf* assignee, transferee
CFDT (=Confédération française du travail) *f* socialist trade union
CGI (=Code général des impôts) *m* general tax code
CGT (=Confédération générale du travail) *f* Communist trade union
CH Nº (=chèque numéro) cheque No.
chaîne de fabrication *f* production line
chaîne de montage *f* assembly line
chaland *m* client
Chambre de commerce *f* Chamber of Commerce
Chambre de commerce internationale *f* International Chamber of Commerce
charge: être à la charge de [*appel, etc.*] to be chargeable to
charge constatée d'avance *f* prepayment
charge fictive *f* fictitious cost
charge opérationnelle *f* overhead, operating cost
charge à payer *f* sum payable
chargé: être chargé de to be in charge of
charges courantes *fpl* current expenses
charges exceptionnelles *fpl* exceptional costs

charges exceptionnelles sur opérations de gestion *fpl* extraordinary losses on operations
charges financières *fpl* interest and other finance charges
charges fixes *fpl* fixed costs
charges incorporables *fpl* product expenses, product charges
charges locatives *fpl* [*de locaux*] rental charges, rental expenses; [*de téléphone, électricité*] standing charges; [*de matériel*] lease charges
charges nettes *fpl* net costs
charges patronales *fpl* employer contributions
charges sociales *fpl* social security charges, welfare charges *Am*
charges sociales patronales *fpl* employer contributions
charges sociales salariales *fpl* employee contributions
charges variables *fpl* variable costs
charges à payer *fpl* accrued expenses, accruals
charges d'exploitation *fpl* operating costs, running costs
charges de structure *fpl* fixed costs
chasseur de têtes *m* head hunter
chef *m* [*dans hiérarchie*] superior; [*de service*] manager, head; [*d'employé*] boss
chef comptable *m* chief accountant
chef d'exploitation *m* operations manager
chef de bureau *m* senior clerk, office manager
chef de fabrication *m* production manager, manufacturing manager
chef de file *m* lead manager
chef de groupe *m* group supervisor, group manager, group leader
chef de produit *m* product manager

chef de service *m* head of department, departmental manager

chef de zone *m* area manager

chef des études *m* research manager

chef des exploitations *m* operations manager

chef des informations *m* PR manager, Public Relations manager

chef des traitements *m* DP manager, Data Processing manager

chef des ventes *m* sales manager

chèque *m* cheque, check *Am*

chèque bancaire *m* bank cheque

chèque barré *m* crossed cheque

chèque bloqué *m* blocked cheque

chèque certifié *m* certified cheque

chèque compensé *m* cleared cheque

chèque nominatif *m* cheque made out to name

chèque postal *m* post office cheque

chèque retourné *m* returned cheque

chèque au porteur *m* cheque made out to bearer, bearer cheque

chèque d'entreprise *m* company cheque

chèque de banque *m* banker's draft, cashier's check *Am*

chèque de virement *m* transfer cheque

chèque en blanc *m* blank cheque

chèque en bois *m* rubber cheque

chèque non endossable *m* non-negotiable cheque

chèque sans provision *m* cheque that bounces, rubber cheque

chéquier *m* cheque book

chevalier blanc *m* white knight

chevronné *m* experienced

chiffrage *m* adding up, totalling

chiffre *m* figure; *en chiffres* [*montant*] in figures

chiffre d'affaires *m* sales, turnover

chiffre d'affaires annuel *m* annual sales figures, annual turnover

chiffre d'affaires critique *m* breakeven point

chiffre d'affaires global *m* total sales

chiffre de vente *m* sales figures

chiffré [*codé*] coded

chiffrer to quantify

se chiffrer à to add up to, to total

chirographaire unsecured

chômage *m* unemployment; *être au chômage* to be unemployed

chômage partiel *m* short time (working)

chômé: jour chômé *m* bank holiday

chômeur *m* unemployed worker; *les chômeurs* the unemployed

chronogramme *m* planner

chronologique chronological

chute des prix *f* drop in prices

circuit de commercialisation *m* marketing network

circuit de distribution *m* distribution network

circulation monétaire *f* circulation of money

circulation des capitaux *f* circulation of capital

circulation des devises *f* circulation of currency

citation *f* summons

classe *f* class; [*comptabilité*] group of accounts

classement *m* classification; [*rangement*] filing

classer to classify; [*ranger*] to file

classification *f* classification

classifier to classify

clause compromissoire *f* arbitration clause

clause contractuelle *f* clause of a/the contract

clause dérogatoire *f* derogatory clause

clause pénale *f* penalty clause

clause à ordre: to order:

clause au porteur *f* pay to bearer clause

clause d'annulation *f* cancellation clause

clause d'arbitrage *f* arbitration clause

clause d'exonération *f* exemption clause

clause d'indexation *f* cost escalation clause, indexation clause

clause de franchise *f* excess clause

clause de non-concurrence *f* non-competition clause

clause de réserve de propriété *f* retention of title clause

clause de résiliation *f* termination clause, cancellation clause

clause de sauvegarde *f* safeguard clause

client *m* customer, client

client douteux *m* doubtful debt, possible bad debt

clientèle *f* customers, clientele

clignotants économiques *mpl* economic indicators

clore un compte to close an account

clôture annuelle des livres *f* year-end closing of accounts

clôture de compte *f* closing of account

clôture de l'exercice *f* end of the financial year

clôturer to close

clôturer à perte to close at a loss

CNPF (=Conseil national du patronat français) *m equivalent to* CBI

coacquéreur *m* joint purchaser

coadministrateur *m* co-director

coassocié *m* co-partner

cocontractant *m* contracting partner

code affectation *m* department code

code assujetti TVA *m* VAT registration number

code banque *m* bank sort code

code client *m* customer code, customer reference number

code général des impôts *m* general tax code

code guichet *m* bank branch code

code taxe *m* tax code

code du travail *m* employment code, employment law, labor code *Am*, labor laws *Am*

codébiteur *m* joint debtor

coder to code

codétenteur *m* joint holder

codification *f* coding

codifier to code

codirecteur *m* co-director

coefficient *m* coefficient

coefficient d'exploitation *m* performance ratio, operating ratio

coefficient de liquidité *m* current ratio

coefficient de rotation *m* stock turnover ratio

coefficient de solvabilité *m* risk asset ratio

cogérance *f* co-management, joint management

cogérer to manage jointly

cogestion *f* co-management, joint management

collaborateur *m* [*dans entreprise*] colleague

collaborer to collaborate

collectif collective

collectivité publique *f* government organization

collègue *mf* colleague

colonne *f* column

colonne créditrice *f* credit column
colonne débitrice *f* debit column
cols blancs *mpl* white-collar workers
combler [*déficit, perte*] to make good
combler un retard to make up for lost time
comité consultatif *m* advisory board
comité d'entreprise *m* works committee
comité d'hygiène et de sécurité *m* health and safety committee
comité de direction *m* management committee, executive committee
commande *f* order
commandement *m* ordering
commander to order
commanditaire *mf* limited partner
commandité *m* general partner, partner with unlimited liability
commerçant *m* merchant
commerce *m* trade; [*vente et achat*] commerce; [*fonds de commerce*] business
commercer to trade
commercial business; [*droit*] commercial; [*embargo, tribunal*] trade
commercialisation *f* marketing
commercialiser to market
commettant *m* principal
commis *m* clerk
commis principal *m* senior clerk
commissaire aux comptes *mf* government auditor
commission *f* fee
commission bancaire *f* bank commission, bank charge, bank fee
Commission bancaire *f* Banking Commission
commission consultative *f* advisory committee
Commission européenne *f* European Commission

commission paritaire *f* joint committee
commission permanente *f* standing committee
commission d'acceptation *f* acceptance fee
commission d'arbitrage *f* arbitration board, arbitration committee
commission d'encaissement *f* collection charge, collection fee
commission d'enquête *f* board of inquiry
commission de change *f* exchange commission
commission de confirmation *f* confirmation fee, confirmation commission; [*pour crédit*] facility fee
commission de garantie *f* guarantee commission
commission de paiement *f* collection charge, collection fee
commissionnaire *mf* agent
communautaire Community
Communauté économique européenne *f* European Economic Community
compagnie *f* company
compagnie mère *f* parent company
compagnie d'assurances *f* insurance company
comparatif comparative
compensable à to be cleared at
compensation *f* [*de chèque*] clearing
compenser to clear
compétitif competitive
compétitivité *f* competitiveness
complémentaire additional
compression de crédit *f* credit squeeze
compression de personnel *f* staff redundancies, staff layoffs, reduction in staff

compromis *m* compromise

compromis de vente *m* sale agreement, agreement to sell

compta *f* accounting

comptabilisation *f* entering into the accounts; [*dénombrement*] counting; *la comptabilisation de l'actif d'une société* the recording of the assets of a company in the accounts

comptabiliser to record in the accounts, to enter in the accounts; [*dénombrer*] to count

comptabilité *f* accounts; [*discipline*] accountancy; [*système*] accounting; *qui est-ce qui fait votre comptabilité ?* who does your accounts?

comptabilité analytique *f* cost accounting

comptabilité commerciale *f* business accounting

comptabilité générale *f* general accounts; [*système*] financial accounting

comptabilité-gestion financière *f* financial management accounting

comptabilité informatisée *f* computerized accounts

comptable *mf* accountant

comptage *m* counting

comptant: au comptant [*achat*] cash; [*acheter*] for cash

compte *m* account; *avoir un compte en banque* to have a bank account

compte bancaire *m* bank account

compte bloqué *m* escrow account, frozen account, blocked account

compte centralisateur *m* central account

compte chèque *m* current account, checking account *Am*

compte chèque postal *m* post office cheque account

compte client *m* account receivable, trade debtor

compte collectif *m* adjustment account, summary account

compte courant *m* current account, checking account *Am*

compte courant bancaire *m* current account with a bank

compte créditeur *m* [*compte payable*] account payable; [*à la banque*] account in credit, credit balance

compte débiteur *m* account receivable; [*à la banque*] account in debit, debit balance

compte divisionnaire *m* divisional account

compte joint *m* joint account

compte livret *m* deposit account

compte postal *m* Post Office account

compte rendu *m* [*rapport*] report; [*procès-verbal*] minutes

compte spécial *m* special account

compte-titres *m* share account

compte à découvert *m* overdrawn account

compte d'actif *m* assets account

compte d'attente *m* suspense account

compte d'exploitation générale *m* trading account

compte d'immobilisations *m* fixed asset account

compte de bilan *m* balance sheet account

compte de charges *m* expense account

compte de chèque bancaire *m* current account, checking account *Am*

compte de contrepartie *m* contra account

compte de correspondant *m* correspondent bank account

compte de dépôt *m* deposit account

compte de passif *m* liabilities account

compte de pertes et profits *m* profit and loss account, income statement *Am*

compte de produits *m* income account, revenue account

compte de régularisation *m* [*de l'actif*] prepayments and accrued income; [*du passif*] accruals and deferred income

compte de réserve *m* reserve account

compte de résultat *m* profit and loss account, income statement *Am*

compte de stock *m* inventory account

compte de l'exploitant *m* owner's capital account

compte en devises étrangères *m* foreign currency account

compter to count

comptes analytiques d'exploitation *mpl* operational cost accounts

comptes annuels *mpl* annual accounts

comptes approuvés *mpl* certified accounts

comptes d'exploitation *mpl* trading accounts

comptes de gestion *mpl* management accounts

comptes de tiers *mpl* other debtors and creditors

comptoir d'escompte *m* discount house

concéder to grant

concession *f* concession; [*agence*] agency; [*contrat de franchisage*] franchise

concession commerciale *f* agency

concession de franchise *f* grant of franchise

concessionnaire *mf* agent; [*de licence*] licensee; [*de brevet*] patentee; [*de contrat de franchisage*] franchisee

conclure [*accord, contrat*] to enter into

conclure un marché to strike a deal

conclusion d'un contrat *f* signing of a contract

concours bancaire *m* bank borrowings

concurrence *f* competition

concurrence acharnée *f* cut-throat competition

concurrence déloyale *f* unfair competition

concurrencer to compete with

concurrent *m* competitor

concurrentiel competitive

conditions d'un contrat *fpl* terms and conditions of a contract

conditions de paiement *fpl* terms of payment

conditions de travail *fpl* working conditions

conduite *f* [*d'entreprise*] management

conférence *f* meeting; [*à grande échelle*] conference

conférence de presse *f* press conference

confidentialité *f* confidentiality

confidentiel confidential

confirmation *f* confirmation; *en confirmation de* in confirmation of

confirmer to confirm

conflit *m* conflict

conflit salarial *m* pay dispute

conflit du travail *m* industrial

dispute

congé *m* leave; [*vacances*] holiday, vacation *Am*; **être en congé** to be on leave

congédiement *m* dismissal

congédier to dismiss

congés payés *mpl* paid leave

conjointement jointly

conjointement et solidairement jointly and severally

conjoncture *f* economic circumstances

conjoncture économique *f* economic situation

conjoncturel [*chômage*] cyclical

connaissement *m* bill of lading, waybill

conseil économique *m* economic council

conseil fiscal *m* tax consultant

conseil juridique *m* legal adviser

Conseil national du patronat français *m equivalent to* Confederation of British Industry

conseil syndical *m* trade union council

conseil d'administration *m* board, board of directors

conseil d'entreprise *m* works committee

conseil de prud'hommes *m* industrial tribunal

conseil de surveillance *m* supervisory board

conseiller to advise

conseiller *m* consultant

conseiller économique *m* economic adviser

conseiller fiscal *m* tax consultant

conseiller juridique *m* legal adviser

conseiller du travail *m* personnel consultant

conseiller en gestion

(**d'entreprise**) *m* management consultant

consensuel by mutual consent

consensus *m* consensus

consentement *m* consent

consentir un prêt to grant a loan

conséquence: agir en conséquence to take appropriate action

consigne *f* [*mot d'ordre*] instruction

consigner une somme to deposit a sum of money

consolidation de bilan *f* balance sheet consolidation

consolider une dette to consolidate a debt

consommations de l'exercice *fpl* total annual expenses

consortium de banques *m* banking consortium

constatation de stock *f* stock take

constaté d'avance [*charge*] prepaid

constater to note; [*par écrit*] to record

constituer une société to set up a company

constitution de société *f* setting up of a company

consultant *m* consultant

consulter to consult

contact *m* contact

contentieux *m* litigation; [*service*] legal department

contestation *f* dispute

contester to contest

continuité d'exploitation *f* going-concern status

contractant *m* contracting party

contracter des dettes to incur debts, to contract debts

contracter des obligations to enter into commitments

contracter une assurance to take out insurance

contraire au contrat contrary to the terms of the contract

contraire aux statuts contrary to the articles of association

contrat *m* contract

contrat collectif *m* collective agreement

contrat notarié *m* notarized contract

contrat à durée déterminée *m* fixed term contract

contrat à durée indéterminée à temps plein *m* permanent full-time contract

contrat à temps partiel *m* part-time contract

contrat à temps plein *m* full-time contract

contrat d'achat *m* purchase contract, bill of sale

contrat d'agence *m* agency contract

contrat d'assurance *m* insurance contract

contrat de bail *m* lease contract

contrat de couverture à terme *m* forward contract

contrat de crédit-bail *m* lease-purchase contract

contrat de mission d'intérim *m* temporary contract

contrat de prêt *m* loan agreement

contrat de travail *m* contract of employment

contrat de travail à durée déterminée *m* fixed term contract

contravention *f* [*de loi*] violation

contre-offre *f* counter-offer

contre-passation *f* journal entry, contra entry

contre-performance *f* poor performance

contresigner to countersign

contribuable *mf* taxpayer

contribuer à to contribute to

contribution *f* contribution

Contribution sociale généralisée *f* general social security contribution

contributions directes *fpl* direct taxation

contributions indirectes *fpl* indirect taxation

contrôle *m* [*de document*] check

contrôle bancaire *m* banking controls

contrôle de comptes *m* audit

contrôle des changes *m* exchange controls

contrôle du bilan *m* audit

contrôler [*surveiller*] to monitor; [*maîtriser*] to control

contrôleur financier *m* financial controller

contrôleur de gestion *m* controller

contrôleur des contributions *m* inspector of taxes

contrôleur du crédit *m* credit controller

convenir de to agree on

convention *f* agreement

convention collective *f* collective agreement

convenu: comme convenu as agreed

conversion d'entreprise *f* change in the line of business

conversion d'un emprunt *f* conversion of loan notes, conversion of loan stock

convertible convertible

convertir to convert

convertir des valeurs to convert securities

convertir un emprunt to convert loan notes, to convert loan stock

convocation *f* [*message*] notice of a/ the meeting

convocation à une réunion *f* notice of a meeting

convocation d'une assemblée *f* calling of a meeting

convoquer les actionnaires to call the shareholders to a meeting

convoquer une assemblée générale to call a general meeting

convoyeur de fonds *m* armed security escort

coopératif co-operative

coopération *f* co-operation

coopérer to co-operate

coordinateur *m* coordinator

coordination *f* coordination

coparticipant *m* co-partner

coparticipation *f* co-partnership

coposséder to have joint ownership of, to own jointly

copossession *f* joint ownership, co-ownership

copropriétaire *mf* joint owner, co-owner

copropriété *f* joint ownership, co-ownership

corporatif corporate

corporation de droit public *f* public corporation, public body

corporel [*immobilisation*] tangible

corps de métier *m* guild, trade association

corrigé en fonction des variations saisonnières seasonally adjusted

corriger to correct

cosignataire *mf* co-signatory

cotation *f* quotation

cote officielle *f* official list

cote de clôture *f* closing price

coté en Bourse quoted on the Stock Exchange; [*société*] listed on the Stock Exchange

coté, daté et paraphé numbered, dated and signed

cotisation *f* contribution

cotisation chômage *f* unemployment contribution

cotisation patronale *f* employer's contribution

cotisation vieillesse *f* pension contribution

cotisation de sécurité sociale *f* social security contribution

cotisations ouvrières *fpl* employee contributions

cotisations salariales *fpl* employee contributions

cotiser to contribute

coupon attaché cum dividend

coupon échu ex dividend

coupure *f* denomination

Cour d'appel *f* Court of Appeal

Cour de justice *f* Court of Justice

courant d'affaires *m* business trend

courbe de coût *f* cost curve

cours *m* [*boursier*] price

cours acheteur *m* bid price

cours vendeur *m* offer price

cours d'achat *m* bid price

cours d'ouverture *m* opening price

cours de clôture *m* closing price

cours de compensation *m* clearing price

cours des changes *m* exchange rates

cours du change *m* rate of exchange

coursier *m* courier

court: à court terme short-term

courtage *m* brokerage

courtage officiel *m* official brokerage

courtier *m* broker

courtier d'assurances *m* insurance broker

coût complet unitaire *m* total unit cost

coût différentiel *m* differential cost

coût fixe total *m* total fixed cost

coût préétabli *m* standard cost

coût standard *m* standard cost

coût unitaire *m* unit cost

coût unitaire moyen pondéré *m* weighted average unit cost

coût unitaire de travail *m* unit labour cost

coût d'achat *m* purchase cost; [*sur bilan*] cost of goods purchased

coût d'acquisition *m* acquisition cost

coût de développement *m* development costs

coût de distribution *m* distribution costs

coût de fonctionnement *m* running cost

coût de production *m* production cost

coût de revient *m* cost price

coûts administratifs *mpl* administrative costs

coûts constatés *mpl* actual costs

coûts cumulés *mpl* cumulative costs

coûts fixes *mpl* fixed costs

coûts opératoires *mpl* operating costs

coûts prévisionnels *mpl* estimated costs

coûts variables *mpl* variable costs

couvert [*par assurance*] covered; [*emprunt*] secured

couverture *f* [*d'assuré*] cover

couverture suffisante *f* adequate cover

couverture à terme *f* term insurance cover

couverture du risque de crédit *f* loan risk cover

couvrir [*frais*] to cover; [*emprunt*] to secure

couvrir un découvert to cover an overdraft

couvrir un déficit to cover a loss

créance *f* debt

créance contestée *f* contested debt

créance douteuse *f* doubtful debt, possible bad debt

créance garantie *f* secured debt

créance impayée *f* unpaid debt, unrecovered debt

créance litigieuse *f* contested debt

créance principale *f* principal debt

créance privilégiée *f* preferred debt

créance recouvrable *f* recoverable debt

créances *fpl* receivables, accounts receivable

créances clients *fpl* accounts receivable, trade debtors

créancier *m* creditor

créancier hypothécaire *m* mortgagee

créancier nanti *m* secured creditor

créancier ordinaire *m* ordinary creditor, unsecured creditor

créancier privilégié *m* preferred creditor

création d'entreprise *f* setting up of a business

crédit *m* credit; *à crédit* credit; *acheter à crédit* to buy on credit

crédit-acheteur *m* buyer credit

crédit back to back *m* back to back credit

crédit-bail *m* lease

crédit bancaire *m* bank credit; *un crédit bancaire* a bank loan

crédit bloqué *m* frozen credit

crédit confirmé *m* confirmed credit

crédit cumulé *m* cumulative credit

crédit documentaire *m* documentary credit, letter of credit

crédit-fournisseur *m* supplier credit

crédit immobilier *m* mortgage

crédit "red clause" *m* red clause credit

crédit revolving *m* revolving credit

crédit (à) court terme *m* short-term

credit
crédit (à) long terme *m* long-term credit
crédit (à) moyen terme *m* medium-term credit
crédit à reporter *m* credit to be carried forward
crédit de campagne *m* stock financing loan
crédit de droits *m* delay in payment of indirect taxes
crédit de TVA *m* VAT credit
crédité de credited with
créditer to credit
créditeur [*solde, etc.*] credit; [*concernant créditeurs*] creditor; *être créditeur* to be in credit
crédits de développement *mpl* development loans
créer une entreprise to set up a business

créer une hypothèque to create a mortgage
créneau *m* niche
crise *f* crisis
crise de main-d'œuvre *f* manpower crisis
croissance économique *f* economic growth
croissance zéro *f* zero growth
CSG (=Contribution sociale généralisée) *f* general social security contribution
culture d'entreprise *f* corporate culture
curateur *m* trustee
curriculum vitae *m* curriculum vitae, resumé *Am*
cycle économique *m* economic cycle
cycle d'exploitation *m* operating cycle

D

DADS (=déclaration annuelle des données sociales) *f* PAYE and NIC return
date *f* date; *en date de ce jour* dated this day; *votre lettre en date du* your letter of; *à date fixe* on a fixed date
date limite *f* deadline

date limite de paiement *f* deadline for payment
date d'achèvement *f* completion date, date of completion
date d'échéance *f* [*de dû*] maturity date; [*de terme*] expiry date
date d'exigibilité *f* due date
date d'expiration *f* expiry date

date d'ouverture de l'exercice *f*
first day of the financial year

date de valeur *f* value date

daté: lettre datée du letter dated the

dater to date; *à dater de ce jour* from today

dation en paiement *f* payment in kind

débauchage *m* laying off

débaucher to lay off

débit *m* debit; *au débit de* to the debit of

débit cumulé *m* cumulative debit

débit de caisse *m* cash debit

débiter to debit

débiter un compte to debit an account

débiter un compte d'une somme to debit a sum to an account

débiteur *m* debtor

débiteur [*solde*] debit

débiteur concordataire *m* bankrupt who has reached a settlement with his debtors

débiteur insolvable *m* insolvent debtor

débiteur principal *m* primary debtor, principal debtor

débiteur solidaire *m* joint and several debtor

déblocage des prix *m* unfreezing of prices

débloquer des fonds to release funds, to make funds available

déboursement *m* disbursement

débourser to pay

débrayage *m* stoppage

débrayer to down tools

décaissable [*charge*] payable

décaissement *m* cash expenditure, cash disbursement

décaisser [*montant*] to pay, to pay out; [*TVA*] to pay

décentralisation *f* decentralization

décentraliser to decentralize

décharge aux administrateurs *f* discharge granted to directors

décharger qn d'une dette to discharge sb from a debt

déchéance *f* [*de droits*] forfeiture; *tomber en déchéance* to lapse

décider qch to decide on sth

décideur *m* decision-maker

décision *f* decision

décision arbitrale *f* arbitration ruling, decision by arbitration

décision de justice *f* court ruling

déclarant de TVA *m* VAT-registered person

déclaration *f* [*écrite*] return

déclaration annuelle de résultats *f* annual statement of results

déclaration annuelle de salaires *f* annual salaries return

déclaration annuelle des données sociales *f* PAYE and NIC return

déclaration fiscale *f* tax return

déclaration sociale *f* PAYE and NIC return

déclaration de créance impayée *f* statement of claim for an unpaid debt

déclaration de résultats *f* statement of results, financial statement

déclaration de revenus *f* income tax return

déclaration de TVA *f* VAT return

déclarations annuelles *fpl* annual returns

déclaré declared

déclarer un dividende to declare a dividend

déclarer une entreprise en faillite to declare a business bankrupt

déclinant declining

décommander to cancel

décomposition des résultats *f*
breakdown of the results

décompte *m* count; [*calcul*]
calculation; [*déduction*] deduction

décompte d'une somme *m*
deduction of a sum

décompter [*somme*] to deduct

déconfiture *f* insolvency; [*débâcle*]
collapse

décote de TVA *f* VAT rebate

découvert: à découvert overdrawn

découvert bancaire *m* bank
overdraft

découvert d'un compte *m* overdraft

décréter un moratoire to declare a
moratorium

dédit *m* forfeit

dédommagé: être dédommagé de to
be compensated for

dédommagement *m* compensation

dédommager to compensate

déductibilité *f* deductibility

déductible deductible

déductible des impôts tax deductible

déduction *f* deduction

déduction fiscale *f* tax allowance

déduire to deduct

défaillance *f* [*d'acheteur*] default

défaillance d'entreprise *f* business
failure

défaillant defaulting

défalcation *f* deduction

défalquer une somme to deduct a
sum of money

défaut de paiement *m* default on
payment

défavorable unfavourable

déficit *m* deficit

déficit budgétaire *m* budget deficit

déficit reportable *m* loss carry
forward

déficitaire loss-making, unprofitable

définition de poste *f* job description

déflation *f* deflation

déflationniste deflationary

dégagement de fonds *m* release of
funds

**dégagement de fonds de
roulement** *m* decrease in working
capital

dégager des crédits to make credit
available

dégager un bénéfice to show a profit

dégeler des crédits to unfreeze
credits

dégraisser les effectifs to lay off
staff

degré *m* degree

dégrèvement *m* tax relief

dégrèvement fiscal *m* tax relief

déjeuner d'affaires *m* business
lunch

déjeuner de travail *m* working lunch

délai *m* period; [*date limite*]
deadline; *dans un délai de* within;
dans les plus brefs délais as soon
as possible

délai-congé *m* period of notice

délai d'exécution *m* deadline; [*de
livraison, de production*] lead time

délai de carence *m* waiting period

délai de grâce *m* days of grace

délai de paiement *m* credit period,
payment term

délai de règlement *m* settlement
period

délai de rigueur *m* strict deadline;
délai de rigueur : at the latest:

délai de validité *m* period of validity

délais légaux *mpl* legal time limit

délégation *f* delegation

délégation d'une dette *f* assignment
of a debt

délégation de pouvoir *f* delegation
of power

délégué *m* delegate

délégué syndical *m* shop steward, union representative

délégué du personnel *m* employee representative, personnel representative

déléguer to delegate

délibération *f* [*d'une assemblée*] vote, resolution

délibérer [*sur une question*] to confer

délit d'abus de biens sociaux *m* misappropriation of corporate funds

délivrance *f* issue

délivrance d'un certificat *f* issue of a certificate

délivrer to issue; [*licence*] to grant

délocaliser to shift, to relocate

demande *f* [*d'emploi, de congé*] application; [*offre et demande*] demand; *sur demande* on request; *à la demande de* at the request of

demande croissante *f* increasing demand

demande d'intervention *f* request for action

demande d'ouverture de crédit *f* credit application, loan application

demande de règlement *f* request for payment

demande de renseignements *f* enquiry, request for information

demande en dommages-intérêts *f* claim for damages

demander [*renseignements*] to ask for; [*paiement*] to request, to demand; [*dédommagements*] to claim

demandeur d'emploi *m* job seeker

démarche collective *f* joint representations

démarche de sélection *f* selection procedure

démarrage *m* [*d'entreprise*] start-up

démarrer un travail to start a job

démettre qn de ses fonctions to remove sb from his/her post

démission *f* resignation; *donner sa démission* to hand in one's resignation

démissionner to resign

démotivation *f* demotivation

deniers *mpl* money, monies

deniers publics *mpl* public funds, public money

dénominateur *m* denominator

dénomination commerciale *f* [*de produit*] trade name

dénomination sociale *f* company name

dénommé: ci-après dénommé hereinafter referred to as

dénoncer un contrat to terminate a contract, to cancel a contract

dénotage *m* downrating

départ volontaire *m* voluntary redundancy

département *m* department

dépassement de coût *m* cost overrun

dépasser to exceed

dépasser un crédit to exceed a credit limit

dépenser to spend

dépenses *fpl* [*débours*] expenditure

dépenses-amortissement *fpl* depreciation expenses

dépenses courantes *fpl* current expenditure(s)

dépenses diverses *fpl* sundry expenses

dépenses extraordinaires *fpl* extraordinary expenses

dépenses publicitaires *fpl* advertising expenditure

dépenses supplémentaires *fpl* additional expenses

dépenses d'exploitation *fpl* operating costs

dépenses de caisse *fpl* cash expenditure

dépenses de fonctionnement *fpl* operating costs

dépenses de formation professionnelle des salariés *fpl* employee training costs

déplafonner un crédit to raise the ceiling on a credit, to raise a credit limit

déposant *m* depositor

déposer to deposit

déposer son bilan to file a petition in bankruptcy

déposer une caution to lodge security, to deposit security

dépôt *m* deposit

dépôt à terme *m* term deposit

dépôt à vue *m* demand deposit, sight deposit

dépôt d'espèces *m* cash deposit

dépôt d'une somme *m* deposit of a sum of money

dépôt de bilan *m* petition in bankruptcy

dépôts à court terme *mpl* short-term deposits

dépréciation *f* depreciation

dépréciation de créances *f* write-down of accounts receivable

se **déprécier** to depreciate

dépt (=département) dept

dérogation *f* exception; *dérogation à* departure from, exception to

désaccord *m* disagreement

désapprovisionné [*compte*] overdrawn

description de poste *f* job description

désendettement *m* reduction in borrowings, reduction in gearing

déséquilibre budgétaire *m* budget imbalance

désignation *f* description

désigner qn à la position de to appoint sb to the position of

désinvestir des capitaux to divest

désinvestissement *m* divestment

dessous-de-table *m* backhander

destinataire *mf* [*de document*] addressee

destiné à [*lettre*] addressed to

déstockage *m* destocking, reduction in stocks

déstockage de production *m* [*poste de bilan*] decrease in stocks

déstocker des marchandises to destock goods, to reduce stocks

détaillé [*facture*] itemized

détailler to itemize

détaxe *f* tax refund

détenir en garantie to hold as security

détenteur *m* holder

détenteur d'obligations *m* bondholder

détenteur de titres *m* shareholder

détention *f* holding

détournement d'actifs *m* embezzlement of assets

détournement de fonds *m* embezzlement of funds

détourner de l'argent to embezzle money

dette *f* debt

dette consolidée *f* consolidated debt

dette foncière *f* property charge; [*hypothécaire*] mortgage debt

dette privilégiée *f* preferred debt

dette véreuse *f* bad debt

dettes fiscales et sociales *fpl* taxes and social security charges

dettes fournisseurs *fpl* accounts payable

dettes à court terme *fpl* current
  liabilities
devancer ses concurrents to be
  ahead of one's competitors, to be
  ahead of the competition
développement *m* development
développer to develop
devis *m* estimate, quote
devis estimatif *m* estimate
devise *f* currency
devise-titre *f* foreign security
  exchange currency
devises étrangères *fpl* foreign
  currency
devoir to owe
devoir de l'argent to owe money
diagramme *m* diagram
diagramme circulaire *m* pie chart
diagramme à barres *m* bar chart
diagramme à secteurs *m* pie chart
diagramme des flux *m* flowchart
diagramme en bâtons *m* bar chart
différé deferred
différence de cours *f* difference in
  prices, price difference
**différences positives/négatives de
  change** *fpl* foreign exchange gains/
  losses
différend *m* dispute, disagreement
différentiel differential
différer le paiement to defer
  payment
difficultés de trésorerie *fpl* cashflow
  difficulties
diffuser to distribute
diffusion *f* distribution
dilapider des fonds to squander
  funds
dilution de capital *f* dilution of
  capital
diminuer le capital to reduce capital
diminution *f* reduction, decrease
diminution des bénéfices *f* drop in

profits, decrease in profits
diminution des dépenses *f* cutting
  down of expenses
diminution des salaires *f* reduction
  in salaries
diminution du capital *f* reduction of
  capital
diplôme *m* diploma
diplômé qualified
direct direct
directeur *m* manager; [*plus haut
  dans hiérarchie*] director
directeur adjoint *m* deputy
  manager; [*plus haut dans
  hiérarchie*] deputy director
directeur administratif *m* executive
  director
directeur commercial *m*
  commercial manager; [*en chef*]
  commercial director
directeur export *m* export manager;
  [*en chef*] export director
directeur financier *m* financial
  manager; [*en chef*] financial
  director, finance director
directeur général *m* [*d'entreprise*]
  managing director, chief executive
  officer
directeur général adjoint *m* deputy
  managing director
directeur gérant *m* executive
  director
directeur intérimaire *m* temporary
  manager, interim manager, acting
  manager; [*en chef*] temporary
  director
directeur régional *m* regional
  manager, area manager; [*en chef*]
  regional director, area director
directeur technique *m* technical
  manager; [*en chef*] technical
  director
directeur d'agence *m* branch

manager

directeur de banque *m* bank manager

directeur de marketing *m* marketing manager; [*en chef*] marketing director

directeur de production *m* production manager; [*en chef*] production director

directeur de produit *m* product manager, brand manager

directeur de succursale *m* branch manager

directeur de l'exploitation *m* operations manager

directeur de la clientèle *m* customer relations manager

directeur de la communication *m* communications manager; [*en chef*] communications director

directeur du personnel *m* personnel manager; [*en chef*] personnel director

direction *f* management; [*service*] department

direction collégiale *f* collegiate management

direction commerciale *f* sales management

direction financière *f* financial management; [*service*] finance department

direction générale *f* senior management

direction mercatique *f* marketing department

direction de l'exploitation *f* operations management; [*service*] operations department

direction de la production *f* production control

direction des crédits *f* credit management

direction des entreprises *f* business management

direction du contentieux *f* legal department

direction du personnel *f* personnel management; [*service*] personnel department

direction du trésor *f* finance department

directive *f* instruction; [*de gouvernement, CEE*] directive

directive européenne *f* EC directive

directoire *m* executive board

directorial management

dirigeant *m* manager

dirigeant syndical *m* union leader

diriger [*entreprise*] to run, to manage

discours *m* speech

discuter une question to discuss an issue

disparité des salaires *f* disparity in salaries

disponibilité *f* availability

disponibilités *fpl* liquid assets

disponibilités en caisse et en banque *fpl* cash on hand and at bank

disponible *m* liquid assets

disponible available; [*actif*] liquid

disposer d'une somme to have a sum of money at one's disposal

disposer un chèque sur to draw a cheque on

disposition fiscale *f* tax provision

disposition à vue *f* sight clause

dissolution *f* dissolution

dissolution d'une société *f* winding up of a company

dissoudre to wind up, to dissolve

distribuer to distribute

distribuer un dividende to pay a dividend

distributeur *m* distributor

distributeur agréé *m* authorized dealer, authorized distributor

distributeur automatique *m* cash dispenser

distribution *f* distribution

distribution d'un bénéfice *f* distribution of profit

distribution de dividende *f* payment of a dividend

diversification *f* diversification

diversifier to diversify

dividende *m* dividend

dividende brut *m* gross dividend

dividende cumulatif *m* cumulative dividend

dividende final *m* final dividend

dividende net *m* net dividend

dividende supplémentaire *m* extra dividend

dividende d'action *m* share dividend

dividendes accrus *mpl* accrued dividends

diviser to divide

division *f* division

division du travail *f* division of labour

document comptable *m* accounting document

document interne à l'entreprise *m* internal company document

document légal *m* legal document

document publicitaire *m* publicity document

document transmissible *m* transferable document

document-type *m* form document

document d'assurance *m* insurance document

document de synthèse *m* financial statements

document de travail *m* working document

documents commerciaux *mpl* business documents

doit et avoir *m* debits and credits

domaine financier *m* financial field

domaine de compétence *m* field, area of expertise, area of competence

domicile fiscal *m* tax domicile

domiciliataire *m* [*d'effet*] paying agent; [*de chèque*] paying bank

domiciliation *f* domiciliation

domiciliation bancaire *f* paying bank

domicilier to domicile

dommages-intérêts *mpl* damages

dommages-intérêts compensatoires *mpl* compensation

dommages punitifs *mpl* punitive damages

données nominatives *fpl* personal data

données d'inventaire *fpl* inventory details

donner son congé to give notice

donneur d'aval *m* guarantor

dos d'un effet *m* back of a bill

dotation aux amortissements *f* depreciation provision, allowance for depreciation, charge to depreciation

dotation aux provisions *f* charge to provisions

dotation en capital *f* capital contribution

dotation en effectifs *f* staff increase

doter une provision to make a provision

double *m* duplicate

doubler to double

dresser to draw up

droit *m* law; [*prérogative*] right; [*imposition*] duty; [*taxe*] tax

droit bancaire *m* banking law

droit civil *m* civil law

droit communautaire *m* Community law

droit fiscal *m* tax law

droit fixe *m* fixed rate of duty

droit au bail *m* [*bien incorporel*] leasehold; [*comme bien incorporel*] right to a lease; [*poste de bilan*] leasehold acquisition costs

droit d'accès *m* right of access

droit d'usage *m* right of use

droit de courtage *m* brokerage (fee)

droit de rachat *m* repurchase right, buyback right

droit de souscription *m* subscription fee

droit des sociétés *m* company law

droit du travail *m* labour laws

droite *f* [*de graphe*] line

droits d'enregistrement *mpl* registration fees

droits de douane *mpl* customs duties, duty

droits de garde *mpl* safe custody fees

droits de tirage *mpl* drawing rights

dû due, owing; **en due forme** in due form

ducroire *m* del credere; [*agent*] del credere agent

dûment duly

duplicata *m* duplicate

durée *f* duration; [*de contrat*] term

durée d'amortissement *f* depreciation period

durée de crédit *f* term of loan

durée de validité *f* period of validity

durée de vie *f* useful life

écart *m* spread, variance

écart net *m* net variance

écart type *m* standard deviation

écart de prime *m* option spread

écarts de conversion *mpl* exchange adjustments

écarts de réévaluation *mpl* revaluation reserve

échange de lettres *m* exchange of letters

échanger to exchange

échanges commerciaux *mpl* trade

échanges internationaux *mpl* international trade

échappatoire fiscale *f* tax loophole

échapper à l'impôt to avoid tax

échapper à la faillite to avoid bankruptcy

échéance *f* [*de lettre de change*] maturity; [*de bail*] expiry date

échéance emprunt *f* loan maturity

échéance à vue *f* sight maturity

échéance de contrat *f* expiry date of a contract

échéance de police *f* maturity of a policy

échéances de fin de mois *fpl* end of month payments

échéancier *m* due date file, aged debtor schedule

échec des négociations *m* breakdown of negotiations

échelle mobile *f* sliding scale; [*clause*] escalator clause

échelle de temps *f* time scale

échelle des salaires *f* salary scale

échelon directorial *m* managerial level

échelonner des paiements to stagger payments, to spread out payments

échoir to fall due

école de commerce *f* business school

économie *f* economy

économie d'entreprise *f* business management, business studies

économie de frais *f* cost savings

économie de main-d'œuvre *f* labour saving

économie de temps *f* time saving

économies *fpl* savings

économies d'échelle *fpl* economies of scale

économique economic

économiser to save

économiste *mf* economist

écoulement de stocks *m* disposal of stocks

écrit *m* written document; *par écrit* in writing

écriture *f* [*comptabilité*] entry

écriture regroupement *f* consolidated entry

écriture d'inventaire *f* closing entries

écriture de clôture *f* closing entry

écriture de régularisation *f* adjusting entry

écritures comptables *fpl* accounting entries

effectif *m* number of employees, employees, staff

effectuer des démarches to take steps

effectuer un paiement to make a payment

effet *m* bill

effet endossé *m* endorsed bill

effet escompté *m* discounted bill

effet à courte échéance *m* short, short-dated bill

effet à date fixe *m* fixed-term bill

effet à longue échéance *m* long, long-dated bill

effet à vue *m* sight bill

effet à l'encaissement *m* bill for collection

effet au porteur *m* bill made out to bearer, bearer bill

effet de commerce *m* bill, commercial bill

effets à ordre *mpl* promissory notes

effets à payer *mpl* bills payable

effets à recevoir *mpl* bills receivable

efficience *f* efficiency

effritement des cours *m* erosion of prices

égalité des chances *f* equal opportunities

égalité des salaires *f* equal pay

élaborer to draw up

élasticité de l'offre *f* elasticity of supply

élasticité de la demande *f* elasticity of demand

élection du bureau *f* election of officers

éléments constitutifs du prix de revient *mpl* cost price factors, cost price contributors, cost factors

élévation du prix d'un produit *f* rise in the price of a product

élever to raise

élire to elect

émarger [*parapher*] to initial

embauche *f* recruitment, hiring

embaucher to recruit, to hire

émetteur d'une traite *m* issuer of a draft

émettre [*chèque, billets de banque*] to issue

émettre des avis to express opinions

émettre un emprunt to issue loan stock, to make a bond issue

émission *f* [*de chèque, billets de banque*] issue

émission d'actions *f* share issue

émission d'obligations *f* bond issue

émoluments *mpl* emoluments

emplacement *m* location, site

emploi *m* employment; [*poste*] job

emploi vacant *m* vacancy

emploi de fonds *m* use of funds

employé *m* employee

employé aux écritures *m* book-keeper

employé de bureau *m* office worker

employer des fonds to use funds

employer des ouvriers to employ workers

employeur *m* employer

emprunt *m* loan

emprunt garanti *m* secured loan

emprunt indexé *m* indexed loan

emprunt obligataire *m* bond issue, loan stock; [*titre*] debenture bond

emprunt obligataire convertible *m* convertible loan stock

emprunt à court terme *m* short-term loan

emprunt à long terme *m* long-term loan

emprunter to borrow

emprunter de l'argent à to borrow money from

emprunter sur to borrow against

emprunteur *m* borrower

emprunts et dettes financières *mpl* bank and other financial borrowings

emprunts à court terme *mpl* short-term borrowings

emprunts à long terme *mpl* long-term borrowings

encadrement *m* [*cadres*] executives; *fonctions d'encadrement* executive functions

encadrement du crédit *m* credit restriction, credit squeeze

encaissable cashable

encaisse *f* cash in till

encaissement *m* collection; [*de chèque*] paying in, encashment *Br*

encaisser to collect; [*chèque*] to cash, to encash *Br*

encaisser de l'argent to receive money; [*sur son compte*] to pay in cash

enchérissement de qch *m* increase in the price of sth

encourir des frais to incur expenses

encourir des risques to run risks

encours *m* loans outstanding, exposure

encours de production de biens *m* work-in-progress

endetté in debt

endettement *m* indebtedness, gearing

s'endetter to get into debt

endos *m* endorsement

endossable endorsable

endossataire *mf* endorsee

endossement *m* endorsement

endosser to endorse
endosser en blanc to blank endorse
endosser la responsabilité to assume responsibility
endosseur *m* endorser
engagement *m* commitment; [*de personnel*] hiring
engagement antérieur *m* prior engagement
engagement écrit *m* written undertaking
engagement à court terme *m* short-term undertaking
engager [*employé*] to take on
engager des capitaux to invest capital
engager des négociations to enter into negotiations
engager sa parole to give one's word
enquête *f* [*pour déterminer les faits*] investigation; [*pour recueillir les avis*] survey
enregistrement *m* [*de données, etc.*] recording, entering, logging
enregistrement comptable *m* accounting entry
enregistrement d'une commande *m* recording of an order, entering of an order, logging of an order
enregistrer to record, to enter, to log
enrichissement *m* [*d'entreprise*] increase in capital
entamer des négociations to open negotiations
entamer des poursuites to take legal proceedings
entamer son capital to break into one's capital
entente *f* agreement
entériner [*accord*] to ratify
enterrer [*projet*] to scrap
entité *f* item

entraîner des dépenses to involve expenditure
entrée d'argent *f* cash received
entrepreneur *m* entrepreneur
entreprise *f* business
entreprise commerciale *f* business operation
entreprise commune *f* joint venture
entreprise exportatrice *f* export company
entreprise familiale *f* family business
entreprise industrielle *f* manufacturing concern, manufacturing company
entreprise prestataire de services *f* service company
entreprise privée *f* private company
entreprise publique *f* public company
entreprise unipersonnelle *f* one-man business, sole trader
entreprise unipersonnelle à responsabilité limitée *f* sole trader with limited liability
entreprise en participation *f* joint venture
entrer en fonction to take up one's duties
entrer en liquidation to go into liquidation
entretenir [*comptes*] to keep in order
entretenir des relations to maintain relations
entretenir une correspondance to keep up a correspondence
entretien *m* [*entrevue*] interview
entrevue *f* interview
enveloppe budgétaire *f* budget, allotted budget, budget allocation
environnement commercial *m* business environment
envisager un chiffre d'affaires to

forecast turnover

envoi contre paiement cash with order

envoi de fonds *m* remittance of funds

épargne *f* saving

épargner to save

éponger des dettes to absorb debts

épuiser to use up

équation *f* equation

équilibrer to balance

équilibrer un budget to balance a budget, to break even

équipe commerciale *f* marketing team

équipe dirigeante *f* management team

équipe de vente *f* sales team, sales force

équipement *m* equipment

équipement industriel *m* industrial plant

équipements *mpl* equipment

erreur de calcul *f* miscalculation

escomptable discountable

escompte *m* discount

escompte commercial *m* trade discount

escompte officiel *m* bank discount rate

escompte de caisse *m* cash discount

escompte de règlement *m* discount for early payment, settlement discount

escompter to discount

escompter une hausse to anticipate an increase

espèces *fpl* cash

espèces en caisse *fpl* cash on hand

espionnage industriel *m* industrial espionage

essai *m* trial, test

essor de l'industrie *m* industrial expansion

estimation approximative *f* rough estimate

estimation des frais *f* estimate of costs

établir les comptes to draw up the accounts

établir un chèque to make out a cheque, to write a cheque

établir un chèque à l'ordre de to make a cheque payable to

établir une facture to draw up an invoice

établir une moyenne to work out an average

établir une société to set up a company

établissement *m* institution

établissement bancaire *m* bank

établissement déclarant *m* company making the return

établissement financier *m* financial institution

établissement payeur *m* paying bank

établissement d'un compte *m* opening an account, setting up an account

établissement de crédit *m* credit institution

établissement du bilan *m* drawing up of a balance sheet

établissement du prix de revient *m* calculation of the cost price

étalement *m* spreading, staggering

étaler sur plusieurs exercices to spread (out) over several financial years

étalon monétaire *m* monetary standard

étalon-or *m* gold standard

état imprimé *m* printed statement

état récapitulatif *m* [*comptabilité*] final assessment, adjustment account

état TVA *m* VAT statement, VAT return

état d'un compte *m* statement of account

état de caisse *m* cash statement

état de compte *m* position on an account

état de fortune *m* personal wealth statement, personal financial statement

état de rapprochement *m* reconciliation statement

état de situation *m* status report, state-of-play report

état des lieux *m* inventory of fixtures

état du marché *m* state of the market

éteindre une dette to pay off a debt

étendue *f* [*de variable*] range

étroitesse du marché *f* limited market

Ets (=établissements): Ets Lavency Lavency

étude *f* study

étude comparative *f* comparative study

étude de faisabilité *f* feasibility study

étude de marché *f* market research; *une étude de marché* a market study

étude des besoins *f* needs study, needs analysis

études de marché *fpl* market research studies

étudier un projet to analyse a project

EURL (=entreprise unipersonnelle à responsabilité limitée) *f* sole trader with limited liability

eurochèque *m* eurocheque

eurodevise *f* eurocurrency

eurodollar *m* eurodollar

eurofranc *m* eurofranc

évaluation *f* valuation

évaluation du coût *f* cost assessment

évaluer to evaluate, to assess

évasion fiscale *f* tax evasion

évasion de capitaux *f* flight of capital

éventail de produits *m* range of products

éviter la faillite to avoid bankruptcy

examen contradictoire *m* examination made in the presence of both parties to a contract

examiner to examine

excédent *m* surplus

excédent budgétaire *m* budget surplus

excédent de caisse *m* cash overs

excéder to exceed

exécuter to carry out

exécuter un contrat to execute a contract, to perform a contract

exécution *f* [*d'un contrat*] execution

exemplaire *m* copy; *en deux exemplaires* in duplicate

exemplaire d'un contrat *m* copy of a contract

exempt d'impôts tax exempt

exempter d'impôts to exempt from tax

exemption d'impôts *f* tax exemption

exercer des fonctions to carry out duties

exercer un contrôle sur to exercise control over

exercer un droit to exercise a right

exercice *m* financial year, fiscal year *Am*; [*d'un droit*] exercise

exercice bénéficiaire *m* profitable year

exercice budgétaire *m* financial year, fiscal year *Am*

exercice comptable *m* financial year, fiscal year *Am*, accounting year

exercice écoulé *m* last financial year

exercice financier *m* financial year, fiscal year *Am*

exercice fiscal *m* tax year

exercice en cours *m* current financial year, current fiscal year *Am*

exiger to demand

exigibilité: date d'exigibilité *f* due date

exigibilité immédiate immediately due

exigibilité de taxe *f* tax liability

exigible payable

existences en caisse *fpl* cash on hand

exonération fiscale *f* tax exemption

exonération d'impôts *f* tax exemption

exonération de responsabilité *f* exemption from liability

exonération de TVA *f* exemption from VAT

exonérer to exempt

exonérer d'impôt to exempt from tax

expansion *f* expansion

expansion industrielle *f* industrial expansion

expérimenté experienced

expert *m* expert

expert-comptable *m* chartered accountant, certified public accountant *Am*

expert financier *m* financial expert

expert fiscal *m* tax expert

expert-répartiteur *m* loss adjuster, average adjuster

expertise *f* valuation

expertise contradictoire *f* valuation made in the presence of both parties to a contract

expertiser [*des marchandises*] to value

expiration *f* expiry

expirer to expire

explicite explicit

exploitant *m* operator; *les risques courus par l'exploitant* the risks taken by the person running the business

exploitation *f* operation

exploitation commerciale *f* business concern

exploitation industrielle *f* industrial concern

exploitation d'un brevet *f* commercialization of a patent

exploiter [*commerce*] to operate, to run; [*employés*] to exploit

exposé de la situation de l'entreprise *m* statement of the company's position

expropriation *f* expropriation

exproprier to expropriate

extension *f* [*d'un contrat*] extension

extension du commerce *f* business expansion

externe outside

extinction d'une dette *f* discharge of a debt

extra-comptable [*ajustement*] off-balance sheet

extrait de compte *m* statement of account; [*banque*] bank statement

F

FAA (=frais accessoires d'achat) *mpl* incidental acquisition expenses

fabricant *m* manufacturer

fabrication *f* manufacture

fabrication en série *f* mass production

fabriquer to manufacture

face: faire face à la demande to meet demand

facilité d'écoulement *f* [*d'un produit*] saleability

facilités de paiement *fpl* payment facilities, easy terms

facteur *m* factor

facteur coût *m* cost factor

facteurs de la production *mpl* production factors

factoriel factorial

facturation *f* invoicing, billing

facture *f* invoice, bill

facture commerciale *f* commercial invoice

facture originale *f* original invoice

facture pro forma *f* pro forma invoice

facture provisoire *f* pro forma invoice

facture rectificative *f* amended invoice

facture d'achat *f* purchase invoice

facture d'avoir *f* credit note

facture de débit *f* debit note

facture de doit *f* debit note

facture de vente *f* sales invoice

facturer to invoice for

facturer qch à qn to invoice sb for sth

facturier *m* invoice clerk

facturier d'entrée *m* [*livre*] purchase ledger; [*employé*] purchase ledger clerk

facturier de sortie *m* [*livre*] sales ledger; [*employé*] sales ledger clerk

faiblir [*cours de la Bourse*] to weaken

failli *m* bankrupt

failli concordataire *m* bankrupt who has reached a settlement with his debtors

failli réhabilité *m* discharged bankrupt

faillite *f* bankruptcy; *faire faillite* to go bankrupt; *être en faillite* to be bankrupt

faire jouer une garantie to invoke a guarantee, to call a guarantee

faire des affaires to do business

faire des frais to run up expenses

faire du commerce to trade

faire la culbute to go bust

faire un prix to quote a price

fait générateur de taxe *m* event giving rise to a tax liability, tax event

fait en double exemplaire duplicate

falsifier to forge

fausse facture *f* false invoice
faute professionnelle *f* professional misconduct
faute de paiement for non-payment
faute de provision for lack of funds
faux chèque *m* forged cheque
faux frais *mpl* incidental expenses
faux en écritures *mpl* forgeries
FAV (=frais accessoires de vente) *mpl* incidental selling expenses
faveur: en faveur de in favour of
favorable favourable
fax *m* fax (machine)
faxer to fax
FDM (=fin de mois) end of month
FED (=Fonds européen de développement) *m* EDF
FEDER (=Fonds européen de développement régional) *m* ERDF
femme cadre *f* female executive
femme d'affaires *f* businesswoman
ferme firm; *acheter ferme* to make a firm purchase
fermer to close
fermeté des cours *f* steadiness of the market
fermeté des prix *f* steadiness of prices
fermeté du marché *f* steadiness of the market
fermeture *f* closing
fermeture d'un compte *f* closing of an account
feuille d'avancement *f* flow sheet
feuille d'impôts *f* tax return
feuille de liquidation *f* settlement note
feuille de paie *f* payroll; [*de l'employé*] pay slip
feuille de présence *f* attendance sheet
feuille de versement *f* paying-in slip

feuillet *m* sheet
fiche d'imputation *f* data entry form
fiche d'imputation comptable *f* accounts record form
fiche de paie *f* pay slip
fiche de stock *f* stock sheet
fictif fictitious
fiduciaire fiduciary
figurer to appear
figurer dans les livres to appear in the books
filiale *f* subsidiary
filiale consolidée *f* consolidated subsidiary
filiale de distribution *f* marketing subsidiary
filiale de vente *f* sales subsidiary
fin: de fin de mois end-of-month
fin de l'exercice *f* end of the financial year; *de fin d'exercice* year-end; *en fin d'exercice* at the end of the financial year
finance *f* finance
financement *m* financing, funding
financement à court terme *m* short-term financing
financement à long terme *m* long-term financing
financement à moyen terme *m* medium-term financing
financement des exportations *m* export financing
financer to finance, to fund
financier *m* financier
financier financial
financièrement financially
firme *f* firm, business
fisc *m* Inland Revenue, Internal Revenue *Am*, tax man
fiscaliste *mf* tax consultant
fiscalité *f* tax system
fiscalité excessive *f* excessive taxation

fiscalité des entreprises *f* corporate taxation

fixation de l'impôt *f* tax assessment

fixe fixed

fixer un plafond to set a ceiling

fléchir to fall

fléchissement des prix *m* fall in prices

flotter to float; *faire flotter* to float

fluctuation *f* fluctuation

fluctuation des cours *f* exchange rate fluctuation; price fluctation

fluctuation des prix *f* price fluctuation

fluctuer to fluctuate

flux *m* flow

flux monétaire *m* cashflow

flux de fonds *m* flow of funds

flux de trésorerie *m* cashflow

FMI (=Fonds monétaire international) *m* IMF

FNGS (=Fonds de garantie des salaires) *m* national guarantee fund for the payment of salaries

fonction *f* function; *être fonction de* to be a function of

fonctionnaire *mf* official, civil servant

fonctionnement *m* running

fonctions *fpl* [*de l'entreprise*] functions; [*d'employé*] duties, responsibilities

fonctions d'encadrement *fpl* executive functions

fondateur *m* founder

fondation d'une entreprise *f* setting up of a business

fondé de pouvoir *m* [*mandant*] proxy; [*directeur de banque*] manager with signing authority

fonder [*entreprise*] to set up

fonds commercial *m* goodwill

fonds commun de placement *m* investment trust, mutual fund

Fonds européen de développement *m* European Development Fund

Fonds européen de développement régional *m* European Regional Development Fund

Fonds monétaire international *m* International Monetary Fund

fonds propres *mpl* equity

fonds publics *mpl* government funds; [*valeurs*] government stocks

Fonds social européen *m* European Social Fund

fonds de chômage *m* unemployment fund

fonds de clientèle *mpl* customer base

fonds de commerce *m* goodwill; [*boutique, etc.*] business

fonds de garantie *m* guarantee fund

Fonds de garantie des salaires *m* national guarantee fund for the payment of salaries

fonds de grève *m* strike fund

fonds de prévoyance *m* contingency fund

fonds de réserve *m* reserve funds

fonds de roulement *m* working capital

fonds de secours *m* emergency fund

force majeure *f* force majeure, act of God

force de travail *f* workforce

force de vente *f* sales force

forcé forced

forclusion *f* foreclosure

forfait *m* lump sum

forfaitage *m* forfaiting

forfaitaire in one amount, lump sum

forfaitairement in a lump sum; [*facturer*] in one amount

formalité *f* formality

formation *f* training

formation continue *f* continuous training

formation permanente *f* continuous training

formation du capital *f* capital formation

forme sociale *f* type of company

former un employé to train an employee

former une société to form a company

formulaire *m* form

formule de calcul *f* mathematical formula

formule de chèque *f* cheque form

formule de crédit *f* credit application form

forte hausse *f* sharp rise

forte somme *f* large sum of money

fourchette de prix *f* price range

fournir à la dépense to defray expenses

fournir des fonds to provide funds

fournir des renseignements to supply information

fournir une caution to give a guarantee, to provide security

fournisseur *m* supplier

fourniture *f* supply(ing)

fournitures *fpl* supplies

foyer fiscal *m* tax domicile

fraction *f* fraction

fraction d'intérêt *f* interest accrued

frais *mpl* expenses, costs

frais accessoires *mpl* incidental costs, incidental expenses

frais accessoires d'achat *mpl* incidental acquisition expenses

frais accessoires de vente *mpl* incidental selling expenses

frais financiers *mpl* interest charges, financial costs

frais fixes *mpl* fixed charges

frais généraux *mpl* overheads, overhead *Am*

frais variables *mpl* variable costs

frais d'achat *mpl* purchase costs

frais d'administration *mpl* administrative costs; [*en échange d'un service*] handling charge

frais d'administration générale *mpl* general overheads, general overhead *Am*, general administration costs

frais d'entretien *mpl* maintenance costs

frais d'établissement *mpl* startup costs

frais d'exploitation *mpl* operating costs

frais de banque *mpl* bank charges

frais de bureau *mpl* office expenses

frais de commission *mpl* commission costs

frais de constitution *mpl* [*de société*] startup costs; [*de compte*] set-up fee

frais de déplacement *mpl* travel expenses

frais de douane *mpl* customs duties

frais de fabrication *mpl* manufacturing costs, production costs

frais de gestion *mpl* administration costs

frais de représentation *mpl* entertainment expenses

frais de tenue de compte *mpl* account charges; [*compte bancaire*] bank charges

franc or *m* gold value of the franc

franc d'impôts tax free, free of tax

franchisage *m* [*contrat*] franchising

franchise *f* franchise; *en franchise de TVA* zero-rated, free of VAT

franchise douanière *f* exemption from customs duty

franchise de TVA *f* VAT exemption, zero-rating

franchisé *m* franchisee, franchise holder

franchisé franchised

franchiseur *m* franchisor

frapper qch d'un impôt to impose tax on sth

frapper qch d'une amende to impose a fine on sth

fraude fiscale *f* tax evasion

fraude sur les produits *f* product fraud

frauder le fisc to evade tax

frauduleusement fraudulently

frauduleux fraudulent

frein à l'expansion *m* brake on growth

freiner to slow down

frictionnel [*chômage*] temporary

frontière *f* border

fructueux profitable

fuite de capitaux *f* flight of capital

fusion *f* merger

fusionner to merge

G

gage mobilier *m* mortgage over assets, mortgage over property

gagé pledged

gager qch to deposit sth as security, to pledge sth as security

gageur *m* pledgor

gagiste *mf* pledgee

gagner gros to make large profits

gagner de l'argent to earn money

gain *m:* **obtenir des gains de compétitivité** to become more competitive

gain latent *m* unrealized gain

gain d'argent *m* financial gain

gain de change *m* exchange gain

gamme de prix *f* price range

gamme de produits *f* product range

garant *m* guarantor

garant solidaire *m* joint and several guarantor

garantie *f* guarantee; [*de produit*] guarantee, warranty; *sous garantie* under guarantee, under warranty

garantie bancaire *f* bank guarantee

garantie contractuelle *f* contractual guarantee

garantie conventionnelle *f* contractual cover

garantie inconditionnelle *f* unconditional guarantee

garantie totale *f* total guarantee

garantie à première demande *f* first

demand guarantee

garantie de bonne exécution *f* performance bond

garantie de bonne fin *f* performance bond

garantie de solvabilité *f* liquidity guarantee

garantir un emprunt to secure a loan

garde en dépôt de titres *f* safe custody

gaspillage d'argent *m* waste of money

GATT *m* GATT

gel de crédits *m* credit freeze

gelé frozen

genre d'affaires *m* line of business

gens d'affaires *mpl* business people

gérance *f* management

gérance libre *f* rented business

gérance salariée *f* salaried management

gérant *m* manager

gérant majoritaire *m* manager with a controlling interest

gérant minoritaire *m* manager with a minority interest

gérant d'affaires *m* business manager

gérant non associé *m* salaried manager, manager with no holding in a business

gérer to manage

gérer un compte to manage an account

gérer une affaire to handle a matter

gestion *f* management

gestion administrative *f* administration

gestion financière *f* financial management

gestion qualité *f* quality control, quality management

gestion d'entreprise *f* business management

gestion de biens *f* asset management

gestion de crédit *f* credit management

gestion de portefeuille *f* portfolio management

gestion de production *f* production management

gestion de stocks *f* stock control, inventory management

gestion de trésorerie *f* cashflow management

gestion des sociétés *f* business management

gestionnaire *mf* manager

GIE (=Groupement d'intérêt économique) *m* intercompany partnership

global: somme globale *f* lump sum

gonflement *m* increase

gonflement du volume du crédit *m* increase in bank lending

gouverner une entreprise to manage a business

grand livre *m* ledger

grand livre général *m* nominal ledger, general ledger

grand livre de paie *m* wages ledger

grand livre des achats *m* purchase ledger

grand livre des comptes *m* accounts ledger

grand livre des ventes *m* sales ledger

graphe *m* graph

graphique *m* diagram, *m* chart

graphique à secteurs *m* pie chart

graphique à tuyaux d'orgue *m* bar chart

gratification *f* bonus

gratification de fin d'année *f* end of year bonus

gratuit free, free of charge
grève *f* strike; *faire (la) grève* to go on strike
grève générale *f* general strike
grève partielle *f* partial strike
grève sauvage *f* wildcat strike
grève surprise *f* lightning strike
grève tournante *f* staggered strike
grève de protestation *f* protest strike
grève de solidarité *f* sympathy strike
grève du zèle *f* work to rule, go-slow
grevé de dettes saddled with debts
grever un budget to put a strain on a budget
gréviste *mf* striker
grille d'analyse par fonction *f* functional analysis chart

grille d'imputation *f* table of account codes
grille des salaires *f* salary scale
groupe de pression *m* pressure group
groupe de travail *m* work group, working party
groupement *m* group
groupement professionnel *m* trade association
groupement d'intérêt économique *m* intercompany partnership
guerre économique *f* economic warfare
guerre des prix *f* price war
guerre des tarifs *f* price war

H

H. (=hors) TVA net of VAT
habilité à signer [*employé de banque*] authorized to sign
habillage de bilan *m* window-dressing of a balance-sheet
hausse subite *f* sudden rise
hausse de prix *f* price rise
hausse des cours *f* stock market rise
hausser les prix to raise prices, to increase prices
haut: à haute valeur ajoutée high value added

haut fonctionnaire *m* senior official
haut de bilan *m* [*fonds propres*] shareholders' funds
haute direction *f* senior management
haute finance *f* high finance
hauteur: à hauteur de [*s'engager*] up to
hebdomadaire weekly
heure-machine *f* machine-hour
heure d'ouverture *f* opening time
heure de fermeture *f* closing time
heures supplémentaires *fpl*

overtime
heures d'ouverture *fpl* opening hours
heures de bureau *fpl* office hours
heures de travail *fpl* hours of work, working hours
hiérarchie administrative *f* administrative hierarchy
hiérarchique: par la voie hiérarchique through official channels
hiérarchisation des fonctions *f* grading of jobs
hiérarchiser les emplois to grade jobs
histogramme *m* bar chart, histogram
holding *m* holding company
homme d'affaires *m* businessman
homologation *f* approval
homologue *mf* counterpart, opposite number
homologuer to approve
honoraire honorary
honoraires *mpl* fees
honorer to honour

honorifique honorary
horaire flexible *m* flexible hours, flexitime
horaire variable *m* flexible hours, flexitime
hors bilan off-balance sheet
hors comptabilité off-balance sheet
hors cote: marché hors cote *m* unlisted market, over-the-counter market
hors taxe net of tax; [*exempt de taxe*] tax free
hors TVA net of VAT
hôtesse d'accueil *f* receptionist
HT (=hors taxe) before tax, exclusive of tax; *le montant HT de la facture* the invoice value net of tax
huissier *m* bailiff
hypothécable mortgageable
hypothécaire mortgage
hypothèque de premier rang *f* first legal mortgage
hypothéquer un bien to mortgage an asset

illégal illegal
illégalité *f* illegality
illimité unlimited
image fidèle *f* true and fair view

image de marque *f* brand image
immatriculation *f* registration
immatriculer to register
immobilier *m* property

immobilisation *f* fixed asset

immobilisation de capitaux *f* tied up capital, capital assets

immobilisations corporelles *fpl* tangible fixed assets

immobilisations financières *fpl* long-term investments

immobilisations incorporelles *fpl* intangible fixed assets

immobilisations non financières *fpl* physical fixed assets

immobilisations en cours *fpl* fixed assets in progress

immobiliser [*fonds*] to tie up

impasse *f* deadlock

impayé *m* unpaid bill

impayé unpaid

impense *f* property improvement expense

*s'***implanter à l'étranger** to set up overseas

implicite implied

importance d'un crédit *f* size of a loan

importateur *m* importer

importateur importing

importations *fpl* imports

importer to import

imposable taxable

imposer un blocage des prix to impose a price freeze

imposition *f* taxation

impôt *m* tax

impôt direct *m* direct tax

impôt foncier *m* property tax

impôt indirect *m* indirect tax

impôt progressif *m* graduated income tax

impôt sur le capital *m* capital tax

impôt sur le chiffre d'affaires *m* turnover tax, sales tax

impôt sur le revenu *m* income tax

impôt sur les bénéfices *m* corporation tax

impôt sur les traitements et salaires *m* tax on wages and salaries

imprimé *m* [*formulaire*] form

imprimé fiscal *m* tax return

improductif [*capital*] non-productive, idle

imputable chargeable

imputation rationnelle *f* practical capacity cost allocation

imputation à *f* charge to

imputer qch sur to charge sth to

imputer une dépense sur un chapitre du budget to charge an expense to a budgeted account

inabordable unaffordable

inacquitté unpaid

inactif [*marché*] slack

inanimé [*marché boursier*] sluggish

incessibilité *f* non-transferability

incessible non-transferable

incidence fiscale *f* tax implications

incitation fiscale *f* tax incentive

inclusivement inclusive

inconvertible non-convertible

incorporation des réserves au capital *f* capitalization of reserves

incorporel [*actif*] intangible

incoté unquoted

indéfectible non-wasting

indemnisable compensable

indemnisation *f* compensation

indemniser to compensate

indemniser qn de qch to compensate sb for sth

indemnité *f* compensation

indemnité compensatrice *f* compensation

indemnité compensatrice de congés payés *f* pay in lieu of holidays

indemnité compensatrice de préavis *f* compensation in lieu of notice

indemnité complémentaire *f*
additional allowance

indemnité conventionnelle *f*
contractual allowance

indemnité journalière *f* daily
allowance

indemnité de chômage *f*
unemployment benefit

indemnité de clientèle *f*
compensation for loss of custom

indemnité de déplacement *f* travel
allowance

indemnité de licenciement *f*
severance pay

indemnité de logement *f*
accommodation allowance

indemnité de maladie *f* sickness
benefit

indemnité de représentation *f*
entertainment allowance

indemnité de retard *f* late payment
penalty

indemnité de rupture *f* severance
pay

indemnité de rupture abusive *f*
compensation for breach of
contract

indemnité de séjour *f* living
expenses

indemnité de transport *f* transport
allowance

indemnité de vie chère *f* cost-of-
living allowance

indépendant [*travailleur*] self-
employed

indexation *f* index-linking

indexation des salaires *f* index-
linking of salaries

indexé index-linked

**indexer une retraite sur le coût de
la vie** to index-link a pension to the
cost of living

indicateur économique *m* economic
indicator

indice boursier *m* share index

indice CAC 40 *m equivalent to* FTSI

indice des cours d'actions *m* share
price index

indice des prix *m* price index

indice des prix de détail *m* retail
price index

indice des prix de gros *m* wholesale
price index

indice des prix et des salaires *m*
wage and price index

indice du coût de la vie *m* cost-of-
living index

indiquer un prix to quote a price

indisponible unavailable

indivis: par indivis in joint
ownership

indivision *f* joint possession

indûment incorrectly

industrialisation *f* industrialization

industrialiser to industrialize

industrie *f* industry

industriel *m* manufacturer,
industrialist

industriel industrial

inéchangeable non-exchangeable

inescomptable undiscountable

inexécution d'un contrat *f* non-
performance of a contract

inexigible not due

inexploité untapped

inflation *f* inflation

inflation galopante *f* galloping
inflation

inflation rampante *f* rampant
inflation

inflation des prix *f* price inflation

inflation des salaires *f* wage
inflation

inflation par la demande *f* demand-
pull inflation

inflation par les coûts *f* cost-push inflation

inflationniste inflationary

infrastructure organisationnelle *f* organizational structure

ingénieur civil *m* civil engineer

ingénieur-conseil *m* consulting engineer

ingénieur technico-commercial *m* sales engineer

ingénieur des ventes *m* sales engineer

initial initial

injecter des capitaux dans une entreprise to inject capital into a business

injection d'argent *f* injection of money

innovation *f* innovation

innover to innovate

inscription *f* registration

inscription comptable *f* accounting entry

inscription hypothécaire *f* registration of a mortgage

inscription sur le registre du commerce *f* registration in the trade register

inscriptions nominatives *fpl* registered shares

s'inscrire en baisse to fall

s'inscrire en hausse to rise

insolvabilité *f* insolvency

insolvable insolvent

inspecteur des contributions *m* tax inspector

Inspection générale des Finances *f* department responsible for auditing public bodies

Inspection de la Sécurité sociale *f* Social Security Inspectorate

instabilité des cours *f* unsteadiness of prices

instable [*marché boursier*] unsettled

installations techniques *fpl* plant and machinery

installer to install

instances dirigeantes *fpl* governing body

instaurer des mesures to bring in new measures

institut de crédit *m* credit institution

institution de crédit *f* credit institution

institutionnel institutional

instruction *f* instruction

instrument de crédit *m* credit instrument

instrument de paiement *m* payment instrument

insuffisance de provision *f* insufficient funds

intangible intangible

intégralement libéré fully paid up

intégrer to integrate

intégrer une somme dans une facture to include a sum in an invoice

interbancaire interbank

interdit: frapper d'interdit to impose a ban on

intéressement aux résultats *m* employee profit-sharing scheme

intéresser les employés aux bénéfices to provide an employee profit-sharing scheme

intérêt *m* interest

intérêt bancaire *m* bank interest

intérêt couru *m* accrued interest

intérêt fixe *m* fixed interest

intérêt simple *m* simple interest

intérêt variable *m* variable-rate interest

intérêt de retard *m* interest on arrears

intérêts compensatoires *mpl*

damages

intérêts composés *m* compound interest

intérêts dus *mpl* interest due

intérêts échus *mpl* accrued interest

intérêts exigibles *mpl* interest due and payable

intérêts moratoires *mpl* default interest, penalty interest

intérêts à échoir *mpl* accruing interest

intérimaire *mf* temporary worker, temp

intérimaire temporary; *directeur intérimaire* acting director

intermédiaire intermediate

interne internal; [*de la société*] in-house

interprétation d'un contrat *f* interpretation of a contract

intersyndical inter-union

intersyndicale *f* inter-union group

intitulé *m* title; [*de compte*] title, heading

introduire en Bourse to introduce on the Stock Exchange

introduire sur le marché to bring onto the market, to launch

introduire une action en justice to start legal proceedings, to bring action

introduire une instance to start legal proceedings

inventaire *m* inventory

inventaire comptable *m* book inventory

inventaire effectif *m* physical inventory

inventaire intermittent *m* periodical

inventory

inventaire permanent *m* perpetual inventory

inventaire théorique *m* theoretical inventory

inventorier to list

investir to invest

investir à court terme to make a short-term investment

investir à long terme to make a long-term investment

investir à moyen terme to make a medium-term investment

investir des capitaux to invest capital

investissement *m* investment

investissement à court terme *m* short-term investment

investissement à l'étranger *m* overseas investment, foreign investment

investissement de capitaux *m* capital investment

investissements privés *mpl* private investment

investissements productifs *mpl* interest-bearing investments

investisseur *m* investor

investisseur institutionnel *m* institutional investor

investisseur privé *m* private investor

irrachetable [*obligation*] irredeemable

irrécouvrable unrecoverable

irrégularités *fpl* irregularities

irrégulier [*marché boursier*] unsteady

irremboursable [*obligation*] irredeemable

J

jetons de présence *mpl* director's fees

jeu de bourse *m* stock market gamble

joint venture *f* joint venture

jouer en bourse to speculate

jouissance d'intérêts *f* entitlement to interest

jour: à jour up to date; *mettre à jour* to update; *mise à jour* update; *à 30 jours fin de mois* 30 days from the end of the month; *payer dans les 30 jours* to pay (at) thirty days

jour chômé *m* public holiday

jour férié *m* public holiday

jour franc *m* clear day

jour ouvrable *m* working day

jour ouvré *m* working day

jour de bourse *m* trading day

jour de grâce *m* day of grace

jour de liquidation *m* settlement day

jour de paiement *m* payment day

jour de valeur *m* value date

journal *m* ledger

journal analytique *m* analysis ledger

journal factures-clients *m* sales invoice ledger

journal factures-fournisseurs *m* purchase invoice ledger

journal d'entreprise *m* company magazine

journal de banque *m* bank book

journal de bord *m* log book

journal de caisse *m* cash book

journal de paie *m* wages ledger

journal des achats *m* purchase ledger

journal des effets à payer *m* bills payable ledger

journal des effets à recevoir *m* bills receivable ledger

journal des rendus *m* returns ledger, returns book

journal des ventes *m* sales ledger

journée de huit heures *f* eight-hour day

journée de travail *f* working day

jours d'intérêt *mpl* interest days

judiciaire [*vente*] court-ordered

jugement *m* judgement

jugement déclaratif de faillite *m* adjudication in bankruptcy

juguler l'inflation to check inflation

jumelage d'entreprises *m* twinning of companies

juridique legal

juriste *mf* lawyer

justificatif de paiement *m* proof of payment

K

kilofranc *m* thousand francs
krach boursier *m* Stock Market crash

L

label *m* [*marque*] trademark
lancer des titres sur le marché to issue shares
lancer un emprunt to issue a bond
lancer une nouvelle entreprise to launch a new company
l/c (=lettre de crédit) *f* L/C
LCR (=lettre de change relevé) *f* bills of exchange statement
légal legal
légaliser des documents to certify documents
légaliser une signature to authenticate a signature
législation *f* legislation
législation financière *f* financial legislation
législation fiscale *f* tax legislation

législation du travail *f* employment legislation
lettre commerciale *f* business letter
lettre d'avis *f* advice note
lettre de change *f* bill of exchange, B/E
lettre de change relevé *f* bills of exchange statement
lettre de confirmation *f* letter of confirmation
lettre de convocation *f* notice of meeting
lettre de crédit *f* letter of credit
lettre de crédit irrévocable *f* irrevocable letter of credit
lettre de garantie *f* letter of guarantee
lettre de garantie bancaire *f* bank guarantee

49

lettre de licenciement *f* letter of dismissal

lettre de poursuite *f* debt chasing letter

lettre de rappel *f* reminder

lettre de recommandation *f* reference

lettre de relance *f* follow-up letter

lettre de relance des impayés *f* debt chasing letter

levée des impôts *f* collection of taxes

levée des titres *f* taking delivery of shares

lever des impôts to collect taxes

levier financier *m* financial leverage

libellé au porteur [*chèque*] made out to bearer

libellé en [*chèque*] made out in; [*cours*] quoted in, given in

libeller à l'ordre de to make out to the order of, to make payable to

libeller un chèque to make out a cheque, to write a cheque

libeller une facture to make out an invoice

libération d'une action *f* paying up of a share

libérer entièrement une action to pay up a share in full

libérer un débiteur to discharge a debtor, to release a debtor

licence *f* licence

licenciement avec préavis *m* dismissal with notice

licenciement sans préavis *m* dismissal without notice

licencier un travailleur to dismiss a worker

lié par contrat bound by contract

lier qn to be binding on sb

lieu d'émission *m* place of issue

lieu de paiement *m* place of payment

ligne de crédit *f* line of credit, credit line

limitatif [*clause*] restrictive

limite d'âge *f* age limit

limite d'endettement *f* borrowing limit

limite de crédit *f* credit limit

limiter la production to limit production

liquidateur *m* liquidator

liquidation *f* [*d'entreprise*] liquidation; [*de dette, compte*] settlement

liquidation judiciaire *f* official receivership

liquidation de fin de mois *f* end of month settlement

liquidation de quinzaine *f* fortnightly settlement

liquidation des biens *f* liquidation of assets

liquide liquid

liquider une dette to pay off a debt

liquider une société to wind up a business

liquidité *f* liquidity

liquidités *fpl* liquid assets

liquidités internationales *fpl* international liquid assets

liste des actionnaires *f* list of shareholders

litige *m* legal dispute

litigieux [*contrat*] in dispute

livraison des titres *f* delivery of securities

livre-journal *m* book of original entry

livre d'achats *m* purchase ledger

livre d'actionnaires *m* register of shareholders

livre d'inventaire *m* annual accounts ledger

livre de caisse *m* cash book

livre de commandes *m* order book

livre de comptes *m* book of

accounts, journal
livre de dépenses *m* cash book
livre de paie *m* wages ledger
livre des créanciers *m* accounts
  payable book/ledger
livre des débiteurs *m* accounts
  receivable book/ledger
livre des effets à payer *m* bills
  payable book/ledger
livre des effets à recevoir *m* bills
  receivable book/ledger
livre des entrées *m* purchase book/
  ledger
livre des inventaires *m* stock book
livre des réclamations *m* claims book
livre des rendus *m* returns book/
  ledger
livre des sorties *m* sales ledger
livre des ventes *m* sales ledger
livret de compte *m* bank book
locataire *mf* tenant, lessee
locateur *m* lessor
locatif rental
location *f* rental, lease
location-bail *f* leasing

location gérance *f* rented business
location-vente *f* hire purchase,
  installment plan *Am*
locaux commerciaux *mpl* business
  premises
lock-out *m* lock-out
logistique *adj* logistic
loi fiscale *f* tax law, fiscal law
loi de l'offre et de la demande *f* law
  of supply and demand
loi des finances *f* finance act
loi sur les sociétés anonymes *f*
  public company law
louer [*locaux*] to rent, to lease *Am*;
  [*équipement*] to lease
loyaux coûts *mpl* [*frais de contrat*]
  costs arising from execution of a
  deed
loyer arriéré *m* rent arrears
loyer commercial *m* commercial rent
loyer nominal *m* nominal rent
loyer de l'argent *m* cost of money
lu et approuvé read and approved
lucratif: sans but lucratif non-
  profit-making

macro-économique macro-
  economic
mailing *m* mailshot
main courante *f* day book

main-d'œuvre *f* work force,
  manpower, labour
main-d'œuvre qualifiée *f* skilled
  labour

mainlevée d'une saisie *f* lifting of an execution order

se **maintenir** [*cours de bourse*] to hold up, to hold steady

maison mère *f* parent company

maison de commerce *f* company

majoration *f* markup

majoration de prix *f* price markup

majorer [*prix*] to mark up; [*salaires*] to increase

majorité absolue *f* absolute majority

majorité relative *f* relative majority

malus *m* [*assurance*] loss of no-claims bonus

malversation *f* embezzlement

management *m* management

manager *m* manager

mandant *m* principal

mandat *m* mandate

mandataire *mf* agent

manier de l'argent to handle money

manque à gagner *m* loss of earnings

manque de caisse *m* cash unders

manque de fonds *m* lack of funds

manuel manual

marasme économique *m* economic stagnation

marc: au marc le franc pro rata

marchand *m* dealer

marchand market

marchandisage *m* merchandizing

marché *m* market; [*affaire, transaction*] deal

Marché commun *m* Common Market

marché financier *m* financial market

marché monétaire *m* money market

marché officiel *m* official market

Marché unique *m* Single Market

marché à terme *m* futures market

marché de l'Eurodevise *m* euromarket

marché des capitaux *m* capital market

marché des changes *m* foreign exchange market

marché des titres *m* securities market

marché des valeurs mobilières *m* share market

marché du travail *m* labour market

marché hors cote *m* unlisted market, over-the-counter market, OTC market

marge *f* margin

marge bénéficiaire *f* profit margin

marge brute d'autofinancement *f* cashflow, funds generated by operations

marge commerciale *f* gross profit margin

marge commerciale moyenne *f* average gross profit margin

marge nette *f* net margin

marge supplémentaire *f* additional margin

marge de crédit *f* credit margin

marge de négociation *f* room for negotiation

marge de sécurité *f* safety margin

marge sur coûts variables *f* contribution

marginal marginal

marque *f* trademark

marque déposée *f* registered trademark

marque protégée *f* registered trademark

marque de commerce *f* trademark

marque de fabrique *f* trademark

masse active *f* assets

masse monétaire *f* money supply

masse passive *f* liabilities

masse salariale *f* staff costs

matérialiser to realize

matériel industriel *m* plant

matières *fpl* material

matières consommables *fpl* supplies, consumables

matières premières *fpl* raw materials

matricule *m* number

matriculer to register

maturité *f* maturity; ***arriver à maturité*** to mature

maximum maximum

MBA (=marge brute d'autofinancement) cashflow, funds generated by operations

médiateur d'entreprises *m* mediator

médiation *f* mediation

membre actif *m* active member

membre fondateur *m* founding member

membre honoraire *m* honorary member

membre du comité *m* committee member

membre du conseil d'administration *m* member of the board, board member

mémoire *m* report

mémorandum *m* memo

mensualiser to make payable by the month

mensualités *fpl* monthly instalments

mensuel monthly

mensuellement monthly

menus frais *mpl* petty expenses, incidental expenses

mercatique *f* marketing

message télex *m* telex (message)

messagerie *f* [*électronique*] electronic mail

méthode à échelles *f* daily balance interest calculation

méthode de financement *f* funding method

méthode de travail *f* work method

méthode par échelles *f* daily balance interest calculation

mettre à jour to update

mettre au point [*plan d'action*] to finalize

mettre en inventaire to inventory

minimum minimum

ministère *m* department, ministry

ministère de l'Economie et des Finances *m* Treasury

ministère des Finances *m* Exchequer *Br*

ministère du Commerce et de l'Industrie *m* Department of Trade and Industry

minoration *f* reduction

minorer des impôts to reduce taxes

mise à jour *f* update

mise à pied *f* dismissal

mise de fonds *f* investment

mise en circulation *f* [*de billets*] issue

mise en demeure *f* formal notice; [*de paiement*] formal demand

mise en exploitation *f* [*de machine*] commissioning

mise en service *f* commissioning

mise en vente *f* putting up for sale

mission *f* [*d'employé*] assignment

mission commerciale *f* business assignment

mi-temps: à mi-temps part-time

mobilisable [*créance*] discountable

mobilisation de fonds *f* raising of funds

mobiliser [*des créances*] to discount

mobiliser de l'argent to raise money

mobilité *f* mobility

modalités de paiement *fpl* methods of payment

mode opératoire *m* modus operandi

mode de codification *m* coding method

mode de paiement *m* method of payment

mode de règlement *m* method of payment

modération d'impôt *f* tax reduction

modification d'un contrat *f* amendment of a contract

moins less, minus

moins-disant *m* lowest bidder

moins-perçu *m* short payment

moins-value *f* capital loss

monétaire monetary

monnaie scripturale *f* deposit money

monnaie de compte *f* money of account

monnaie de papier *f* paper money

monnaie de réserve *f* reserve currency

montant *m* amount

montant brut *m* gross (amount)

montant exonéré de TVA *m* VAT exempt amount

montant maximum *m* maximum amount

montant minimum *m* minimum amount

montant net *m* net (total)

montant total *m* total amount

montant du retour net *m* net return

monter en flèche to soar

monter une entreprise to set up a business

moratoire *m* moratorium

mouvement ascensionnel *m* upward movement

mouvement boursier *m* stock market movement

mouvement d'un compte *m* account movement

mouvement de baisse *m* downward movement

mouvement des capitaux *m* movement of capital

mouvement des cours *m* price fluctuation

mouvement des devises *m* currency fluctuation

mouvement des prix *m* price fluctuation

mouvement des valeurs *m* share movements

mouvements monétaires *mpl* monetary fluctuations

moyennant paiement in exchange for payment, subject to payment

moyenne *f* average; [*en statistique*] mean

moyenne annuelle *f* yearly average

moyenne mensuelle *f* monthly average

moyenne pondérée *f* weighted average

moyenne simple *f* simple average

moyens disponibles *mpl* available means

moyens financiers *mpl* financial means

moyens liquides *mpl* liquid resources

moyens de paiement *mpl* means of payment

multilatéral multilateral

multinationale *f* multinational

multiplier to multiply

multisectoriel multisector

mutuel mutual

mutuelle *f* mutual insurance company

N

nantir des valeurs to deposit shares as security

nantir un prêt to secure a loan

nantissement *m* pledge, guarantee, security

nationalisation *f* nationalization

nationalisé nationalized

nationaliser to nationalize

naufrage *m* [*d'entreprise*] failure

négociabilité d'un titre *f* negotiability of an instrument

négociable negotiable

négociant *m* merchant

négociation *f* negotiation

négociation collective *f* collective bargaining

négociations précontractuelles *fpl* precontractual negotiations

négociations à prime *fpl* options trading

négociations à terme *fpl* futures trading

négociations au comptant *fpl* spot trading

négocier to negotiate

net net

net commercial *m* net profit

net financier *m* net interest income; [*à payer*] net interest charges; [*prix net*] net price, net

net à payer *m* net payable

net d'impôt net of tax

niveau des prix *m* price levels

niveau des salaires *m* salary levels

niveler par le bas to level down

nom commercial *m* trade name

nominal *m* [*d'action*] nominal value; [*d'obligation*] par value

nominal nominal, par

nomination à un poste *f* appointment to a post

nommer qn directeur to appoint sb manager

non dilué undiluted

non-exécution *f* [*d'un contrat*] non-performance

non-paiement *m* non-payment

non-salarié unsalaried

non-syndiqué *m* non-union worker

non-valeur *f* [*créance*] worthless amount

non vérifié unaudited

norme de travail *f* work standard

notarié certified by a notary; [*acte*] notarized

notation *f* rating

note de commission *f* commission note, fee note

note de couverture *f* cover note

note de crédit *f* credit note

note de débit *f* debit note

note de frais *f* expense account; [*présentée après coup*] expenses

note de rappel *f* reminder

note de service *f* memo

notification *f* notification

notifier qn de qch to notify sb of sth

nouveaux emprunts *mpl* new borrowings

nouvelle émission *f* [*d'actions*] new issue

noyau dur *m* hard core

nu-propriétaire *m* reversionary owner

nue-propriété *f* reversionary ownership

nul et non avenu null and void

nullité d'un contrat *f* invalidity of a contract

numéraire *m* cash

numéraire cash

numéro d'identité bancaire *m* bank sort code

numéro d'ordre *m* order number

numéro de compte *m* account number

numéro de référence *m* reference number

obérer de dettes to burden with debt

objectif à terme *m* short-term objective

objet d'un contrat *m* object of a contract

obligataire *m* debenture bond

obligataire debenture

obligation *f* bond, debenture

obligation cautionnée *f* secured bond

obligation contractuelle *f* contractual obligation

obligation convertible *f* convertible bond

obligation garantie *f* guaranteed bond

obligation hypothécaire *f* mortgage bond

obligation indexée *f* index-linked bond

obligation nominative *f* registered bond

obligation à intérêt variable *f* floating rate bond

obligation à revenu fixe *f* fixed rate bond

obligation à revenu variable *f* floating rate bond

obligation à taux progressif *f* step-up bond

obligation au porteur *f* bearer bond

obligations *fpl* loan stock, loan notes

obligatoire compulsory

observer un contrat to comply with a contract

obtention d'un prêt *f* obtaining of a loan

occupation principale *f* main occupation

occuper un emploi to hold a job

OCDE (=Organisation de coopération et de développement économique) *f* OECD

octroi *m* granting

octroyer un prêt to grant a loan

office de publicité *m* advertising agency

offre *f* offer; [*dans appel d'offres*] bid; [*offre et demande*] supply

offre commerciale *f* bid

offre publique d'achat *f* takeover bid

offre d'emploi *f* job offer, offer of employment

oisif [*capital*] idle

OIT (=Organisation internationale du travail) *f* ILO

OPA (=offre publique d'achat) *f* takeover bid

opération courante *f* normal business transaction

opération financière *f* financial transaction

opération imposable *f* taxable transaction

opération en capital *f* capital transaction

opérations courantes *fpl* ordinary activities

opérations fermes *fpl* firm transactions

opérations de Bourse *fpl* Stock Exchange transactions

opérations en commun *fpl* joint ventures

opérer un virement to make a transfer

opposition: faire opposition à un chèque to stop a cheque

option *f* option

option d'achat *f* option to buy; [*Bourse*] call

option de change *f* foreign currency option

option de vente *f* option to sell; [*Bourse*] put

or en barres *m* (gold) bullion

or en lingots *m* (gold) bullion

ordonnance *f* order

ordonnance de paiement *f* order to pay

ordonnancement *m* [*de paiement*] order to pay; [*mise en ordre*] scheduling

ordonnancer un paiement to order a payment, to authorize a payment

ordonnateur *m* payer; [*Bourse*] giver of an order

ordre *m* order; *à l'ordre de* payable to (the order of)

ordre ferme *m* firm order

ordre à terme *m* futures order

ordre au comptant *m* cash order

ordre d'achat *m* purchase order

ordre de paiement *m* payment order

ordre de prélèvement permanent *m* standing order

ordre de vente *m* order to sell

ordre de virement *m* transfer order

ordre du jour *m* [*de réunion*] agenda

organigramme *m* organization chart

organigramme de production *m* production flowchart

organisation *f* organization

Organisation internationale du travail *f* International Labour Organization

organisation scientifique du travail *f* time and motion studies

Organisation de coopération et de développement économique *f* Organization for Economic Cooperation and Development

organiser to organize
organisme *m* body
organisme professionnel *m* professional body
organisme de crédit *m* credit institution
orientation de la Bourse *f* stock market trend
orienté à la baisse [*marché boursier*] falling
orienté à la hausse [*marché boursier*] rising
original *m* original
osciller to fluctuate
OST (=organisation scientifique du travail) time and motion studies
outil de gestion *m* management tool
ouverture d'un compte *f* opening of an account
ouverture de crédit *f* granting of a loan
ouvrier *m* manual worker
ouvrier qualifié *m* skilled worker
ouvrier spécialisé *m* semi-skilled worker
ouvrir un compte to open an account
ouvrir un crédit to grant a loan

P

paie *f* pay
paiement anticipatif *m* advance payment, payment in advance, prepayment
paiement anticipé *m* advance payment, payment in advance, prepayment
paiement arriéré *m* payment in arrears
paiement comptant *m* cash payment, payment in cash
paiement différé *m* deferred payment
paiement échelonné *m* staged payments, staggered payments
paiement électronique *m* electronic payment, payment by electronic transfer
paiement intégral *m* payment in full
paiement mensuel *m* monthly payment
paiement partiel *m* partial payment, part payment
paiement progressif *m* increasing payments
paiement à échéance *m* payment at maturity
paiement à vue *m* payment at sight

paiement au comptant *m* cash payment, payment in cash

paiement d'avance *m* advance payment, payment in advance

paiement du solde *m* payment of the balance

paiement en espèces *m* cash payment

paiement en nature *m* payment in kind

paiement par acomptes *m* payment by instalments

paiement par anticipation *m* payment in advance

paiement par chèque *m* payment by cheque

paiements internationaux *mpl* international payments

paiements périodiques *mpl* periodic payments

panier de monnaies *m* basket of currencies

panique boursière *f* stock market panic

papier bancable *m* bankable paper

papier commercial *m* commercial paper

papier-monnaie *m* paper money

papier négociable *m* negotiable paper

papier à ordre *m* instrument to order

papier à vue *m* sight paper

papier au porteur *m* bearer paper

papiers valeurs *mpl* securities

paquet de valeurs *m* block of shares

paradis fiscal *m* tax haven

parafiscal [*taxe*] exceptional

parafiscalité *f* special taxation

paraphe *m* initials

parapher to initial

parité *f* parity

parité des monnaies *f* monetary parity

parités du change *fpl* exchange rate parity

Parlement européen *m* European Parliament

parquet *m* [*de la bourse*] floor

parrainage *m* sponsorship

parrainer to sponsor

part sociale *f* share of capital, capital share

part aux bénéfices *f* share of profits

part de marché *f* market share

partage de voix *m* division of votes, breakdown of votes

partager le bénéfice to share the profits

partenaires commerciaux *mpl* trading partners

partenaires sociaux *mpl* workers and management

partenariat *m* partnership

participant *m* participant

participation *f* holding

participation croisée *f* cross holding

participation majoritaire *f* majority holding

participation aux bénéfices *f* profit sharing

participation des salariés *f* employees' holdings

participer à to take part in

participer à une entreprise to have an interest in a business

participer aux bénéfices to have a share in the profits

partie double *f* double entry; *en partie double* double entry

partie prenante *f* party concerned; [*dans un projet*] participant

passation d'écriture *f* journal entry

passation d'un dividende *f* payment of a dividend

passation de commande *f* placing of an order

passe de caisse *f* cashier error allowance

passer commande à qn to place an order with sb

passer commande de qch to place an order for sth

passer en compte to enter

passer par pertes et profits to transfer to profit and loss

passer un marché to sign a deal

passer un montant to post an amount

passer une commande to place an order

passible d'impôts liable to tax

passible de taxe liable to tax

passif *m* liabilities

passif exigible *m* current liabilities

patrimoine *m* property, wealth; [*actif net*] net worth

patron *m* boss

patronage: sous le patronage de under the sponsorship of

patronal employer's

patronat *m* employers

patronner une entreprise to back a business

payable comptant payable in cash

payable à l'échéance payable at maturity

payable à la banque payable at the bank

payé d'avance prepaid

payer à tempérament to pay by instalments

payer à vue to pay at sight

payer au comptant to pay cash

payer en espèces to pay in cash

payer par chèque to pay by cheque

payez au porteur pay to bearer

pays hors communauté *m* non-EC country

PC (=pièce de caisse) *f* cash voucher

PCG (=plan comptable général) *m* chart of accounts

PDG (=Président-directeur général) *m* Chairman and Managing Director, CEO, Chief Executive Officer, President *Am*

pécuniaire pecuniary

pénalité *f* penalty

pénalité libératoire *f* full and final penalty payment

pénalité de retard *f* late payment penalty; late delivery penalty

pension: mise en pension *f* borrowing against securities, pledging

pension de retraite *f* retirement pension

pénurie de capitaux *f* shortage of capital

pénurie de main-d'œuvre *f* labour shortage

PER (=plan d'épargne retraite) *m* retirement savings plan

percepteur *m* tax collector

perception *f* collection

perception à la source *f* tax deduction at source

perception de dividende *f* receipt of a dividend

percevoir [*impôts*] to collect

percevoir l'allocation chômage to receive unemployment benefit

percevoir une commission to receive a commission

perdre sur to lose on

péréquation *f* equalization

performance *f* performance

performant [*entreprise*] efficient

période comptable *f* financial period, fiscal period *Am*

période d'amortissement *f* depreciation period

période d'essai *f* trial period

périodique periodic(al)

permis de travail *m* work permit

personne morale *f* body corporate, corporate body, legal entity

personnel *m* staff, personnel

personnel administratif *m* administrative staff

personnel qualifié *m* qualified personnel

personnel de bureau *m* office staff

perspectives d'avenir *fpl* prospects

perspectives de reprise *fpl* outlook for recovery

perte *f* loss; *à perte* at a loss

perte brute *f* gross loss

perte envisagée *f* estimated loss

perte indemnisable *f* compensable loss

perte latente *f* unrealized loss

perte nette *f* net loss

perte partielle *f* partial loss

perte supportée *f* loss attributable

perte transférée *f* loss transferred

perte d'intérêts *f* loss of interest

perte de bénéfice *f* loss of profit

perte de change *f* foreign exchange loss

perte en capitaux *f* capital loss

pertes et profits *mpl* profit and loss

petite annonce *f* classified ad

petite caisse *f* petty cash

petites et moyennes entreprises *fpl* small (and medium-sized) businesses

petites et moyennes industries *fpl* small (and medium-sized) industries

phase de production *f* stage of production

PIB (=produit intérieur brut) *m* GDP

pièce justificative *f* voucher

pièce de caisse *f* cash voucher

pièces justificatives *fpl* documentary evidence

pignoratif with a repurchase option

piloter [*projet*] to be in charge of

piquet de grève *m* picket

place bancaire *f* banking centre

place boursière *f* stock market

place financière *f* financial centre

place marchande *f* market place

place monétaire *f* money market

placement *m* investment

placement avantageux *m* good investment

placement court terme *m* short-term investment

placement temporaire *m* temporary investment

placement à court terme *m* short-term investment

placement à long terme *m* long-term investment

placement à revenus fixes *m* fixed income investment

placement à revenus variables *m* variable income investment

placer to place; [*argent*] to invest

placer à court terme to invest short-term

placer à intérêts to invest at interest

plafond du crédit *m* credit ceiling

plafonner to level out, to level off

plainte *f* complaint

plan comptable *m* chart of accounts

plan comptable général *m* chart of accounts

plan d'amortissement *m* depreciation schedule

plan d'épargne retraite *m* retirement savings plan

plan de comptes *m* chart of accounts

plan de financement *m* funding plan, financial plan

plan de marchéage *m* marketing mix

plan de production *m* production plan

planification *f* planning

planification à long terme *f* long-term planning

planifier to plan

planning *m* plan, schedule

planning de fabrication *m* manufacturing plan, manufacturing schedule

planning des charges *m* expenditure plan

plaquette publicitaire *f* advertising brochure

plein emploi *m* full employment

plein tarif *m* full price

plein temps: à plein temps full-time

plus plus

plus-value *f* capital gain

PME (=petites et moyennes entreprises) *fpl* small (and medium-sized) businesses; *une PME* a small business

PMI (=petites et moyennes industries) *fpl* small (and medium-sized) industries

PNB (=produit national brut) *m* GNP

poids de la fiscalité *m* tax burden

point: faire le point to take stock

point mort *m* breakeven point

police tous risques *f* comprehensive policy

police d'assurance *f* insurance policy

politique commerciale *f* trade policy

politique économique *f* economic policy

politique monétaire *f* monetary policy

politique de crédit *f* credit policy

politique de plein emploi *f* full employment policy

politique des prix *f* pricing policy

politique des salaires *f* wages policy

ponction fiscale *f* taxation

pondération *f* weighting

pondéré weighted

pondérer une moyenne to weight an average

portefeuille *m* portfolio

portefeuille d'assurances *m* insurance portfolio

portefeuille de titres *m* securities portfolio

porte-parole du personnel *m* staff spokesperson

se **porter garant envers** to stand guarantor for, to stand surety for

porter intérêt to yield interest

porter plainte to make a complaint

porter un montant au crédit d'un compte to credit an amount to an account

porter un montant au débit d'un compte to debit an amount to an account

porteur *m* bearer

porteur d'actions *m* bearer of shares

porteur d'une procuration *m* holder of a proxy

porteur d'une traite *m* bearer of a bill

position créditrice *f* credit balance

position débitrice *f* debit balance

position financière *f* financial position

position d'un compte *f* balance of an account

possesseur de valeurs *m* share owner

possession de fait *f* de facto possession

possessions d'une société *fpl* assets of a company

poste *m* [*au bilan*] entry, item

poste créditeur m credit item
poste débiteur m debit item
poste extraordinaire m extraordinary item
poste à pourvoir m vacancy
poste de bilan m balance sheet item
postulant m applicant
postuler un travail to apply for a job
pot-de-vin m backhander, bribe
pour acquit received with thanks
pour cent per cent
pourcentage m percentage
poursuivre qn en justice to sue sb, to take legal action against sb
poussée de f upsurge in
pouvoir m [*procuration*] power of attorney
pouvoir d'achat m purchasing power
pouvoirs publics mpl public authorities
préalables d'un accord mpl pre-contract conditions
préavis m notice
préavis de grève m strike notice
préavis de paiement m payment advice
précédent m precedent
précomptabilisation f preparation of accounting entries
précompte m advance deduction
précompter to withhold
préfacturation f prebilling
préférentiel preferential
préfinancement m pre-financing
pré-imputation f pre-input preparation
prélèvement m withholding, deduction
prélèvement automatique m direct debit
prélèvement bancaire m direct debit
prélèvement fiscal m tax deduction
prélèvement salarial m deduction from wages
prélever to withhold, to deduct
prélever une commission to deduct a commission
première de change f first of exchange
prendre à bail to take out a lease on, to lease
prendre une police d'assurance to take out an insurance policy
preneur de lettre de change m payee of a bill of exchange
préposé m clerk
préretraite f early retirement
prescription f [*ordonnance*] order; [*règlement*] regulation
prescription acquisitive f acquisition of a right due to the passage of time
prescription extinctive f lapse of a right due to the passage of time
prescrire to stipulate
présentation f presentation
présentation à l'acceptation f presentation for acceptance
présentation au paiement f presentation for payment
présenter à l'encaissement to present for collection
présenter des factures to present invoices
présidence d'une société f chairmanship of a company, presidency of a company *Am*
président m chairman, president *Am*
Président-directeur général m Chairman and Managing Director, Chief Executive Officer, President *Am*
Président du conseil m Chairman of the Board
présider une assemblée to chair a meeting

présomption de responsabilité *f*
presumption of liability
presse: la presse the press
pression fiscale *f* tax burden
prestataire de services *m* service
provider, service supplier
prestation de capitaux *f* provision
of capital
prestation de services *f* provision of
services
prestations *fpl* services
prestations en nature *fpl* allowances
in kind
prêt bancaire *m* bank loan
prêt bonifié *m* soft loan
prêt participatif *m* equity loan
prêt personnalisé *m* personal loan
prêt à court terme *m* short-term loan
prêt à intérêts *m* loan at interest
prêt à long terme *m* long-term loan
prêt à taux réduit *m* reduced rate
loan
prêt sans intérêt *m* interest-free loan
prêt sur titres *m* loan against
securities
prête-nom *m* nominee company
prêter à intérêt to lend at interest
prêter de l'argent to lend money
prêter sur titres to lend against
securities
prêteur *m* lender
prévision *f* forecast
prévision (des) ventes *f* sales
forecast
prévisionnel forecast
prévisions budgétaires *fpl* budget
forecasts
prévisions économiques *fpl*
economic forecast
prévoyance *f* contingency, provision
for the future
prévoyance sociale *f* social security
provisions

prime *f* premium
prime annuelle *f* annual premium
prime familiale *f* family allowance
prime d'ancienneté *f* long service
award
prime d'assurance *f* insurance
premium
prime d'émission *f* bond discount
prime d'intéressement *f*
reversionary bonus
prime de fusion *f* merger premium
prime de rendement *f* performance
bonus, success fee
prime de renouvellement *f* renewal
premium
prime de transport *f* transport
allowance
principal et intérêts *m* principal and
interest
principe de la partie double *m*
double entry method
prise de bénéfices *f* profit-taking
prise de décision *f* decision-making
prise en charge *f* charge
privatisation *f* privatization
privatiser to privatize
privé private
privilégié [*créancier*] preferred
prix contractuel *m* contractual price
prix coûtant *m* cost price; *à prix*
coûtant at cost
prix facturé *m* invoice price
prix taxe comprise *m* price inclusive
of tax
prix unique *m* one price, single price
prix unitaire *m* unit price
prix d'achat *m* purchase price
prix d'exercice *m* [*d'option d'achat*]
exercise price, strike price
prix d'offre *m* supply price
prix de détail *m* retail price
prix de gros *m* wholesale price
prix de revient *m* cost price

prix de vente *m* selling price
prix hors taxe *m* price net of tax
procédure de faillite *f* bankruptcy proceedings
procès-verbal *m* report; [*de réunion*] minutes
procuration *f* proxy
producteur *m* producer
productif d'intérêts interest-bearing
production *f* production
production immobilisée *f* fixed assets produced for use by the company
production stockée *f* [*poste de bilan*] stored production, production left in stock
production vendue *f* sales
production de l'exercice *f* production for the period
productivité *f* productivity
produire to produce
produire des intérêts to bear interest
produire une créance to result in an account receivable
produit *m* product
produit brut *m* gross proceeds, gross income
produit constaté d'avance *m* prepaid income
produit intérieur brut *m* gross domestic product
produit national brut *m* gross national product
produit net *m* net proceeds, net income
produit net partiel *m* accrued income
produits annexes *mpl* incidental income
produits courants *mpl* current income
produits exceptionnels *mpl* extraordinary income

produits financiers *mpl* interest dividends and other financial income
produits à recevoir *mpl* accrued income, accruals
produits d'exploitation *mpl* income from operations
produits de gestion courante *mpl* income from operations
produits en cours *mpl* work in progress
profil de poste *m* job description
profit *m* profit
profit espéré *m* anticipated profit
profit réel *m* real profit
profitabilité *f* profitability
pro forma pro forma
programme de formation *m* training programme
progressif [*taux*] graduated, increasing
progressivité *f* [*d'impôt*] graduation
projet *m* project, plan
projet de budget *m* draft budget
projet de contrat *m* draft agreement
prolongation *f* extension
prolonger to extend
promoteur *m* promoter
promotion *f* promotion
promotion immobilière *f* property development
promotion interne *f* internal promotion, promotion from within the company
promotionnel promotional
promouvoir to promote
se **prononcer** to give a decision
proportion *f* proportion
proposer un dividende to propose a dividend
proposition *f* proposal
proposition d'assurance *f* insurance proposal

propriétaire *mf* owner; [*qui loue*] landlord

propriété immobilière *f* property

propriété industrielle *f* industrial property

prorogation *f* [*de séance*] adjournment

proroger une échéance to extend payment terms

protestable protestable

protêt *m* protest

protocole d'accord *m* [*contrat*] outline agreement

provision *f* provision

provision insuffisante *f* [*sur un compte*] insufficient funds

provision pour dépréciation *f* provision for depreciation, allowance for depreciation

provision pour risques et charges *f* contingency and loss provision

provisionnel interim

provisions réglementées *fpl* regulated provisions

provisoire provisional

prud'homme *m* industrial arbitrator

PU (=prix unitaire) *m* UP

publipostage *m* mailshot

purger une hypothèque to redeem a mortgage

qualité *f* [*emploi*] occupation; [*fonction*] position

quantum des bénéfices *m* proportion of profits

quinquennal five-year

quittance *f* receipt; [*facture*] bill

quittance finale *f* final payment, final discharge

quittance d'assurance *f* receipt for payment of insurance monies

quittance pour solde de compte *f* closing account balance

quittancer to receipt

quitte: être quitte d'une dette to be free of a debt

quitus *m* full discharge

quitus fiscal *m* tax clearance

quorum *m* quorum

quorum des votes *m* quorum

quote-part *f* share

quotidien daily

quotient *m* quotient

R

rabais *m* reduction, discount
rabaissement *m* lowering
rabaisser to lower
rabattre [*prix*] to reduce
rachat *m* [*de valeur, police, etc.*] redemption; [*de société*] buyout
rachat forfaitaire des créances *m* lump-sum purchase of accounts receivable
rachetable [*action*] redeemable
racheter [*dette, titres, etc.*] to redeem; [*entreprise*] to buy
racheter une créance to purchase an account receivable
racheter une obligation to retire a bond, to redeem a bond
racheteur *m* purchaser
radiation *f* [*d'article de compte*] striking out
radier to strike out
raison sociale *f* company name
rajustement *m* adjustment
rajuster to adjust
ralentissement *m* slowdown
rallonge budgétaire *f* addition to the budget
rang *m* [*de créance*] rank
rappel de compte *m* reminder of account outstanding
rappel de salaire *m* back pay
rapport *m* report; [*mathématique*] ratio
rapport annuel *m* annual report
rapport mensuel *m* monthly report

rapport d'expertise *m* valuation, expert's report
rapport de gestion *m* report of the board of directors, management report
rapport des affaires sociales *m* social report
rapport des commissaires aux comptes *m* government auditors' report
rapporter de l'argent to be profitable
rapporter des bénéfices to be profitable
rapporter des intérêts to yield interest
rapporter par an to yield annually
rapprochement bancaire *m* bank reconciliation
ratio *m* ratio
ratio d'exploitation *m* performance ratio, operating ratio
ratio de capitalisation *m* p/e ratio, price/earnings ratio
ratio de gestion *m* financial ratio, financial management ratio
ratio de liquidités *m* quick ratio, acid test ratio
ratio de situation *m* financial ratio
ratio de trésorerie *m* cash ratio
rationalisation *f* rationalization
rationaliser to rationalize
réaffecter [*personnel*] to reassign; [*crédits*] to reallocate

réalisation d'un bénéfice *f* making a profit

réaliser to realize

réaliser un bénéfice to make a profit

réapprovisionnement des stocks *m* restocking

réapprovisionner [*un magasin*] to restock

réassurance *f* reinsurance

réassurer to reinsure

réassureur *m* reinsurer

récapitulation *f* summary

récapituler to summarize

recensement *m* stock take

recensement des entreprises *m* company census

recenser des marchandises to inventory goods, to check off goods

récépissé *m* receipt

réception *f* [*de marchandises*] receipt

réceptionniste *mf* receptionist

récession économique *f* economic recession

recette annuelle *f* annual earnings

recette brute *f* gross earnings

recette journalière *f* daily takings

recette nette *f* net receipts

recettes *fpl* receipts

recettes fiscales *fpl* tax revenue

recettes publiques *fpl* government revenue

recettes et dépenses *fpl* revenue and expenditure

receveur des contributions directes *m* tax collector

receveur des impôts *m* tax collector

recherche et développement *f* research and development

réclamer le paiement to demand payment

reclassement professionnel *m* redeployment

reclasser [*salaires*] to regrade

reconductible renewable

reconduction *f* renewal

reconduire un bail to renew a lease

reconnaissance de dette *f* [*document*] debt instrument, IOU

reconstituer des stocks to restock

reconversion industrielle *f* industrial redeployment

se **reconvertir dans** [*industrie*] to move into, to diversify into

recours *m* recourse

recours contentieux *m* litigation, legal recourse

recouvrable [*dette*] recoverable, collectible

recouvrement d'impôts *m* tax collection

recouvrement de créances *m* debt collection

recouvrer [*créance, traite*] to collect

recrutement *m* recruitment

recruter to recruit

rectificatif *m* correction

rectification *f* correction

rectifier to correct

recto *m* [*d'effet*] face

reçu *m* receipt

reçu d'espèces *m* cash receipt

reculer [*cours de Bourse*] to drop

reculer un paiement to defer payment

récupérable recoverable

récupération *f* recovery

récupérer to recover

récupérer ses débours to recoup one's expenditure

recyclage *m* [*de personnel*] retraining

se **recycler** to retrain

reddition de comptes *f* presentation of accounts for audit, reporting

redevable *mf* person liable for tax

rédhibition *f* cancellation of sale due

to a material defect
rédhibitoire [*vice*] material
rédiger to draw up; [*bon de commande*] to make out
redistribuer to redistribute
redistribution *f* [*de personnel*] redeployment
redressement *m* [*comptabilité*] adjustment
redressement économique *m* economic recovery
redressement fiscal *m* demand for tax arrears
redresser [*comptabilité*] to adjust
redresser une entreprise to put a company back on its feet
redû *m* balance due
réduction de capital *f* decrease in capital
réduction de dépenses *f* reduction of expenditure
réduction de personnel *f* staff cutback
réduction des impôts *f* tax cut
réduction des prix *f* price reduction
réduction des salaires *f* wage cut
réduire to reduce
réduire le personnel to cut staff
réduit [*tarif*] reduced
rééchelonnement *m* [*de dette*] rescheduling
rééchelonner une dette to reschedule a debt
réembaucher to rehire
réescompte *m* rediscount
réescompter to rediscount
réévaluation *f* revaluation
réévaluer to revalue
réfaction *f* rebate
références bancaires *fpl* bank references
refinancement *m* [*d'un crédit*] refinancing

refinancer to refinance
refus de paiement *m* non payment; [*de traite*] dishonour
régime simplifié *m* simplified system
régime d'imposition *m* tax system
régime de retraite *m* pension plan
régime du forfait *m* standard assessment system
régime du réel *m* full assessment system
régime du réel simplifié *m* simplified full assessment system
régir des biens to manage assets
registre de présence *m* attendance register
registre des procès-verbaux *m* minutes book
Registre du commerce *m* trade register
règle du décalage d'un mois *f* one month in arrears rule
règlement *m* [*de facture*] settlement, payment; [*statut*] regulation
règlement au comptant *m* payment in cash
règlement par chèque *m* payment by cheque
réglementation *f* regulations
réglementation du change *f* exchange control regulations
réglementation du travail *f* labour legislation
régler [*fournisseur*] to pay; [*compte*] to settle
régler au comptant to pay in cash
régressif [*impôt, tarif*] tapering
régularisation *f* [*de compte, stocks, charges*] adjustment
régulariser [*compte*] to adjust
régularité et sincérité des charges *f* true and fair nature of expenses
réhabilitation d'un failli *f* discharge of a bankrupt

69

réhabiliter un failli to discharge a bankrupt

réimposer to reintroduce tax on

réimposition *f* retaxation

réinstallation *f* relocation

réintégration *f* add-back

réinvestir to reinvest

relance *f* follow-up

relance de l'économie *f* economic revival

relations commerciales *fpl* business relations

relations publiques *fpl* public relations

relations d'affaires *fpl* business relations

relations de travail *fpl* labour relations

relevé d'identité bancaire *m* bank details

relevé de caisse *m* cash statement

relevé de compte *m* bank statement, statement of account

relevé de factures *m* statement of invoices

relevé de fin de mois *m* end-of-month statement

relèvement *m* [*reprise*] recovery; [*augmentation*] raising

relever [*augmenter*] to raise

relever qn de ses fonctions to relieve sb of his/her duties

relever un compte to make out a statement of account

relever une industrie to revive an industry

reliquat *m* balance

reliquat de caisse *m* cash balance

reliquat de compte *m* account balance

remaniement du personnel *m* staff reshuffle

remboursable repayable, refundable

remboursement *m* repayment, refund

remboursement anticipé *m* early repayment

rembourser to repay, to pay back, to refund

remercier un employé to dismiss an employee

remettre à l'encaissement to remit for collection

remettre à l'escompte to remit for discount

remettre une dette to cancel a debt; [*à plus tard*] to defer (payment of) a debt

remise *f* [*rabais*] discount; [*de fonds*] remittance

remise à vue *f* demand deposit

remise d'effets *f* remittance of bills

remise d'une dette *f* cancellation of a debt; [*à plus tard*] deferment of (payment of) a debt

remise de caisse *f* cash discount

remise de fonds *f* remittance of funds

rémunérateur [*placement*] interest-bearing

rémunération *f* remuneration; [*salaire*] pay

rémunération de capital *f* interest on capital

rémunérer to pay, to remunerate

rendement *m* [*d'investissement*] return, yield; [*d'employé*] performance

rendez-vous d'affaires *m* business meeting

rendre 5% to yield 5%

renégociation *f* renegotiation

renégocier to renegotiate

renflouer une entreprise to bail out a company

rengager [*personnel*] to rehire

renonciation *f* waiver
renouvelable renewable
renouveler une traite to renew a bill of exchange
renouvellement *m* renewal
renseignements de crédit *mpl* status enquiry, credit enquiry
rentabiliser des installations to make facilities cost-effective
rentabiliser des investissements to obtain a return on investments
rentabilité *f* profitability; [*d'investissement*] rate of return
rentabilité du capital *f* return on capital
rentable profitable, cost-effective
rentrée d'argent *f* inflow of money
rentrées fiscales *fpl* tax revenue
rentrées journalières *fpl* daily takings
rentrées et sorties de caisse *fpl* cash receipts and payments
rentrer dans ses fonds to recoup one's investment
rentrer dans ses frais to recover one's expenses
renvoi *m* [*à plus tard*] postponement; [*d'employé*] dismissal
renvoyer [*à plus tard*] to postpone; [*employé*] to dismiss
réorganiser to reorganize
réouverture *f* re-opening
répartir [*somme*] to distribute
répartir au prorata to distribute proportionally
répartir des actions to allot shares
répartir les frais to share the costs
répartir les risques to share the risks
répartition des frais *f* allocation of expenses
répartition du bénéfice *f* distribution of profits
répartition du dividende *f* distribution of the dividend
répertorier to list
report *m* [*à plus tard*] postponement, deferral; [*comptabilité*] carrying forward; *"report"* carried forward
report à nouveau carried forward
report à l'exercice suivant carried forward to the next year
report de l'exercice précédent carried forward from the previous year
reporté postponed, deferred
reporter une somme to carry a sum forward
reports et avances sur titres *mpl* collateral loans
repos compensateur *m* time off in lieu
reprendre le travail to return to work
repreneur *m* buyer
représentant *m* representative, agent
représentant syndical *m* union representative
représentant de commerce *m* representative, rep, commercial traveller
représentant du personnel *m* employees' representative
représentation *f* representation; [*agence*] agency
représenter une société to represent a company
représenter une traite à l'acceptation to re-present a bill for acceptance
reprise économique *f* economic recovery
reprise de l'entreprise par ses salariés *f* employee buyout
reprise des affaires *f* business recovery

reprises sur provisions *fpl* recovery of provisions, write-back of provisions

RES (=reprise de l'entreprise par ses salariés) *f* employee buyout

réserve *f* reserve; *sans réserve de retour* non-returnable, no-return

réserve contractuelle *f* contractual reserve

réserve facultative *f* optional reserve

réserve légale *f* legal reserve

réserve réglementée *f* regulatory reserve

réserves *fpl* reserves

réserves statuaires *fpl* statutory reserves

résolutions d'une assemblée *fpl* resolutions of a meeting

résorber un déficit to absorb a deficit

responsabilité civile *f* public liability

responsabilité contractuelle *f* contractual liability

responsabilité limitée *f* limited liability

responsabilité patronale *f* employer's liability

responsabilité solidaire et indivise *f* joint and several liability

responsable *mf* person in charge

responsable client *mf* account manager

responsable produit *mf* product manager

responsable syndical *m* union leader

responsable des ventes *mf* sales manager

responsable du service commercial *mf* sales and marketing manager

resserrement du crédit *m* credit squeeze

ressource *f* resource

ressources financières *fpl* financial resources

ressources humaines *fpl* human resources

restant *m* remainder, balance

restant de compte *m* account balance, account surplus

restant en caisse *m* cash surplus

restituer to restore

restrictif restrictive

restructuration *f* restructuring

restructurer to restructure

résultat *m* result, profit or loss

résultat courant *m* profit before tax and extraordinary items

résultat exceptionnel *m* extraordinary profit or loss

résultat financier *m* financial profit or loss

résultat d'exploitation *m* operating profit or loss

résultat de l'exercice *m* profit or loss for the financial year

résultat de la période *m* profit or loss for the financial period

résumé *m* abstract, summary

retard delay; *en retard* late

retarder le paiement to delay payment

retenu à la source deducted at source

retenue *f* deduction, withholding

retenue sur salaire *f* wage deduction; [*mensuel*] salary deduction

retenues patronales *fpl* employer's contributions

retenues salariales *fpl* wage deductions, employee's contributions

retirer to withdraw

retirer sa participation d'une société to sell one's shares in a

company, to sell out
retour *m* return; *par retour du courrier* by return (of mail)
retour net *m* net return
retour sur l'investissement *m* return on investment
retour sur ventes *m* return on sales
retourner un effet to return a bill
retrait *m* withdrawal
retrait d'espèces *m* cash withdrawal
retraite *f* retirement
retraite complémentaire *f* supplementary pension
rétribuer to pay
rétribution *f* payment
rétroactif back-dated, retroactive
rétroaction *f* [*réaction*] feedback
rétroaction d'une augmentation de salaire *f* backdating of a rise, making a rise retroactive
rétrospective *f* review
réunion d'actionnaires *f* shareholders' meeting
réunion de comité *f* committee meeting
réunion des créanciers *f* creditors' meeting
réunion du conseil *f* board meeting
réunion du conseil d'administration *f* board meeting
réunir [*capitaux, somme d'argent*] to raise
revendications syndicales *fpl* union demands
revenu annuel *m* annual income
revenu disponible *m* disposable income
revenu imposable *m* taxable income
revenu net *m* net income
revenu d'entreprise *m* corporate

income, company earnings
revenus accessoires *mpl* incidental income
revenus actuels *mpl* current earnings
reversement *m* additional payment
reverser [*impôt*] to pay
revêtir un accord d'une signature to put one's signature to an agreement
réviser to revise
réviseur interne *m* internal auditor
révocable [*crédit*] revocable, callable
révoquer to dismiss
revue d'entreprise *f* company magazine
RIB (=relevé d'identité bancaire) *m* bank details
ristourne de fidélité *f* regular customer rebate
rôle des contributions *m* tax roll
rompu aux affaires with business experience
rotation *f* rotation
rotation des capitaux *f* capital turnover
rotation des stocks *f* stock turnover, stock turnaround, inventory turnover
rouge: dans le rouge in the red
roulement de capitaux *m* turnover of capital
roulement du personnel *m* staff turnover
royalties *fpl* royalties
RRR (=remise, rabais, ristourne) discounts and allowances
rupture de stock *f* stock outage; *être en rupture de stock* to be out of stock

S

SA (=**société anonyme**) *f* plc
saisie-arrêt *f* attachment
saisir to seize
saisonnier seasonal
salaire *m* wage; [*mensuel*] salary
salaire annuel garanti *m* annual guaranteed wage/salary
salaire brut *m* gross wage/salary
salaire indirect *m* benefit in kind
salaire plafond *m* maximum wage/salary
salaire plafonné *m* wage/salary ceiling
salaire réel *m* real wage/salary
salaire d'appoint *m* second salary
salaire de base *m* basic wage/salary
salarial wage; [*mensuel*] salary
salarié *m* wage earner; [*payé mensuellement*] salaried employee
salariés *mpl* [*de société*] employees
salle de conférence *f* conference room
salle du conseil *f* board room
SARL (=**société à responsabilité limitée**) *f* Ltd
savoir-faire *m* expertise, know-how
SCA (=**société en commandite par actions**) *f* partnership limited by shares
schéma *m* diagram
schéma d'entreprise *m* organization chart
schématiser to make a diagram of
SCI (=**société de commerce international**) *f* international trading corporation
scinder une société to break up a company, to split a company
scission d'actifs *f* divestment of assets, hive-off of assets
scission d'une entreprise *f* break-up of a company
SCS (=**société en commandite simple**) *f* limited partnership
séance *f* session
séance de concertation *f* policy meeting
secrétaire *mf* secretary
secrétaire général *m* company secretary
secrétaire de direction *mf* executive secretary
secrétaire de séance *mf* meetings secretary
section syndicale d'entreprise *f* union branch
Sécurité sociale *f* social security, welfare *Am*
semaine de cinq jours *f* five-day week
semainier *m* diary
semestre *m* six months, half year
semestriel six-monthly, half-yearly
service *m* [*direction*] department
service administratif *m* administration (department)
service après-vente *m* [*direction*] after-sales (department); [*service rendu*] after-sales service

service clientèle *m* [*direction*] customer service (department); [*service rendu*] customer service

service commercial export *m* export department

service comptable *m* accounts (department)

service contrôle qualité *m* quality control (department)

service financier *m* finance (department)

service lancement *m* product launch department

service d'un emprunt *m* servicing a loan

service de recouvrement *m* collection department

service de l'expédition *m* shipping (department)

service de la dette *m* debt servicing

service de la prospection *m* marketing (department)

service des achats *m* purchasing (department); [*très grand*] procurement (department)

service du courrier *m* mail room

service du personnel *m* personnel (department)

seuil de rentabilité *m* breakeven (point)

SICAV (=société d'investissement à capital variable) *f* unit trust, mutual fund *Am*

siège administratif *m* administrative headquarters

siège principal *m* head office

siège social *m* registered office, head office

siège à pourvoir au conseil d'administration *m* vacancy on the board

siège d'exploitation *m* operational headquarters

siéger au conseil d'administration to have a seat on the board, to be on the board

sigle *m* [*d'entreprise*] logo

signataire *mf* signatory

signature par procuration *f* signature by proxy

signer par procuration to sign by proxy, to pp

simulation *f* [*prévision*] forecast

SIRET: No SIRET company registration number

situation financière *f* financial situation

situation nette *f* net worth

situation de compte *f* account balance, account position

situation de la banque *f* bank balance

situation de la caisse *f* cash balance, cash position

SME (=Système monétaire européen) *m* EMS

SMIC (=salaire minimum interprofessionnel de croissance) *m* minimum wage

smicard *m* minimum wage earner

SNC (=société en nom collectif) *f* commercial/industrial partnership

société *f* company

société affiliée *f* affiliated company

société anonyme *f* public limited company, corporation *Am*

société commerciale *f* company

société commune *f* joint venture

société fiduciaire *f* trust company

société mère *f* parent company

société nationalisée *f* nationalized company

société à responsabilité limitée *f* limited liability company

société d'affacturage *f* factoring company

société de commerce international *f* international trading corporation

société de gestion *f* holding company

société de négoce *f* trading company

société de personnes *f* partnership

société en commandite *f* form of partnership limited by shares

société en commandite simple *f* limited partnership

société en commandite par actions *f* partnership limited by shares

société en nom collectif *f* commercial/industrial partnership

société en participation *f* joint venture

solde *m* balance

solde actif *m* credit balance

solde bénéficiaire *m* credit balance

solde créditeur *m* credit balance

solde débiteur *m* debit balance

solde déficitaire *m* debit balance

solde disponible *m* available balance

solde passif *m* debit balance

solde de tout compte *m* final settlement

solde en caisse *m* cash balance

solder [*compte, livres*] to close, to balance

solliciter un emploi to apply for a position

solvabilité *f* solvency

solvable solvent

somme due *f* amount due

somme nette *f* net (amount)

sortant [*administrateur*] outgoing

sortie *f* [*de capitaux, devises*] outflow

sorties de caisse *fpl* cash payments

sorties de fonds *fpl* outgoings

sorties de trésorerie *fpl* cash outflow

souffrance: en souffrance outstanding

soumettre à l'impôt to subject to tax

soumettre un rapport to submit a report

source de revenus *f* source of revenue

sous-capitalisé undercapitalized

sous-compte *m* subsidiary account, sub-account

souscripteur *m* [*d'effet de commerce*] drawer; [*d'emprunt*] subscriber

souscription *f* [*de société*] subscribed capital

sous-directeur *m* assistant manager; [*plus haut dans la hiérarchie*] assistant director

sous-emploi *m* under-employment

sous-total *m* subtotal

soustraire to subtract

spécialisé specialized; [*ouvrier*] semi-skilled

spécification *f* specification

spécification de la fonction *f* job description

spéculateur *m* speculator

spéculatif speculative

spéculation *f* speculation

spéculer to speculate

sphères de la finance *fpl* financial circles

spirale inflationniste *f* inflationary spiral

spirale des prix et des salaires *f* wage and price spiral

stable stable

staff de direction *m* managerial staff

stage *m* training period

stagiaire *mf* trainee

stagnant stagnant

stagnation *f* stagnation

statisticien *m* statistician

statistiques *fpl* statistics

statut juridique *m* legal status

statut légal *m* legal status

statutaire statutory
statuts de société *mpl* memorandum and articles of association, bylaws *Am*, articles of incorporation *Am*
stipulation *f* stipulation
stock *m* stock
stock final *m* closing stock
stock initial *m* opening stock
stock stratégique *m* perpetual inventory
stock de sécurité *m* perpetual inventory
stocker des marchandises to stock goods
stratégie de l'entreprise *f* corporate strategy
structure de l'entreprise *f* company structure, corporate structure
subalterne *mf* junior
subdiviser to subdivide
subdivision *f* subdivision
subir des pertes to suffer losses
subordonné *m* subordinate
subside *m* subsidy, grant
subvention *f* subsidy, grant
subvention d'exploitation *f* operating subsidy
subventionner une entreprise to subsidize a company
succursale *f* branch
superbénéfice *m* sum of directors' percentage of profit and super dividend
superdividende *m* super dividend
supérieur [*cadre*] senior
superviser une entreprise to supervise a company
supervision *f* supervision
suppléance *f* temporary replacement
suppléant *m* replacement; [*de directeur*] deputy
suppléer qn to replace sb; [*directeur*] to deputize for sb

supplément d'imposition *m* additional taxes
supplément de prix *m* additional charge
supplétif additional
suppression d'emplois *f* shedding of jobs
supprimer des emplois to shed jobs
supprimer un poste to abolish a position
suraccumulation de capital *f* over-accumulation of capital
surcapitalisation *f* overcapitalization
surcapitaliser to overcapitalize
surcharge *f* surcharge
surcharger d'impôts to overburden with taxes .
surcoût *m* cost overrun
surcroît de dépenses *m* additional expenditure
sureffectif *m* overmanning; *en sureffectif* surplus
surenchère *f* overbid
surendettement *m* over-indebtedness, over-gearing
surestimation *f* overestimate
surestimer to overestimate
sûreté en garantie d'une créance *f* surety for a loan
surévaluation *f* over-valuation
surévaluer to over-value
surprime *f* additional premium
surprofit *m* excess profit
sursis de paiement *m* extra time to pay
surtaxe *f* [*postale*] surcharge
surveillant *m* supervisor
suspendre les paiements to stop payments, to suspend payment
suspension *f* [*de séance*] adjournment
suspension d'un paiement *f* stopping of a payment

77

suspension de paiements *f* moratorium on payment

syndic de faillite *m* official receiver

syndicaliste *mf* trade unionist

syndicat *m* trade union

syndicat financier *m* financial syndicate

syndicat ouvrier *m* trade union

syndicat patronal *m* employers' organization

syndicat professionnel *m* trade association, professional association

syndicat de faillite *m* official receivership

syndiqué *m* trade union member; *être syndiqué* to be a member of a trade union

syndiquer to unionize

synopsis *m* synopsis

synthétique [*bilan*] summary

système comptable *m* accounting system

système fiscal *m* tax system

Système monétaire européen *m* European Monetary System

système d'inventaire *m* inventory method

système de participation aux bénéfices *m* profit-sharing scheme

système de prévoyance *m* system of benefits

système de relance *m* follow-up system

système de retraite *m* pension scheme

T

table ronde *f* round table

tableau *m* table

tableau récapitulatif *m* summary table

tableau synoptique *m* synopsis, summary

tableau d'amortissement *m* depreciation schedule

tableau d'avancement de commandes *m* order flowchart

tableau de bord *m* management report

tableau de conversion *m* conversion table

tableau de financement *m* statement of sources and uses of funds; [*planning*] finance plan

tableau de roulement *m* statement of changes in working capital

tableau des emplois et ressources de fonds *m* statement of sources and applications of funds

tantième *m* percentage
tantième des administrateurs *m* directors' fee
tarif *m* [*prix*] rate
tarif dégressif *m* tapering rate, declining rate
tarif différentiel *m* differential rate
tarif export *m* export tariff
tarif horaire *m* hourly rate
tarif préférentiel *m* preferential rate
tarif progressif *m* increasing rate
tarif à forfait *m* all-in price
tarif de base *m* basic rate
tarifaire tariff
tarifer to set the rate of
tarification *f* setting of rates
taux *m* rate
taux intermédiaire *m* intermediate rate
taux linéaire *m* straight-line rate
taux normal *m* standard rate
taux officiel *m* official rate
taux préférentiel *m* prime rate
taux privé *m* market rate
taux réduit *m* reduced rate
taux uniforme *m* uniform rate, flat rate
taux d'accroissement *m* rate of increase, rate of growth
taux d'actualisation *m* net present value rate, NPV rate
taux d'amortissement *m* rate of depreciation, depreciation rate
taux d'échange *m* rate of exchange, exchange rate
taux d'escompte *m* discount rate
taux d'inflation *m* rate of inflation, inflation rate
taux d'intérêt *m* interest rate, rate of interest
taux d'usure *m* penal rate
taux de base bancaire *m* bank base rate

taux de capitalisation *m* price/earnings ratio, p/e ratio
taux de change *m* rate of exchange, exchange rate
taux de conversion *m* conversion rate
taux de croissance *m* growth rate, rate of growth
taux de marge *m* mark-up ratio
taux de TVA *m* VAT rate, rate of VAT
taxable taxable
taxation *f* taxation
taxation différentielle *f* differential taxation
taxe *f* tax; *toutes taxes comprises* inclusive of tax
taxe foncière *f* property tax
taxe locale *f* local tax
taxe parafiscale *f* indirect tax, excise tax
taxe régionale *f* local tax
taxe à l'exportation *f* export tax
taxe d'apprentissage *f* percentage of annual gross payroll paid by companies to finance technical training
taxe de luxe *f* luxury tax
taxe sur la valeur ajoutée *f* value added tax
taxe sur le revenu *f* income tax
taxe sur les salaires *f* employment tax
taxer to tax
TCA (=taxe sur le chiffre d'affaires) *f* sales tax
technicien *m* technician
temporaire temporary
temps: à temps complet full-time; *à temps partiel* part-time
temps de cycle *m* business cycle
tendance *f* trend
tendance ascensionnelle *f* upward trend

tendance à la baisse *f* downward trend

tenir à bail to hold a lease on

tenir les livres à jour to keep the books up to date

tenir une réunion to hold a meeting

tenue d'une réunion *f* holding a meeting

tenue de caisse *f* petty cash management

tenue des livres *f* bookkeeping

tenue des stocks *f* stock keeping

terme: à terme échu on the due date; **à terme fixe** fixed-term

terme d'échéance *m* [*d'effet*] maturity date

terme de bail *m* term of lease

terme de liquidation *m* account period, settlement period

termes de paiement *mpl* terms of payment

terrains *mpl* land

tête d'entreprise *f* head of a/the company

thésaurisation *f* hoarding

thésauriser to hoard

tiers détenteur *m* third party holder

tiers porteur *m* [*d'effet*] holder in due course

tiers possesseur *m* third party owner

tiers provisionnel *m* interim payment of tax

timbre fiscal *m* tax stamp

timbre-quittance *m* receipt stamp

tirage *m* [*de chèque*] drawing; [*de prêt*] draw down

tirages annuels *mpl* annual drawings

tiré *m* drawee

tirer à découvert to overdraw

tirer à vue to draw at sight

tirer un bénéfice to take a profit

tirer un chèque sur to draw a cheque on

tirer une traite sur to draw a bill on

tireur *m* drawer

titre *m* security

titre nominatif *m* registered security

titre participatif *m* equity loan

titre universel de paiement *m* universal payment order

titre au porteur *m* bearer bond

titre d'action *m* share certificate

titre d'obligation *m* loan note, bond note

titre de créance *m* loan note, debt instrument

titre de participation *m* equity investment

titre de propriété *m* title deed

titre de rente *m* government bond

titres *mpl* securities, stock *Am*

titres émis *mpl* issued securities

titres libérés *mpl* fully paid-up securities

titres à revenu fixe *mpl* fixed income securities

titres à revenu variable *mpl* floating rate securities

titres à terme *mpl* futures

titres de placement *mpl* marketable securities

titulaire *mf* [*de compte, police*] holder

titulaire d'action *mf* shareholder

total général *m* grand total

total à payer *m* total payable

total des recettes *m* total receipts

totaliser to total

toucher ses appointements to draw one's salary

toucher un chèque to cash a cheque

toucher un intérêt to receive interest

tout compris all-in

toutes taxes comprises inclusive of tax

trafiquer les comptes to fiddle the

accounts

traite *f* draft; [*lettre de change*] bill of exchange

traite bancaire *f* bank draft

traite documentaire *f* documentary bill

traite pro forma *f* pro forma bill

traite à courte échéance *f* short-dated bill

traite à date fixe *f* time bill

traite à longue échéance *f* long-dated bill

traite à vue *f* sight draft

traite contre acceptation *f* acceptance bill

traite de complaisance *f* accommodation bill

traite "sans frais" *f* bill "without protest"

traitement *m* salary

traitement fixe *m* fixed salary

traitement initial *m* starting salary

traitement de base *m* basic salary

tranche d'imposition *f* tax bracket

tranche de paiement *f* instalment

transaction *f* transaction

transactions bancaires *fpl* bank transactions

transactions boursières *fpl* Stock Exchange transactions

transactions commerciales *fpl* business transactions

transcrire to transcribe

transcrire des écritures to transcribe entries

transférable transferable

transférer to transfer

transfert d'actions *m* transfer of shares

transfert de capitaux *m* transfer of capital

transfert de charges *m* expense transfer, transfer of charges

transfert de créances *m* assignment of accounts receivable

transfert de devises *m* currency transfer

transfert de fonds *m* transfer of funds

transfert des frais *m* transfer of costs

translation de propriété *f* transfer of title

transmissible par endossement transferable by endorsement

transmission par endossement *f* transfer by endorsement

travail *m* work; [*poste*] job

travail administratif *m* administrative work

travail à mi-temps *m* part-time work

travail à plein temps *m* full-time work

travail à temps partiel *m* part-time work

travail d'équipe *m* teamwork

travail en équipes *m* teamwork

travailler to work

travailleur *m* worker

travailleur indépendant *m* self-employed person

travailleur manuel *m* manual worker

travailleur salarié *m* salaried worker

travailleur à temps réduit *m* person on short time

treizième mois *m* amount equal to one-thirteenth of annual salary paid at Christmas

Trésor public *m* Treasury Department

trésorerie *f* cashflow; [*service d'entreprise*] accounts (department)

trésorier *m* treasurer

tribunal *m* court

tribunal arbitral *m* arbitration tribunal

tribunal de commerce *m* trade tribunal

tribunal des prud'hommes *m* industrial tribunal

trimestre *m* quarter

trimestriel quarterly

triple: en triple exemplaire in triplicate

trop-perçu *m* overpayment of tax

trucage *m* [*de comptes*] window-dressing

truquer [*comptes*] to window-dress

trust commercial *m* commercial monopoly

trust industriel *m* industrial monopoly

truster *vi* to form a monopoly

truster *vt* to form into a monopoly

TTC (=toutes taxes comprises) inclusive of tax

TUP (=titre universel de paiement) *m* universal payment order

TVA (=taxe sur la valeur ajoutée) *f* VAT

TVA encaissée *f* output tax

TVA récupérée *f* input tax

union patronale *f* employers' organization

unité administrative *f* administrative unit

unité monétaire *f* monetary unit

unité de compte *f* unit of account

URSSAF (=Union de recouvrement des cotisations de sécurité sociale et d'allocations familiales) *f* organization which collects social security and family allowance payments

usine *f* factory, plant

usine clés-en-main *f* turnkey plant

usine pilote *f* pilot plant

usufruit *m* usufruct, life interest

utilisable [*crédit*] available

V

valable valid
valeur *f* [*d'objet*] value, worth
valeur actualisée *f* present value
valeur actuelle *f* current value
valeur assurée *f* insured value
valeur brute *f* gross value
valeur compensée *f* cleared value
valeur comptable *f* book value
valeur comptable nette *f* net book value
valeur locative *f* rental value
valeur marchande *f* market value
valeur nominale *f* [*d'obligation*] par value; [*d'action*] nominal value
valeur résiduelle *f* residual value
valeur transactionnelle *f* settlement value
valeur vénale *f* fair market value
valeur à l'échéance *f* maturity value
valeur à l'encaissement *f* value for collection
valeur d'achat *f* purchase value
valeur d'inventaire *f* balance sheet value, break-up value
valeur d'origine *f* original value
valeur de bilan *f* book value
valeur de rachat *f* [*de police*] surrender value
valeur en bourse *f* stock market value
valeurs cotées *fpl* quoted securities
valeurs émises *fpl* securities issued
valeurs étrangères *fpl* foreign securities

valeurs mobilières *fpl* securities
valeurs mobilières de placement *fpl* marketable securities
valeurs négociables *fpl* marketable securities
valeurs nominatives *fpl* registered securities
valeurs réalisables *fpl* realizable securities, marketable securities
valeurs à revenu fixe *fpl* fixed income securities
valeurs à revenu variable *fpl* floating rate securities
valeurs de bourse *fpl* quoted securities
valeurs de placement *fpl* marketable securities
validation *f* authentication
valider to authenticate
validité *f* validity
valoir to be worth
valorisation *f* [*d'inventaire*] valuation
valoriser to increase the value of
variable *f* variable
variation saisonnière *f* seasonal variation
variation de stock *f* stock variation, change in stock
vendre à crédit to sell on credit
vendre à perte to sell at a loss
vendre à terme to sell forward
vendre au comptant to sell for cash

vendre de gré à gré to sell privately
vente f sale
vente directe f direct selling
vente-marketing f sales and marketing
vente à crédit f credit sale
vente à terme f forward sale
vente à l'amiable f sale by private agreement
vente en gros f wholesaling
ventes fpl sales, turnover
ventilation f [de chiffres] breakdown
ventiler to break down
vérificateur m auditor
vérification (comptable) f audit
vérification à rebours f audit trail
vérifier to verify; [comptes] to audit
versement m instalment, payment
versement d'espèces m cash deposit
versements échelonnés mpl staggered payments
verser to pay; [à la banque] to deposit, to pay in
verser qch au crédit de qn to credit sb with sth
verser un acompte to make a down payment
VI (=valeur d'inventaire) f balance sheet value, break-up value
viabiliser une entreprise to make a business viable
viabilité f viability
viable viable
vice-présidence f vice-chairmanship, vice-presidency Am
vice-président m vice-chairman, vice-president Am
virement bancaire m bank transfer

virement postal m post office transfer
virement SWIFT m SWIFT transfer
virement par courrier m mail transfer
virement par télex m telex transfer
virer to transfer
viser des livres de commerce to certify the books
viser un effet to stamp a bill
VMP (=valeurs mobilières de placement) fpl marketable securities
voie: par voie hiérarchique through official channels
voix consultative f consultative role
voix délibérative f vote
voix prépondérante f casting vote
volume annuel de production m annual (volume of) production
volume des affaires m volume of business
volume des ventes m sales volume, volume of sales
vote à main levée m vote by a show of hands
vote au scrutin secret m secret ballot
vote par procuration m proxy
voter une proposition to vote in favour of a proposal
voyage d'affaires m business trip
voyager pour affaires to travel on business
voyageur de commerce m commercial traveller
vu et approuvé seen and approved
vue: à vue at sight; [dépôt] demand

absenteeism absentéisme *m*
absolute majority majorité absolue *f*
to **absorb a deficit** résorber un déficit
to **absorb debts** éponger des dettes
abstract résumé *m*
abuse abus *m*
accelerated depreciation amortissement dégressif *m*
acceptance acceptation *f*
acceptance bill traite contre acceptation *f*
acceptance fee commission d'acceptation *f*
accommodation allowance indemnité de logement *f*
accommodation bill traite de complaisance *f*
account compte *m*; *payment on account* acompte *m*; *to make a payment on account* donner un acompte
account balance [*status*] situation de compte *f*; [*after audit*] reliquat de compte *m*
account charges frais de tenue de compte *mpl*
account credit avoir de compte *m*
account holder titulaire de compte *mf*
account management charges [*banking*] frais de tenue de compte *mpl*

account manager responsable client *mf*
account movement mouvement de compte *m*
account number numéro de compte *m*
account payable compte créditeur *m*, dette fournisseur *f*
account period terme de liquidation *m*
account position situation de compte *f*
account receivable compte client *m*, compte débiteur *m*
account surplus restant de compte *m*
accountancy comptabilité *f*, compta *f*
accountant comptable *mf*
accounting comptabilité *f*, compta *f*
accounting document document comptable *m*
accounting entry écriture comptable *f*
accounting entry sheet/form bordereau de codification *m*, bordereau d'imputation *m*, bordereau de saisie *m*
accounting firm cabinet d'expertise comptable *m*
accounting method procédé comptable *m*, mode comptable *m*
accounting period période comptable *f*
accounting record form fiche d'imputation comptable *f*

accounting system système comptable *m*

accounting year année comptable *f*

accounts comptes *mpl*; [*accounting*] comptabilité *f*; *to enter in the accounts* comptabiliser; *who does your accounts?* qui est-ce qui fait votre comptabilité ?

accounts (department) service comptable *m*

accounts clerk aide-comptable *mf*

accounts ledger grand livre des comptes *m*

accounts payable dettes fournisseurs *fpl*

accounts payable ledger livre des créanciers *m*

accounts receivable créances *fpl*, créances clients *fpl*

accounts receivable ledger livre des débiteurs *m*

accruals [*accrued expenses*] charges à payer *fpl*; [*accrued income*] produits à recevoir *mpl*

accruals and deferred income compte de régularisation *m*

accrued dividends dividendes accrus *mpl*

accrued income produit à recevoir *m*

accrued interest intérêts échus *mpl*

accruing interest intérêts à échoir *mpl*

to **accumulate** accumuler

accumulation accumulation *f*

acid test ratio ratio de liquidité immédiate *m*

to **acknowledge receipt of** accuser réception de

acknowledgement of debt reconnaissance de dette *f*

acknowledgement (of receipt) accusé de réception *m*

acquisition acquisition *f*

acquisition cost coût d'acquisition *m*

across-the-board increase augmentation générale *f*

act of God force majeure *f*; *an act of God* un cas de force majeure

acting intérimaire, par intérim

acting director directeur intérimaire *m*

action action *f*; [*legal*] action (en justice) *f*

active member membre actif *m*

activity activité *f*

actual costs coûts constatés *mpl*

actuarial actuariel

actuary actuaire *mf*

to **adapt** adapter

to **add** ajouter; [*figures*] additionner

to **add up to** se chiffrer à

add-back réintégration *f*

adding up addition *f*

addition addition *f*

additional complémentaire, supplémentaire

additional charge supplément de prix *m*

additional clause amendement *m*

additional expenditure surcroît de dépenses *m*

additional expenses dépenses supplémentaires *fpl*

additional margin marge supplémentaire *f*

additional premium surprime *f*

additional taxes supplément d'imposition *m*

addressed to destiné à

addressee destinataire *mf*

adequate cover couverture suffisante *f*

adjournment suspension *f*

adjudication in bankruptcy jugement déclaratif de faillite *m* *to* **adjust** ajuster; [*wages*] rajuster; [*in accounts*] régulariser

to **adjust to** s'adapter à

adjusting entry écriture de régularisation *f*

adjustment ajustement *m*; [*of wages*] rajustement *m*; [*in accounts*] régularisation *f*

adjustment account compte collectif *m*

admin administration *f*, gestion administrative *f*; [*work*] travail administratif *m*

administration administration *f*, gestion administrative *f*; [*work*] travail administratif *m*

administration costs frais d'administration *mpl*, frais de gestion *mpl*

administration (department) service administratif *m*

administrative administratif

administrative costs coûts administratifs *mpl*

administrative expenses frais administratifs *mpl*

administrative headquarters siège administratif *m*

administrative hierarchy hiérarchie administrative *f*

administrative staff personnel administratif *m*

administrative unit unité administrative *f*

administrative work travail administratif *m*

administrator administrateur *m*

advance [*of money*] avance (de fonds) *f*; [*down payment*] acompte *m*

advance payment paiement anticipé *m*, paiement d'avance *m*, paiement anticipatif *m*

advertising publicité *f*

advertising agency agence de publicité *f*, bureau de publicité *m*

advertising brochure plaquette publicitaire *f*

advertising campaign campagne publicitaire *f*, campagne de publicité *f*

advertising expenditure dépenses publicitaires *fpl*

advice note avis *m*; [*from bank*] avis de la banque *m*

to **advise** aviser; [*give consultancy*] conseiller

advising bank banque notificatrice *f*

advisory board comité consultatif *m*

advisory capacity: in an advisory capacity en tant que conseiller

advisory committee commission consultative *f*

affidavit affirmation sous serment *f*, acte de notoriété *m*

affiliated affilié

affiliated company société affiliée *f*

affiliated member affilié *m*

after-sales (department) service après-vente *m*

after-sales service service après-vente *m*, SAV *m*

after tax après imposition, après impôt

age limit limite d'âge *f*

aged creditor créancier âgé *m*

aged debt créance âgée *f*

aged debtor schedule échéancier *m*

agency agence *f*; [*right of agency*] concession *f*, concession commerciale *f*

agency contract contrat d'agence *m*

agenda ordre du jour *m*

agent agent *m*, représentant *m*; [*for product distribution*] concessionnaire *mf*

AGM (=Annual General Meeting) AGO f

to **agree** être d'accord; [*figures*] correspondre

to **agree on** convenir de

to **agree with** être d'accord avec

agreed: as agreed comme convenu

agreement accord m; [*formal*] convention f

agreement to sell compromis de vente m

ahead: to be ahead of one's competitors devancer ses concurrents

all-in tout compris

all-in price tarif à forfait m

to **allocate** affecter, allouer

allocation affectation f

allocation of expenses répartition des frais f

to **allot** [*shares*] attribuer, répartir

allotment [*of shares*] attribution f

allowance allocation f; [*for depreciation, bad debts etc*] dotation f

allowances in kind prestations en nature fpl

amended invoice facture rectificative f

amendment modification f, amendement m

amendment of a contract modification d'un contrat f

to **amortize** amortir

amortized amorti

amount montant m, somme f

amount due montant dû m, somme due f

amount exclusive of VAT montant hors TVA m

to **analyse** analyser

analysis analyse f

analyst analyste mf

annual annuel

annual accounts comptes annuels mpl

annual accounts ledger livre d'inventaire m

annual depreciation annuité d'amortissement f

annual drawings tirages annuels mpl

annual earnings [*of company*] recette(s) annuelle(s) f(pl)

annual general meeting assemblée générale ordinaire f, assemblée ordinaire f

annual guaranteed salary salaire annuel garanti m

annual income revenu annuel m

annual meeting assemblée annuelle f

annual premium prime annuelle f

annual report rapport annuel m

annual returns déclarations annuelles fpl

annual salaries return déclaration annuelle des salaires f

annual sales figures chiffre d'affaires annuel m

annual turnover chiffre d'affaires annuel m

annual (volume of) production volume annuel de production m

annual wages return [*by employer*] déclaration annuelle des salaires f

annual writedown annuité d'amortissement f

annually par an

annuity annuité f

to **antedate** antidater

anticipated profit profit espéré m

to **appear** [*on a list*] figurer

to **appear in the books** figurer dans les livres

appendix [*to document*] annexe f

applicant demandeur m, postulant m

application demande f; [*for job*]

candidature *f*

to **apply** appliquer

to **apply for a job** poser sa candidature pour un poste, postuler un travail

to **apply for a position** solliciter un emploi

to **appoint sb manager** nommer qn directeur

to **appoint sb to the position of** désigner qn à la position de

appointment to a post nomination à un poste *f*

appropriate approprié; **to take appropriate action** agir en conséquence

approval approbation *f*; [*of dealer, distributor*] agrément *m*; **on approval** à l'essai

approval of the accounts approbation des comptes *f*

to **approve** approuver; [*dealer, distributor*] agréer

arbiter arbitre *m*

to **arbitrate** arbitrer

arbitration arbitrage *m*

arbitration board commission d'arbitrage *f*

arbitration clause clause d'arbitrage *f*, clause compromissoire *f*

arbitration committee commission d'arbitrage *f*

arbitration ruling décision arbitrale *f*

arbitration tribunal tribunal arbitral *m*

area director directeur régional *m*

area manager directeur régional *m*

area of competence domaine de compétence *m*

area of expertise domaine de compétence *m*

area of operations branche d'activité *f*

argument [*for or against something*] argumentation *f*

arm's length [*relationship*] impartial; [*price*] réaliste

arrangement arrangement *m*; [*with creditors*] accommodement *m*

arrears arrérages *mpl*, arriéré *m*; **in arrears** [*payment*] arriéré

article article *m*

articles of association statuts de société *mpl* _

asap (=as soon as possible) dans les plus brefs délais

to **ask for** demander

assembly line chaîne de montage *f*

to **assess** évaluer

asset actif *m*

asset management gestion de biens *f*

asset-stripping réalisation de l'actif suite au rachat d'une société *f*

assets actif *m*, actifs *mpl*

assignee cessionnaire *mf*

assignment [*of asset*] cession *f*; [*task*] tâche *f*

assignment of accounts receivable transfert de créances *m*

assignment of debts transfert de créances *m*

assistant adjoint *m*

assistant accountant aide-comptable *mf*

assistant director sous-directeur *m*

assistant manager sous-directeur *m*

associate *adj* adjoint

association association *f*

assured [*person insured*] assuré *m*

attached to annexé à

to **attend a meeting** assister à une réunion

attendance register registre de présence *m*

attendance sheet feuille de
  présence *f*
attorney *Am* avocat *m*
audit audit *m*, contrôle du bilan *m*,
  contrôle des comptes *m*,
  vérification *f*
to **audit** apurer, vérifier
audit trail vérification à rebours *f*
auditing apurement *m*
auditor vérificateur *m*; *firm of
  auditors* cabinet d'audit *m*, cabinet
  comptable *m*
auditors' report rapport des
  vérificateurs *m*
to **authenticate** valider, authentifier
to **authenticate a signature** légaliser
  une signature
authentication validation *f*,
  authentification *f*; [*of signature*]
  légalisation *f*
authenticity authenticité *f*
authorization autorisation *f*
to **authorize** autoriser
to **authorize a payment** ordonnancer
  un paiement
authorized autorisé; [*supplier etc*]
  agréé
authorized capital capital autorisé *m*
authorized distributor distributeur
  agréé *m*
authorized representative agent
  mandataire *m*

authorized share capital capital
  autorisé *m*
authorized signatory signataire
  accrédité *m*; *to be an authorized
  signatory* être habilité à signer
authorized to sign habilité à signer
automatically renewable
  renouvelable automatiquement
availability disponibilité *f*
available disponible; *to make funds
  available* débloquer des fonds; *to
  make credit available* dégager des
  crédits
available balance solde disponible *m*
available capital capitaux
  disponibles *mpl*
available means moyens
  disponibles *mpl*
aval aval bancaire *m*
to **avalize** avaliser
average moyenne *f*; *to work out the
  average* établir la moyenne
average *adj* moyen
average adjuster expert-
  répartiteur *m*
average gross profit margin marge
  commerciale moyenne *f*
to **avoid bankruptcy** éviter la
  faillite, échapper à la faillite
to **avoid tax** échapper à l'impôt
award [*of contract*] adjudication *f*
to **award** adjuger

B

to **backdate** antidater
back-dated rétroactif
backhander pot-de-vin *m*, dessous-de-table *m*
back of a bill dos d'un effet *m*
back pay rappel de salaire *m*
back to back credit crédit back to back *m*
backer [*of company*] bailleur de fonds *m*
backwardation déport *m*
bad debt dette véreuse *f*
to **bail out a company** renflouer une entreprise
bailiff huissier *m*
balance solde *m*; [*after audit*] reliquat *m*; [*situation, state*] situation *f*; [*remaining amount*] restant *m*
to **balance** équilibrer
to **balance a budget** équilibrer un budget
to **balance the books** balancer les livres
balance due solde dû *m*
balance of an account [*status*] situation d'un compte *f*; [*after audit*] reliquat d'un compte *m*
balance sheet bilan *m*, bilan comptable *m*
balance sheet account compte de bilan *m*
balance sheet consolidation consolidation de bilan *f*

balance sheet item poste de bilan *m*
balance sheet value valeur de bilan *f*, valeur d'inventaire *f*, VI *f*
bank banque *f*
bank *adj* bancaire, de banque
to **bank with** avoir un compte à
bank account compte bancaire *m*; *to have a bank account* avoir un compte en banque
bank balance situation de compte *f*
bank base rate taux de base bancaire *m*
bank book [*for accounting*] journal de banque *m*, livre de banque *m*; [*of account holder*] livret de compte *m*
bank borrowings emprunts bancaires *mpl*, concours bancaire *m*
bank branch code code guichet *m*
bank charge commission bancaire *f*
bank charges frais de banque *mpl*, agios *mpl*
bank cheque chèque bancaire *m*
bank commission commission bancaire *f*
bank credit avoir en banque *m*, crédit bancaire *m*
bank details relevé d'identité bancaire *m*, RIB *m*
bank discount rate escompte officiel *m*
bank draft traite bancaire *f*

bank guarantee garantie bancaire *f*, caution de banque *f*

bank holiday jour férié *m*, jour chômé *m*

bank interest intérêt bancaire *m*

bank ledger livre de banque *m*, journal de banque *m*

bank loan prêt bancaire *m*

bank manager directeur de banque *m*

banknote billet de banque *m*

bank notification avis de la banque *m*

bank overdraft découvert bancaire *m*

bank reconciliation rapprochement bancaire *m*

bank references références bancaires *fpl*

bank shares valeurs bancaires *fpl*

bank sort code code banque *m*

bank statement extrait de compte *m*, relevé de compte *m*

bank transactions transactions bancaires *fpl*

bank transfer virement bancaire *m*

bank transfer advice avis de virement *m*

bankable paper papier bancable *m*

banker banquier *m*

banker's draft chèque de banque *m*

banking *adj* bancaire, de banque

banking centre place bancaire *f*

Banking Commission Commission bancaire *f*

banking consortium consortium de banques *m*

banking controls contrôle bancaire *m*

banking law droit bancaire *m*

bankrupt failli *m*; *to go bankrupt* faire faillite; *to be bankrupt* être en faillite

bankruptcy faillite *f*; [*fraudulent*] banqueroute *f*

bankruptcy proceedings procédure de faillite *f*

bar chart diagramme à barres *m*, histogramme *m*, graphique à tuyaux d'orgue *m*

base rate [*of banks*] taux de base bancaire *m*

basic rate tarif de base *m*

basic salary traitement de base *m*, salaire de base *m*

basic wage salaire de base *m*

basis base *f*

basis for depreciation base amortissable *f*

basis of calculations base de calcul *f*

basket of currencies panier de monnaies *m*

B/E (=bill of exchange) lettre de change *f*

to **bear interest** produire des intérêts

to **bear the costs** supporter les frais, assumer les frais

bearer porteur *m*; *made out to bearer* libellé au porteur

bearer bill effet au porteur *m*

bearer bond titre au porteur *m*

bearer cheque chèque au porteur *m*

bearer of a bill porteur d'un effet *m*

bearer of shares porteur d'actions *m*

bearer paper papier au porteur *m*

bearer share action au porteur *f*

before tax hors taxe, HT; [*income*] avant impôt

beneficiary bénéficiaire *mf*; [*of family allowance etc*] allocataire *mf*

benefit [*paid by the State*] allocation *f*

benefit in kind avantage en nature *m*

best: at best order ordre au mieux

bid offre *f*, soumission *f*

bid bond caution de soumission *f*

bid price cours d'achat *m*, cours acheteur *m*

bill [*invoice*] facture *f*; [*commercial*] effet *m*

bill for collection effet à l'encaissement *m*

bill of exchange effet *m*, traite *f*, lettre de change *f*

bill of lading connaissement *m*

bill of sale contrat d'achat *m*

bill "without protest" traite "sans frais" *f*

billing facturation *f*

bills of exchange statement lettre de change relevé *f*, LCR *f*

bills payable ledger livre des effets à payer *m*, journal des effets à payer *m*

bills receivable ledger livre des effets à recevoir *m*, journal des effets à recevoir *m*

blank cheque chèque en blanc *m*

to **blank endorse** endosser en blanc

to **block** bloquer

block of shares paquet d'actions *m*

blocked account compte bloqué *m*

blocked cheque chèque bloqué *m*

board [*of company*] conseil *m*, conseil d'administration *m*; *to be on the board* siéger au conseil

board meeting réunion du conseil d'administration *f*, réunion du conseil *f*

board of directors conseil d'administration *m*

board of inquiry commission d'enquête *f*

board room salle du conseil *f*

body organisme *m*

body corporate personne morale *f*

bond obligation *f*

bond holder détenteur d'obligations *m*

bond issue émission d'obligations *f*, emprunt obligataire *m*; *to make a bond issue* émettre un emprunt

bonus bonus *m*

book of original entry livre-journal *m*

book-keeper employé/employée aux écritures *m/f*

book-keeping tenue des livres *f*

book value valeur comptable *f*

to **borrow** emprunter

to **borrow against** emprunter sur

to **borrow money from** emprunter de l'argent à

borrower emprunteur *m*

borrowing against securities pledging mise en pension *f*

borrowing capacity capacité à emprunter *f*, capacité d'endettement *f*

borrowing limit limite d'endettement *f*

borrowings emprunts *mpl*

boss chef *m*, patron *m*

to **bounce: cheque that bounces** chèque sans provision *m*

bound by contract lié par contrat

boycott boycott *m*

to **boycott** boycotter

branch succursale *f*; [*of bank*] agence *f*

branch manager directeur de succursale *m*

branch office succursale *f*, bureau-satellite *m*

brand image image de marque *f*

brand manager directeur de produit *m*

breach of contract rupture de contrat *f*

breach of trust abus de confiance *m*

to **break down** [*figures etc*] ventiler; [*negotiations*] échouer

to **break even: at what level do we break even?** à quel niveau est-ce qu'on rentre dans nos frais ?

to **break into one's capital** entamer son capital

to **break up a company** scinder une société

breakdown [*of figures etc*] ventilation *f*

breakdown of negotiations échec des négociations *m*

breakdown of the results décomposition des résultats *f*

breakeven point seuil de rentabilité *m*, point mort *m*

breakfast meeting réunion au petit déjeuner *f*

break-up of a company scission d'une entreprise *f*

break-up value valeur d'inventaire *f*, VI *f*

bribe pot-de-vin *m*

to **brief** briefer

briefing briefing *m*

to **bring action** introduire une action en justice

to **bring forward** reporter

to **bring in new measures** instaurer des mesures

to **bring onto the market** introduire sur le marché

brochure brochure *f*

broker courtier *m*

brokerage courtage *m*

brokerage (fee) droit de courtage *m*

budget enveloppe budgétaire *f*, budget *m*

budget *adj* budgétaire

budget deficit déficit budgétaire *m*

budget forecasts prévisions budgétaires *fpl*

budget surplus excédent budgétaire *m*

budgeting budgétisation *f*

buffer stock stock de sécurité *m*, stock stratégique *m*

bulletin bulletin *m*

bullion or en barres *m*, or en lingots *m*

business [*affair, matter*] affaire *f*; [*company*] firme *f*, entreprise *f*; [*line of business*] activité *f*; [*activity*] affaires *fpl*; **business for sale** fonds de commerce à vendre; *to be in business* faire des affaires

business *adj* commercial

business accounting comptabilité commerciale *f*

business assignment mission commerciale *f*

business card carte de visite *f*

business concern exploitation commerciale *f*

business cycle temps de cycle *m*

business documents documents commerciaux *mpl*

business enterprise entreprise commerciale *f*

business environment environnement commercial *m*

business expansion extension du commerce *f*

business experience: with business experience rompu aux affaires

business failure défaillance d'entreprise *f*

business letter lettre commerciale *f*

business lunch déjeuner d'affaires *m*

businessman homme d'affaires *m*

business management gestion d'entreprise *f*, gestion des sociétés *f*, direction des entreprises *f*; [*study*] économie d'entreprise *f*

business manager gérant
  d'affaires *m*
business meeting rendez-vous
  d'affaires *m*
business people gens d'affaires *mpl*
business plan programme de
  financement et de gestion *m*
business premises locaux
  commerciaux *mpl*
business recovery reprise des
  affaires *f*
business relations relations
  d'affaires *fpl*, relations
  commerciales *fpl*
business school école de commerce *f*
business studies économie
  d'entreprise *f*
business transactions transactions
  commerciales *fpl*

business trend courant d'affaires *m*
business trip voyage d'affaires *m*
businesswoman femme d'affaires *f*
bust: to go bust faire la culbute
to **buy** acheter; [*company*] racheter
to **buy forward** acheter à terme
to **buy sb out** racheter les parts de qn
buyback right droit de rachat *m*
buyer acheteur *m*; [*of company*]
  repreneur *m*
buyer credit crédit-acheteur *m*
buying department service des
  achats *m*
buyout [*by employees*] rachat de
  société par les salariés *m*; [*by
  management*] rachat de société par
  la direction *m*
bylaws [*Am: of company*] statuts de
  société *mpl*

C/A (=checking account) *Am*
  C/C *m*, CCB *m*
C/A (=cheque account) C/C *m*,
  CCB *m*
C/A (=current account) C/C *m*,
  CCB *m*
to **calculate** calculer
calculation calcul *m*, décompte *m*
calendar year année civile *f*
to **call a general meeting** convoquer

une assemblée générale
to **call a guarantee** faire jouer une
  garantie
to **call (in) a loan** demander le
  remboursement d'un prêt
to **call the shareholders to a
  meeting** convoquer les
  actionnaires
call for capital appel de fonds *m*
call for tenders appel d'offres *m*

call money argent au jour le jour *m*

callable remboursable

called-up (share) capital capital appelé *m*

campaign campagne *f*

to **cancel** annuler; [*appointment*] décommander

to **cancel a contract** annuler un contrat, résilier un contrat

to **cancel a debt** remettre une dette

cancellation annulation *f*; [*of contract*] annulation *f*, résiliation *f*

cancellation clause clause d'annulation *f*, clause de résiliation *f*

capital capital *m*

capital budget budget des investissements *m*

capital contribution apport en capital *m*, dotation en capital *f*, apport de capitaux *m*

capital employed capital engagé *m*

capital equipment biens d'équipement *mpl*

capital expenditure dépenses en immobilisations *fpl*, dépenses en capital *fpl*

capital gain plus-value *f*

capital gains tax impôt sur la plus-value *m*

capital injection injection de capital *f*, injection de capitaux *f*

capital-intensive qui demande un capital important

capital levy impôt sur le capital *m*

capital loss moins-value *f*

capital market marché des capitaux *m*

capital share part sociale *f*

capital tax impôt sur le capital *m*

capital transfer transfert de capitaux *m*

capital transfer tax taxe sur le transfert de capitaux *f*

capital turnover rotation des capitaux *f*

capitalization capitalisation *f*

to **capitalize** capitaliser

card [*business card*] carte de visite *f*

carried forward "report"

carried forward from the previous year report de l'exercice précédent

carried forward to the next year report à l'exercice suivant

to **carry a sum forward** reporter une somme

to **carry out** exécuter

to **carry out duties** exercer des fonctions

carrying forward report *m*

cash argent comptant *m*, argent liquide *m*; [*item on balance sheet*] caisse *f*; *to buy for cash* acheter (au) comptant; *to pay cash* payer (au) comptant

cash *adj* numéraire

to **cash** encaisser

to **cash a cheque** encaisser un chèque

cash at bank avoir en banque *m*

cash balance [*status*] situation de caisse *f*; [*amount remaining*] solde en caisse *m*

cash book livre de caisse *m*, journal de caisse *m*, livre de dépenses *m*, brouillard (de caisse) *m*

cash budget budget de trésorerie *m*

cash contribution apport en numéraire *m*

cash deposit versement d'espèces *m*, dépôt d'espèces *m*

cash discount remise sur paiement au comptant *f*, escompte de caisse *m*

cash dispenser distributeur automatique *m*

cash expenditure dépenses de

caisse *fpl*

cashflow trésorerie *f*; [*in cashflow statement*] marge brute d'autofinancement *f*

cashflow difficulties difficultés de trésorerie *fpl*

cashflow forecast prévision de trésorerie *f*

cashflow management gestion de trésorerie *f*

cashflow statement état des mouvements de la trésorerie *m*

cash in hand argent en caisse *m*

cash in till encaisse *f*

cash ledger journal de caisse *m*

cash on hand argent en caisse *m*

cash on hand and at bank disponibilités en caisse et en banque *fpl*

cash order ordre au comptant *m*

cash outflow sorties de trésorerie *fpl*

cash overs excédent de caisse *m*

cash payment paiement au comptant *m*, paiement comptant *m*, paiement en espèces *m*

cash payments sorties de caisse *fpl*

cash position situation de caisse *f*

cash purchase achat au comptant *m*, achat contre espèces *m*

cash ratio ratio de trésorerie *m*

cash receipt reçu d'espèces *m*

cash receipts and payments rentrées et sorties de caisse *fpl*

cash received [*balance sheet item*] entrée d'argent *f*

cash statement état de caisse *m*, bordereau de caisse *m*, relevé de caisse *m*

cash surplus restant en caisse *m*

cash transaction marché au comptant *m*

cash unders manque de caisse *m*

cash voucher pièce de caisse *f*, PC *f*

cash withdrawal retrait d'espèces *m*

cashable encaissable

cashier error allowance passe de caisse *f*

cashier's check *Am* chèque de banque *m*

casting vote voix prépondérante *f*

CBI (=Confederation of British Industry) *equivalent to* CNPF *m*

to **cease trading** cesser ses activités, cesser toute activité commerciale

ceiling [*limit*] plafond *m*; *to raise the ceiling on a credit limit* déplafonner un crédit

central account compte centralisateur *m*

central bank banque centrale *f*

central buying group centrale d'achat *f*

central purchasing group centrale d'achat *f*

centralization centralisation *f*

to **centralize** centraliser

CEO (=Chief Executive Officer) PDG *m*

certificate certificat *m*

certificate of deposit certificat de dépôt *m*

certificate of dishonour certificat de non-paiement *m*

certificate of incorporation certificat d'enregistrement de société *m*

certificate of transfer acte de cession *m*

certification certification *f*

certified authentique

certified accounts comptes approuvés *mpl*

certified by a notary notarié

certified cheque chèque certifié *m*

certified public accountant *Am* expert-comptable *m*

to **certify** certifier

to **certify documents** légaliser des documents

to **certify the books** viser des livres de commerce

to **chair a meeting** présider une assemblée

chairman président *m*

chairman and managing director Président-directeur général *m*

chairman of the board Président du conseil *m*

chairmanship of a company présidence d'une société *f*

chairperson président *m*, présidente *f*

Chamber of Commerce Chambre de commerce *f*

Chamber of Commerce and Industry Chambre de commerce et de l'industrie *f*

change modification *f*

change in stock variation de stock *f*

change in the line of business conversion d'entreprise *f*

channels: to go through channels passer par la voie hiérarchique

charge: to be in charge of [*matter, question*] être chargé de; [*department*] diriger; *the person in charge* le/la responsable

charge frais *m*; [*banking*] agio *m*; [*to an account*] imputation *f*

charge card carte accréditive *f*

charge to provisions dotation aux provisions *f*

chargeable [*to an account*] imputable; *to be chargeable to* [*payable by*] être à la charge de

chart graphique *m*

chart of accounts plan comptable général *m*

chartered accountant expert-comptable *m*

cheap bon marché, économique

check contrôle *m*; [*Am: for payment*] chèque *m*

to **check** vérifier

to **check inflation** juguler l'inflation

checking account *Am* compte chèque *m*

cheque chèque *m*

cheque book chéquier *m*

cheque card carte bancaire *f*

cheque made out to bearer chèque au porteur *m*

cheque No. (=cheque number) CH N°

cheque number numéro de chèque *m*

chief accountant chef comptable *m*

chief executive officer président-directeur général *m*

chronological chronologique

circulating assets actif circulant *m*

circulation of capital circulation des capitaux *f*

circulation of currency circulation des devises *f*

circulation of money circulation monétaire *f*

civil law droit civil *m*

civil servant fonctionnaire *mf*

claim réclamation *f*; [*insurance*] demande *f*

to **claim** réclamer

claim for damages demande en dommages-intérêts *f*

claims book livre des réclamations *m*

class classe *f*

classification classement *m*, classification *f*

classified ad petite annonce *f*

to **classify** classer, classifier

clause of a/the contract clause contractuelle *f*

clawback récupération *f*

clear: one clear day un jour franc
to **clear** compenser
cleared amount valeur compensée *f*
cleared cheque chèque compensé *m*
clearing compensation *f*
clearing agreement accord de clearing *m*
clearing bank banque compensatrice *f*
clearing price cours de compensation *m*
clerk commis *m*, préposé *m*
client client *m*
clientele clientèle *f*
to **close** [*letter, bank account*] fermer; [*books*] solder
to **close a deal** arrêter un marché
to **close a meeting** mettre fin à une réunion
to **close an account** [*banking*] clore un compte
to **close at a loss** clôturer à perte
to **close off an account** arrêter un compte
closing fermeture *f*
closing balance solde de compte *m*
closing entry écriture de clôture *f*
closing of an account [*banking*] clôture de compte *f*, fermeture de compte *f*
closing (off) of the accounts arrêt des comptes *m*
closing price cours de clôture *m*
closing stock stock final *m*
closing time heure de fermeture *f*
code code *m*
to **code** coder, codifier
coded [*encoded*] chiffré
coding codification *f*
co-director codirecteur *m*, coadministrateur *m*
coefficient coefficient *m*
to **collaborate** collaborer

collaboration collaboration *f*
collapse effondrement *m*
collateral nantissement *m*, caution *f*
collateral loans crédits sur nantissement *mpl*
colleague collègue *mf*, collaborateur *m*
to **collect** [*debts*] recouvrer; [*taxes*] percevoir
collectible [*debt*] recouvrable
collection [*of debts*] recouvrement *m*; [*of bill*] encaissement *m*; [*of taxes*] perception *f*
collection charge commission de paiement *f*, commission d'encaissement *f*
collection fee commission de paiement *f*, commission d'encaissement *f*
collection of taxes levée des impôts *f*
collective collectif
collective agreement contrat collectif *m*, convention collective *f*
collective bargaining négociation collective *f*
column colonne *f*
co-management cogérance *f*
to **come to an agreement on** se mettre d'accord sur
commerce commerce *m*
commercial commercial
commercial bank banque commerciale *f*
commercial bill effet de commerce *m*
commercial director directeur commercial *m*
commercial invoice facture commerciale *f*
commercial law droit commercial *m*
commercial manager directeur commercial *m*

commercial monopoly trust commercial *m*

commercial paper effets de commerce *mpl*

commercial rent loyer commercial *m*

commercial traveller voyageur de commerce *m*

commission commission *f*; [*on exchange*] commission de change *f*

commission costs frais de commission *mpl*

commission note note de commission *f*

commissioning [*of new plant*] mise en exploitation *f*; [*of machine*] mise en service *f*

commitment engagement *m*

committee meeting réunion de comité *f*

committee member membre du comité *m*

Common Market Marché Commun *m*

communications director directeur de la communication *m*

Community *adj* [*EC*] communautaire

Community law droit communautaire *m*

Companies Act Loi sur les sociétés *f*

Companies House *Br* institut où sont enregistrées toutes les informations concernant les entreprises du pays *m*

company société *f*, entreprise *f*, compagnie *f*

company brochure brochure de société *f*

company car voiture de fonction *f*

company cheque chèque d'entreprise *m*

company earnings revenu d'entreprise *m*

company head tête d'entreprise *f*

company law droit des sociétés *m*

company magazine revue d'entreprise *f*, journal d'entreprise *m*

company name raison sociale *f*, dénomination sociale *f*

company policy politique de la société *f*

company registration number numéro d'enregistrement de société *m*

company search audit d'entreprise *m*

company secretary secrétaire général *m*

company structure structure de l'entreprise *f*

comparative comparatif

comparative study étude comparative *f*

compensable indemnisable

compensable loss perte indemnisable *f*

to **compensate** indemniser, dédommager; *to be compensated for* être dédommagé de

to **compensate sb for sth** indemniser qn de qch

compensation indemnisation *f*, dédommagement *m*; [*money*] dommages-intérêts compensatoires *mpl*, indemnité *f*

compensation for loss of custom indemnité de clientèle *f*

compensation for wrongful dismissal indemnité de rupture abusive *f*

compensation in lieu of notice indemnité compensatrice de préavis *f*

compensatory amounts montants compensatoires monétaires *mpl*

to **compete with** concurrencer

competition concurrence *f*; *to be ahead of the competition* devancer ses concurrents

competitive compétitif, concurrentiel

competitiveness compétitivité *f*

competitor concurrent *m*

complaint réclamation *f*, plainte *f*; *to make a complaint* faire une réclamation, porter plainte

to **complete** [*finish*] achever

completion achèvement *m*

completion date date d'achèvement *f*

to **comply with** se conformer à

to **comply with a contract** respecter un contrat

composition [*with creditors*] accommodement *m*

compound interest intérêts composés *mpl*

comprehensive insurance assurance tous risques *f*, assurance multirisque *f*

comprehensive policy police tous risques *f*, police multirisque *f*

compromise compromis *m*

to **compromise** compromettre

compulsory obligatoire

computerized accounts comptabilité informatisée *f*

concession concession *f*

condition [*of contract*] condition *f*, terme *m*

Confederation of British Industry *equivalent to* Conseil national du patronat français *m*

to **confer** délibérer

conference conférence *f*

conference room salle de conférence *f*

confidential confidentiel

confidentiality confidentialité *f*

to **confirm** confirmer, attester

confirmation confirmation *f*; *in confirmation of* en confirmation de

confirmation fee commission de confirmation *f*

confirmed credit crédit confirmé *m*

confirming bank banque confirmatrice *f*

conflict conflit *m*

consensus consensus *m*

consent consentement *m*

to **consent to** consentir à

to **consolidate a debt** consolider une dette

consolidated accounts comptes consolidés *mpl*

consolidated debt dette consolidée *f*

consolidated entry écriture de consolidation *f*

consolidated subsidiary filiale consolidée *f*

to **consult** consulter

consultancy [*firm*] cabinet conseil *m*; [*work*] consultation *f*

consultant conseiller *m*, consultant *m*

consultative role voix consultative *f*

consulting engineer ingénieur-conseil *m*

consumables biens consommables *mpl*

contact contact *m*; [*agent*] agent de contact *m*

to **contest** contester

contested debt créance litigieuse *f*

contingency prévoyance *f*

contingency fund fonds de prévoyance *m*

contra contrepartie *f*

contra account compte de contrepartie *m*

contra entry contre-passation *f*

contract contrat *m*; *to be awarded the contract* être l'adjudicataire *to* **contract debts** contracter des dettes

contract-awarding party adjudicateur *m*

contract of employment contrat de travail *m*

contracting party contractant *m*, cocontractant *m*

contractual allowance indemnité conventionnelle *f*

contractual cover garantie conventionnelle *f*

contractual guarantee garantie contractuelle *f*

contractual liability responsabilité contractuelle *f*

contractual obligation obligation contractuelle *f*

contractual price prix contractuel *m*

contrary to the terms of the contract contraire aux termes du contrat

to **contribute to** contribuer à; [*to pension plan, NIC etc*] cotiser à

contribution contribution *f*; [*to pension plan, NIC etc*] cotisation *f*

contribution in kind apport en nature *m*

contribution (margin) marge sur les coûts variables *f*

control contrôle *m*

to **control** contrôler

controller contrôleur de gestion *m*

controlling factor facteur déterminant *m*

controlling interest participation majoritaire *f*

conversion of loan stock conversion d'un emprunt *f*

conversion rate taux de conversion *m*

conversion table tableau de conversion *m*

to **convert** convertir

to **convert loan stock** convertir un emprunt

to **convert securities** convertir des valeurs

convertible bond obligation convertible *f*

convertible loan stock emprunt obligataire convertible *m*

to **co-operate** coopérer

co-operation coopération *f*

co-operative coopératif

coordination coordination *f*

coordinator coordinateur *m*

co-owner copropriétaire *mf*

co-ownership copropriété *f*

co-partner coparticipant *m*, coassocié *m*

co-partnership coparticipation *f*

copy [*duplicate*] copie *f*; [*sample*] exemplaire *m*

copy of a contract exemplaire d'un contrat *m*

corporate assets biens sociaux *mpl*

corporate body personne morale *f*

corporate culture culture d'entreprise *f*

corporate funds biens sociaux *mpl*

corporate income revenu d'entreprise *m*

corporate infrastructure infrastructure de l'entreprise *f*

corporate strategy stratégie de l'entreprise *f*

corporate taxation fiscalité des entreprises *f*

corporation *Am* société *f*

corporation tax impôt sur les sociétés *m*, IS *m*

to **correct** corriger

correction correction *f*

to **correspond with** correspondre avec

correspondence correspondance *f*
correspondent correspondant *m*
correspondent bank account
    compte de correspondant *m*
co-signatory cosignataire *mf*
cost coût *m*; *at cost* à prix coûtant
to **cost** coûter
to **cost sth** [*calculate costs of*]
    évaluer les coûts de
cost accounting comptabilité
    analytique *f*
cost analysis analyse des coûts *f*
cost assessment évaluation du coût *f*
cost budget budget des charges *m*
cost centre centre d'analyse *m*
cost curve courbe de coût *f*
cost-effective rentable; *to make*
    facilities cost-effective rentabiliser
    des installations
cost escalation clause clause
    d'indexation *f*
cost factor facteur coût *m*
cost-of-living allowance indemnité
    de vie chère *f*
cost-of-living index indice du coût
    de la vie *m*
cost of money loyer de l'argent *m*
cost of sales coût de revient des
    produits vendus *m*
cost overrun dépassement de coût *m*
cost price coût de revient *m*, prix de
    revient *m*, prix coûtant *m*; *at cost*
    price à prix coûtant
cost price factors éléments
    constitutifs du prix de revient *mpl*
cost-push inflation inflation par les
    coûts *f*
cost savings économie de frais *f*
costing évaluation des coûts *f*
costs coûts *mpl*, frais *mpl*
count décompte *m*
to **count** compter
counter-offer contre-offre *f*

counterpart homologue *mf*
to **countersign** contresigner
counting comptage *m*
coupon bon *m*
courier courrier *m*; [*local*] coursier *m*
court tribunal *m*; *out of court* à
    l'amiable
Court of Appeal Cour d'Appel *f*
Court of Justice Cour de Justice *f*
court-ordered [*sale*] judiciaire
court ruling décision de justice *f*
cover couverture *f*
to **cover** couvrir
to **cover a loss** couvrir un déficit
to **cover an overdraft** couvrir un
    découvert
cover note note de couverture *f*
covered couvert
credit crédit *m*; [*in an account*]
    avoir *m*; *on credit* à crédit; *to buy*
    on credit acheter à crédit; *to be in*
    credit être créditeur; *account in*
    credit compte créditeur *m*
credit *adj* [*purchase*] à crédit;
    [*balance*] créditeur
to **credit** créditer
to **credit an account** créditer un
    compte
to **credit an amount to an account**
    porter un montant au crédit d'un
    compte
to **credit sb with an amount** verser
    un montant au crédit de qn
credit advice avis de crédit *m*
credit application demande
    d'ouverture de crédit *f*
credit application form formule de
    crédit *f*
credit balance solde créditeur *m*
credit balance of an account
    position créditrice d'un compte *f*
credit bank banque de crédit *f*
credit card carte de crédit *f*

105

credit ceiling plafond du crédit *m*
credit column colonne créditrice *f*
credit control contrôle du crédit *m*
credit controller contrôleur du crédit *m*
credit facilities facilités de crédit *fpl*
credit freeze gel de crédits *m*
credit guarantee institution caisse de garantie *f*
credit institution institut de crédit *m*, institution de crédit *f*
credit instrument instrument de crédit *m*
credit insurance assurance crédit *f*
credit item poste créditeur *m*
credit limit limite de crédit *f*
credit line ligne de crédit *f*
credit management gestion des crédits *f*, gestion de crédit *f*
credit margin marge de crédit *f*
credit note note de crédit *f*, avoir *m*
credit period délai de crédit *m*, délai de paiement *m*
credit policy politique de crédit *f*
credit purchase achat à crédit *m*
credit restriction encadrement du crédit *m*
credit sale vente à crédit *f*
credit squeeze resserrement du crédit *m*
credit terms conditions de crédit *fpl*
credit to be carried forward crédit à reporter *m*
credit-worthiness solvabilité *f*
credit-worthy solvable
credited with crédité de
creditor créancier *m*, créditeur *m*
creditor *adj* créditeur
creditors' meeting réunion des créanciers *f*
critical path chemin critique *m*
critical path analysis analyse du chemin critique *f*

to **cross a cheque** barrer un chèque
to **cross out** barrer
cross holding participation croisée *f*
crossed cheque chèque barré *m*
to **crystallize** [*a debt*] matérialiser
cum dividend coupon attaché
cumulative costs coûts cumulés *mpl*
cumulative credit crédit cumulé *m*
cumulative debit débit cumulé *m*
cumulative depreciation amortissements cumulés *mpl*
cumulative dividend dividende cumulatif *m*
currency devise *f*
currency fluctuation mouvement des devises *m*
currency transfer transfert de devises *m*
current actuel
current account compte courant *m*, compte chèque *m*
current account with a bank compte courant bancaire *m*
current assets actif circulant *m*
current earnings revenus actuels *mpl*
current expenditure(s) dépenses courantes *fpl*
current expenses charges courantes *fpl*
current financial year exercice en cours *m*
current fiscal year *Am* exercice en cours *m*
current income [*in accounts*] produits courants *mpl*; [*actual earnings*] revenu actuel *m*
current liabilities passif exigible *m*, dettes à court terme *fpl*
current ratio coefficient de liquidité *m*
current value valeur actuelle *f*
curriculum vitae curriculum vitae *m*

curve courbe *f*
customer client *m*
customer code code client *m*
customer credit avoir-client *m*
customer file fichier client *m*
customer follow-up relance client *f*
customer reference number code
  client *m*
customer relations manager
  directeur de la clientèle *m*
customer service service clientèle *m*
customer service (department)

  service clientèle *m*
customers clientèle *f*
customs duties droits de douane *mpl*
to **cut staff** réduire le personnel
cutback dégonflement *m*
cut-throat competition concurrence
  acharnée *f*
cutting down of expenses
  diminution des dépenses *f*
CV (=curriculum vitae) CV *m*
cyclical conjoncturel

D

daily quotidien
daily allowance indemnité
  journalière *f*
daily balance interest calculation
  méthode à échelles *f*, méthode par
  échelles *f*
daily takings recette journalière *f*
damages dommages-intérêts *mpl*,
  intérêts compensatoires *mpl*
data entry form fiche d'imputation *f*
date date *f*; *to date* à ce jour
to **date** dater; *letter dated the ...* lettre
  datée du ...; *dated this day* en date
  de ce jour
date of completion date
  d'achèvement *f*
day book main courante *f*,

  brouillard *m*
day of grace jour de grâce *m*
days of grace délai de grâce *m*
DCF (=discounted cashflow)
  VAN *f*
deadline date limite *f*, délai *m*; *to
  make the deadline* respecter le
  délai
deadlock impasse *f*
deal marché *m*, affaire *f*
to **deal with** [*have dealings with*]
  traiter avec, avoir affaire à; [*look
  after*] s'occuper de
dealer marchand *m*; [*sole
  distributor*] concessionnaire *mf*
debenture obligation *f*
debenture *adj* obligataire

107

debenture bond emprunt
obligataire *m*, obligataire *m*

debit débit *m*; *to the debit of* au débit
de

debit *adj* débiteur

to **debit** débiter

to **debit an account** débiter un
compte

to **debit an amount to an account**
porter un montant au débit d'un
compte, débiter un compte d'un
montant

debit advice avis de débit *m*

debit balance solde débiteur *m*,
solde déficitaire *m*

debit balance of an account position
débitrice d'un compte *f*

debit column colonne débitrice *f*

debit item poste débiteur *m*

debit note facture de débit *f*, note de
débit *f*

debits and credits doit et avoir *m*

debt dette *f*; [*to be recovered*]
créance *f*; *in debt* endetté; *to get
into debt* s'endetter

debt chasing letter lettre de
poursuite *f*, lettre de relance des
impayés *f*

debt collection recouvrement de
créances *m*

debt collection agency agence de
recouvrement de dettes *f*

debt instrument titre de créance *m*

debt servicing service de la dette *m*

debtor débiteur *m*

decentralization décentralisation *f*

to **decentralize** décentraliser

to **decide on sth** adopter une décision
concernant qch

decimal décimal

decision décision *f*; *to give a
decision* se prononcer; *to make a
decision* prendre une décision

decision by arbitration décision
arbitrale *f*

decision-maker décideur *m*

decision-making prise de décision *f*

to **declare a business bankrupt**
déclarer une entreprise en faillite

to **declare a dividend** déclarer un
dividende

to **declare a moratorium** décréter un
moratoire

declared déclaré

declining déclinant

decrease diminution *f*

to **decrease** diminuer

decrease in capital diminution de
capital *f*

decrease in profits diminution des
bénéfices *f*

decrease in stocks [*profit and loss
item*] déstockage de production *m*

decrease in working capital [*on
uses of funds statement*]
dégagement de fonds de
roulement *m*

decree arrêté *m*

to **deduct** déduire

to **deduct a commission** prélever une
commission

to **deduct a sum of money** défalquer
une somme

to **deduct taxes** prélever des taxes

deducted at source retenu à la
source

deductibility déductibilité *f*

deductible déductible

deduction déduction *f*; [*from salary*]
retenue *f*

deduction from wages retenue
salariale *f*, prélèvement salarial *m*

deduction of a sum décompte d'une
somme *m*

deduction of tax at source retenue
salariale à la source *f*

deed acte *m*

deed of acknowledgment acte récognitif *m*

deed of sale acte de vente *m*

deed of transfer acte de cession *m*

de facto possession possession de fait *f*

default interest intérêts moratoires *mpl*

defaulting défaillant

to **defer** renvoyer

to **defer payment** différer le paiement

deferral renvoi *m*

deferred renvoyé

deferred depreciation amortissements différés *mpl*

deferred payment paiement différé *m*

deficit déficit *m*

deflation déflation *f*

deflationary déflationniste

to **defray expenses** fournir à la dépense

degree degré *m*; [*academic*] diplôme *m*

delay retard *m*

to **delay payment** retarder le paiement

del credere ducroire *m*

delegate délégué *m*

to **delegate** déléguer

delegation délégation *f*

delegation of power délégation de pouvoir *f*

to **deliver shares** délivrer des valeurs

delivery livraison *f*

demand demande *f*

demand *adj* à vue

to **demand** demander; [*pay rise, payment*] exiger, réclamer

to **demand payment from sb** sommer qn de payer

demand deposit remise à vue *f*, dépôt à vue *m*

demand-pull inflation inflation par la demande *f*

demotivation démotivation *f*

denomination [*of share, of banknote*] coupure *f*

denominator dénominateur *m*

department service *m*, direction *f*; [*government*] ministère *m*

Department of Trade and Industry ministère du Commerce et de l'Industrie *m*

departmental manager chef de service *m*

departure from dérogation à *f*

deposit [*into bank*] dépôt *m*; [*security*] arrhes *fpl*

to **deposit** déposer, verser; [*into bank*] déposer

to **deposit as security** nantir, gager

to **deposit security** déposer une caution

deposit account compte livret *m*, compte de dépôt *m*

deposit bank banque de dépôt *f*

deposit book livret de dépôts *m*

deposit money monnaie scripturale *f*

deposit of a sum of money dépôt d'une somme *m*

depositor déposant *m*

to **depreciate** se déprécier; [*equipment*] se dévaluer, s'avilir

depreciated amorti

depreciation dépréciation *f*; [*of equipment*] amortissement *m*

depreciation period période d'amortissement *f*

depreciation rate taux d'amortissement *m*

depreciation schedule tableau d'amortissement *m*, plan d'amortissement *m*

dept (=department) dépt
to **deputize for sb** suppléer qn
deputy adjoint *m*, suppléant *m*
deputy director directeur adjoint *m*
deputy manager directeur adjoint *m*
deputy managing director directeur général adjoint *m*
derogatory clause clause dérogatoire *f*
description désignation *f*, description *f*
design department bureau d'études *m*
desk diary agenda *m*
to **destock goods** déstocker des marchandises
destocking déstockage *m*
to **develop** développer
development costs coût de développement *m*
diagram diagramme *m*, schéma *m*; [*chart*] graphique *m*; *to make a diagram of* schématiser
dialogue dialogue *m*
diary agenda *m*; [*showing a week at a time*] semainier *m*
difference in prices [*of shares*] différence de cours *f*
differential différentiel
differential cost coût différentiel *m*
differential rate tarif différentiel *m*
differential taxation taxation différentielle *f*
dilution of capital dilution de capital *f*
diploma diplôme *m*
direct direct
direct cost coût direct *m*
direct debit prélèvement automatique *m*
direct debit advice avis de prélèvement *m*
direct labour costs coûts de main-d'œuvre directe

direct selling vente directe *f*
direct tax impôt direct *m*
direct taxation contributions directes *fpl*
directive directive *f*
director directeur *m*; [*board member*] administrateur *m*
director's fees jetons de présence *mpl*
director's loan account compte courant des administrateurs *m*
disagreement désaccord *m*, différend *m*
disbursement déboursement *m*
to **discharge a bankrupt** réhabiliter un failli
to **discharge a debt** apurer une dette
to **discharge a debtor** libérer un débiteur
to **discharge sb from a debt** décharger qn d'une dette
discharge of a bankrupt réhabilitation d'un failli *f*
discharge of a debt extinction d'une dette *f*
discharged bankrupt failli réhabilité *m*
discount remise *f*; [*bank*] escompte *m*
to **discount** escompter
discount for early payment escompte de règlement *m*
discount house comptoir d'escompte *m*
discount rate taux d'escompte *m*
discountable escomptable
discounted bill effet escompté *m*
discounted cashflow valeur actualisée nette *f*
discounting of a bill escompte commercial *m*
discounts and allowances remise,

rabais, ristourne, RRR
to **discuss an issue** discuter une
question
dishonour refus de paiement *m*
to **dismiss** [*employee*] licencier,
renvoyer, congédier
dismissal [*of employee*]
licenciement *m*, renvoi *m*,
congédiement *m*
dismissal with notice licenciement
avec préavis *m*
dismissal without notice
licenciement sans préavis *m*
dispatch (department)
expéditions *fpl*
disposable income revenu
disponible *m*
disposal [*of goods, property*]
aliénation *f*; *to have a sum of
money at one's disposal* disposer
d'une somme
disposal of assets cession d'actifs *f*
disposals of stocks écoulement de
stocks *m*
dispute différend *m*, contestation *f*;
in dispute litigieux
dissolution [*of company*]
dissolution *f*
to **dissolve** [*company*] dissoudre
to **distribute** diffuser, distribuer
distribution diffusion *f*, distribution *f*
distribution costs coûts de
distribution *mpl*
distribution network réseau de
distribution *m*, circuit de
distribution *m*
distribution of profit distribution
d'un bénéfice *f*
distribution of profits répartition du
bénéfice *f*
distributor distributeur *m*
diversification diversification *f*
to **diversify** diversifier

to **diversify into** se reconvertir dans
divestment désinvestissement *m*
divestment of assets scission
d'actifs *f*
to **divide** diviser; [*money*] répartir
to **divide profits among
shareholders** répartir les bénéfices
entre les actionnaires
to **divide proportionally** répartir au
prorata
dividend dividende *m*
dividend share action de jouissance *f*
division division *f*
division of labour division du
travail *f*
division of votes partage de voix *m*
divisional account compte
divisionnaire *m*
document document *m*
documentary bill traite
documentaire *f*
documentary credit crédit
documentaire *m*
documentary evidence pièces
justificatives *fpl*
documentation documentation *f*
documents documents *mpl*
domicile domicile *m*
to **domicile** domicilier
domiciliation domiciliation *f*
to **double** doubler
double entry partie double *f*
double entry book-keeping
comptabilité en partie double *f*
doubtful debt client douteux *m*,
créance douteuse *f*
**down: to be down 12% as against
last year** être en baisse de 12% par
rapport à l'année précédente
to **down tools** débrayer
down payment acompte *m*; *to make
a down payment* donner un
acompte

downward movement mouvement
de baisse *m*

downward trend tendance à la
baisse *f*

DP (=data processing) manager
chef des traitements *m*

draft [*bill*] traite *f*

draft agreement projet de contrat *m*

draft budget projet de budget *m*

to **draw a bill on** tirer une traite sur

to **draw a cheque on** tirer un chèque
sur, disposer un chèque sur

to **draw at sight** tirer à vue

to **draw one's salary** toucher ses
appointements

to **draw up** rédiger; [*list*] dresser

to **draw up a plan** élaborer un projet

to **draw up an invoice** rédiger une
facture

to **draw up the accounts** établir les
comptes

draw down tirage *m*

drawee tiré *m*

drawer tireur *m*; [*of bill*]

souscripteur *m*

drawing tirage *m*

drawing rights droits de tirage *mpl*

drawing up of a balance sheet
établissement du bilan *m*

to **drop** [*prices*] reculer

drop-deadline délai de rigueur *m*

drop in prices baisse des prix *f*

**DTI (=Department of Trade and
Industry)** ministère du Commerce
et de l'Industrie *m*

due dû; *in due form* en due forme

due date échéance *f*; *on the due date*
à l'échéance, à terme échu

duly dûment

dunning letter lettre de poursuite *f*

duplicate double *m*, duplicata *m*; *in
duplicate* en deux exemplaires

duplicate *adj* fait en double
exemplaire

duration durée *f*

duties [*of employee*] fonctions *fpl*

duty [*tax*] droit *m*; [*excise*] droits de
douane *mpl*

E

early repayment remboursement
   anticipé *m*
early retirement préretraite *f*
to **earn money** gagner de l'argent
easy: to make a job easier faciliter
   un travail
easy terms facilités de paiement *fpl*
EC (=European Community) CEE *f*
EC *adj* de la CEE
EC directive directive européenne *f*
economic adviser conseiller
   économique *m*
economic circumstances
   conjoncture *f*
economic forecast prévisions
   économiques *fpl*
economic policy politique
   économique *f*
economic recovery reprise
   économique *f*, redressement
   économique *m*
economic stagnation marasme
   économique *m*
economic warfare guerre
   économique *f*
economies of scale économies
   d'échelle *fpl*
economist économiste *mf*
economy économie *f*
**EDF (=European Development
   Fund)** FED *m*
**EEC (=European Economic
   Community)** CEE *f*
EEC *adj* de la CEE

efficiency efficience *f*
efficient performant
eight-hour day journée de huit
   heures *f*
elasticity of demand élasticité de la
   demande *f*
elasticity of supply élasticité de
   l'offre *f*
to **elect [sb]** élire
election of officers élection du
   bureau *f*
electronic mail courrier
   électronique *m*, messagerie *f*
electronic payment paiement
   électronique *m*
electronic transfer transfert
   électronique *m*
to **embezzle money** détourner de
   l'argent
embezzlement malversation *f*
embezzlement of assets
   détournement d'actifs *m*
embezzlement of funds
   détournement de fonds *m*
emergency fund fonds de secours *m*
emoluments émoluments *mpl*
to **employ workers** employer des
   ouvriers
employee employé *m*, employée *f*
employee buyout reprise de
   l'entreprise par les salariés *f*, RES *f*
employee contributions cotisations
   salariales *fpl*, charges sociales
   salariales *fpl*

employee profit-sharing scheme intéressement aux résultats *m*

employee file fichier salarié *m*

employee representative délégué du personnel *m*

employee training costs dépenses de formation professionnelle des salariés *fpl*

employee's contributions retenues salariales *fpl*

employees effectif *m*, salariés *mpl*

employees' representative représentant du personnel *m*

employer employeur *m*

employer contributions charges patronales *fpl*, charges sociales patronales *fpl*

employer's patronal

employer's contributions cotisations patronales *fpl*, retenues patronales *fpl*

employer's liability responsabilité patronale *f*

employers patronat *m*

employers' organization syndicat patronal *m*

employment emploi *m*

employment agency agence de placement *f*, bureau de placement *m*

employment law code du travail *m*, législation du travail *f*

employment tax taxe sur les salaires *f*

EMS (=European Monetary System) SME *m*

to **encash** *Br* encaisser

encashment *Br* encaissement *m*

end of month de fin de mois

end of month payments échéances de fin de mois *fpl*

end of month settlement liquidation de fin de mois *f*

end of month statement relevé de fin de mois *m*

end of the financial year fin de l'exercice *f*, clôture de l'exercice *f*; *at the end of the financial year* en fin d'exercice

end of year bonus gratification de fin d'année *f*

endorsable endossable

to **endorse** endosser

endorsed bill effet endossé *m*

endorsee endossataire *mf*

endorsement endos *m*, endossement *m*

endorsement to a policy avenant *m*

endorser endosseur *m*

enquiry demande de renseignements *f*

to **enter** [*to record*] enregistrer

to **enter in an account** passer en compte

to **enter in the accounts** comptabiliser

to **enter into** [*deal, contract*] conclure

to **enter into commitments** contracter des obligations

to **enter into negotiations** engager des négociations

entering [*recording*] enregistrement *m*

entering into the accounts comptabilisation *f*

entering of an order enregistrement d'une commande *m*

entertainment allowance indemnité de représentation *f*

entertainment costs frais de représentation *mpl*

entitlement to interest jouissance d'intérêts *f*

entrepreneur entrepreneur *m*

entry [*in accounts*] poste *m*,

écriture *f*
enumeration énumération *f*
equal opportunities égalité des chances *f*
equal pay égalité des salaires *f*
equation équation *f*
equipment équipement *m*, équipements *mpl*
equity capitaux propres *mpl*
equity loan prêt participatif *m*, titre participatif *m*
ERDF (=European Regional Development Fund) FEDER *m*
escalator clause échelle mobile *f*
escrow account compte bloqué *m*
estimate estimation *f*; [*for work*] devis *m*, devis estimatif *m*
estimated costs coûts prévisionnels *mpl*
estimated loss perte envisagée *f*
estimation of costs estimation des frais *f*
eurocheque eurochèque *m*
eurocurrency eurodevise *f*
eurodollar eurodollar *m*
eurofranc eurofranc *m*
European Commission Commission européenne *f*
European Development Fund Fonds européen de développement *m*
European Economic Community Communauté économique européenne *f*
European Monetary System Système monétaire européen *m*
European Parliament Parlement européen *m*
European Regional Development Fund Fonds européen de développement régional *m*
to **evade tax** frauder le fisc
to **evaluate** évaluer

to **examine** examiner
to **exceed** dépasser
to **exceed a credit limit** dépasser un crédit
exceptional costs charges exceptionnelles *fpl*
excess clause clause de franchise *f*
excess profit surprofit *m*
excessive taxation fiscalité excessive *f*
exchange échange *m*; *in exchange for payment* moyennant paiement
to **exchange letters** échanger des lettres
to **exchange opinions** échanger des opinions
exchange control regulations réglementation du change *f*
exchange controls contrôle des changes *m*
exchange gain gain de change *m*
exchange loss perte de change *f*
exchange of letters échange de lettres *m*
exchange rate taux de change *m*
exchange rate fluctuations fluctuation des cours *f*
exchange rate parity parités du change *fpl*
exchange rates cours des changes *m*
Exchequer *Br* ministère des Finances *m*
excise tax accise *f*
exclusive of tax hors taxe
ex dividend coupon échu
to **execute a contract** exécuter un contrat
execution exécution *f*
executive cadre *m*
executive board directoire *m*
executive committee comité de direction *m*

executive director directeur administratif *m*, directeur gérant *m*

executive functions fonctions d'encadrement *fpl*

executive recruitment agency association pour l'emploi des cadres *f*, APEC *f*

executive secretary secrétaire de direction *mf*

executives encadrement *m*

to **exempt** exonérer

to **exempt from tax** exonérer d'impôt

exempt from exonéré de

exemption clause clause d'exonération *f*

exemption from customs duty franchise douanière *f*

exemption from liability exonération de responsabilité *f*

exemption from VAT exonération de TVA *f*

exercise exercice *m*

to **exercise a right** exercer un droit

to **exercise control over** exercer un contrôle sur

exercise price [*of share*] prix d'exercice *m*

ex gratia payment paiement à titre de faveur *m*

exorbitant exorbitant

expansion expansion *f*

to **expedite a piece of work** expédier un travail

expenditure dépenses *fpl*

expenditure plan planning des charges *m*

expense dépense *f*; [*cost*] charge *f*

expense account note de frais *f*; [*accounting*] compte de charges *m*

expense transfer transfert de charges *m*

expenses frais *mpl*, note de frais *f*

experienced expérimenté, chevronné

expert expert *m*

expert's report rapport d'expertise *m*

expertise savoir-faire *m*

to **expire** expirer, arriver à échéance

expiry expiration *f*

expiry date échéance *f*, date d'échéance *f*, date d'expiration *f*

expiry date of a contract échéance d'un contrat *f*

explicit explicite

to **exploit employees** exploiter des salariés

export company entreprise exportatrice *f*

export department service commercial export *m*

export director directeur export *m*

export financing financement des exportations *m*

export manager directeur export *m*

export tariff tarif export *m*

export tax taxe à l'exportation *f*

exposure encours *m*

to **express opinions** émettre des avis

to **expropriate** exproprier

expropriation expropriation *f*

to **extend** prolonger

to **extend payment terms** proroger une échéance

extension prolongation *f*, extension *f*

external auditor vérificateur externe *m*

external financing financement externe *m*

extra income salaire d'appoint *m*

extra time to pay sursis de paiement *m*

extraordinary expenses dépenses extraordinaires *fpl*

extraordinary general meeting assemblée générale extraordinaire *f*

extraordinary income produits
  exceptionnels *mpl*

extraordinary item poste
  extraordinaire *m*

face [*of letter of exchange*] recto *m*
face value valeur nominale *f*
factor facteur *m*
factoring affacturage *m*
factoring company société
  d'affacturage *f*
factory usine *f*
failure [*of company*] naufrage *m*
fair market value valeur vénale *f*
to **fall** [*shares, rates*] s'inscrire en
  baisse, fléchir
to **fall due** échoir, arriver à échéance
to **fall in value** baisser en valeur
fall in prices chute des prix *f*
falling [*stock market*] orienté à la
  baisse
false invoice fausse facture *f*
family allowance prime familiale *f*
family business entreprise familiale *f*
favour: in favour of en faveur de
favourable favorable
fax (message) télécopie *f*, fax *m*
feasibility study étude de faisabilité *f*
fee note note d'honoraires *f*
feedback rétroaction *f*
fees honoraires *mpl*
female executive femme cadre *f*

fictitious fictif
fictitious asset actif fictif *m*
fictitious cost charge fictive *f*
to **fiddle the accounts** trafiquer les
  comptes
fiduciary fiduciaire
figure chiffre *m*; *in figures* en
  chiffres
file [*computer*] fichier *m*
to **file a petition in bankruptcy**
  déposer son bilan
final demand dernier rappel *m*
final discharge quittance finale *f*,
  quitus *m*
final dividend dividende final *m*
final payment quittance finale *f*
final settlement solde de tout
  compte *m*
to **finalize** mettre au point
finance finance *f*; [*funding*]
  finances *fpl*
to **finance** financer
finance act loi des finances *f*
finance (department) service
  financier *m*
finance director directeur
  financier *m*

finance plan tableau de financement *m*

financed from cash flow autofinancé

financial financier

financial accounting comptabilité générale *f*

financial centre place financière *f*

financial circles sphères de la finance *fpl*

financial controller contrôleur financier *m*

financial costs frais financiers *mpl*

financial department service financier *m*

financial director directeur financier *m*

financial expert expert financier *m*

financial field domaine financier *m*

financial gain gain d'argent *m*

financial institution établissement financier *m*

financial legislation législation financière *f*

financial leverage levier financier *m*

financial management direction financière *f*, gestion financière *f*

financial management accounting comptabilité-gestion financière *f*

financial manager directeur financier *m*

financial market marché financier *m*

financial means moyens financiers *mpl*

financial newspaper journal financier *m*

financial period période comptable *f*

financial position position financière *f*

financial resources ressources financières *fpl*

financial situation situation financière *f*

financial statement bilan financier *m*

financial statements document de synthèse *m*

financial syndicate syndicat financier *m*

financial transaction opération financière *f*

financial transactions flux financier *m*

financial year exercice *m*, exercice comptable *m*, année budgétaire *f*

financially financièrement

financier financier *m*

financing financement *m*

financing plan plan de financement *m*

fine [*punishment*] amende *f*

firm firme *f*

firm *adj* ferme; *to make a firm purchase* acheter ferme

firm of auditors cabinet comptable *m*

firm option option ferme *f*

firm order ordre ferme *m*

firm transactions opérations fermes *fpl*

firmness of the market fermeté des cours *f*

first demand guarantee garantie à première demande *f*

first of exchange première de change *f*

fiscal law loi fiscale *f*

fiscal period *Am* période comptable *f*

fiscal year *Am* exercice *m*, exercice comptable *m*, année budgétaire *f*

five-day week semaine de cinq jours *f*

five-year quinquennal

fixed fixe; *on a fixed date* à date fixe

fixed annual payment annuité constante *f*

fixed asset actif immobilisé *m*

fixed asset account compte

d'immobilisations *m*
fixed assets immobilisations *fpl*
fixed capital capital fixe *m*
fixed charges frais fixes *mpl*
fixed cost centre centre d'analyse de structure *m*
fixed costs charges fixes *fpl*, charges de structure *fpl*, coûts fixes *mpl*
fixed income investment placement à revenus fixes *m*
fixed income securities titres à revenu fixe *mpl*, valeurs à revenu fixe *fpl*
fixed interest intérêt fixe *m*
fixed rate bond obligation à revenu fixe *f*
fixed rate of interest taux d'intérêt fixe *m*
fixed salary traitement fixe *m*
fixed-term à terme fixe
fixed-term bill effet à date fixe *m*
fixed-term contract contrat à durée déterminée *m*
flat rate taux uniforme *m*
flexible hours horaire flexible *m*, horaire variable *m*
flexitime horaire flexible *m*, horaire variable *m*
flight of capital fuite de capitaux *f*, évasion de capitaux *f*, exode des capitaux *m*
to **float** *vi* flotter
to **float** *vt* faire flotter
to **float on the Stock Exchange** introduire en Bourse
floating assets actif circulant *m*
floating capital capital flottant *m*
floating rate bond obligation à intérêt variable *f*, obligation à revenu variable *f*
floating rate securities titres à revenu variable *mpl*, valeurs à revenu variable *fpl*

floor [*of stock market*] parquet *m*, corbeille *f*
flow flux *m*
flowchart organigramme *m*
flow of funds flux de fonds *m*
flow of goods and services flux réel *m*
flow sheet feuille d'avancement *f*
to **fluctuate** fluctuer; [*share price*] osciller
fluctuation fluctuation *f*
fluctuation of a share price oscillation d'une valeur *f*
follow-up letter lettre de relance *f*
follow-up system système de relance *m*
Footsie *equivalent to* indice CAC 40 *m*
force majeure force majeure *f*
forced forcé
forecast prévision *f*
to **forecast turnover** prévoir un chiffre d'affaires
forecast balance sheet bilan prévisionnel *m*
foreclosure forclusion *f*
foreign étranger
foreign currency devises étrangères *fpl*
foreign currency account compte en devises étrangères *m*
foreign currency holding avoir en devises étrangères *m*
foreign currency option option de change *f*
foreign exchange broker cambiste *mf*
foreign exchange gain gain de change *m*
foreign exchange loss perte de change *f*
foreign exchange market marché des changes *m*

foreign investment investissement à l'étranger *m*

foreign securities valeurs étrangères *fpl*

forfaiting forfaitage *m*

forfeit dédit *m*

forfeiture déchéance *f*

to **forge** [*chèque, signature*] falsifier

forged cheque faux chèque *m*

forgeries faux en écriture *mpl*

form formulaire *m*, imprimé *m*

to **form a company** former une société

to **form a monopoly** truster

to **form into a monopoly** truster

formal demand mise en demeure *f*

formal notice mise en demeure *f*

formality formalité *f*

fortnightly settlement liquidation de quinzaine *f*

forward buying achat à terme *m*

forward contract contrat à terme *m*

forward sale vente à terme *f*

founder fondateur *m*

founder's share part de fondateur *f*

founding member membre fondateur *m*

fraction fraction *f*

franchise franchise *f*

franchise holder franchisé *m*

franchised franchisé

franchisee franchisé *m*

franchising franchisage *m*

franchisor franchiseur *m*

fraudulent frauduleux

fraudulently frauduleusement

free: to be free of a debt être quitte d'une dette

free (of charge) gratuit

free of tax franc d'impôts

free of VAT en franchise de TVA

freeze blocage *m*

to **freeze assets** immobiliser des . . actifs

freezing of capital immobilisation de capitaux *f*

fringe benefits avantages sociaux *mpl*

frozen gelé

frozen account compte bloqué *m*

frozen credit crédit bloqué *m*

FTSI (=Financial Times Share Index) *equivalent to* indice CAC 40 *m*

full discharge quitus *m*

full employment plein emploi *m*

full employment policy politique de plein emploi *f*

full payment paiement intégral *m*; *to make full payment for a share* libérer entièrement une action

full price plein tarif *m*

full-time à plein temps, à temps complet

full-time contract contrat à temps plein *m*

full-time work travail à plein temps *m*

fully paid up [*capital*] intégralement libéré

fully paid-up capital apports libérés *mpl*

fully paid-up securities titres libérés *mpl*

function fonction *f*; *to be a function of* être fonction de

functional analysis chart grille d'analyse par fonction *f*

functions fonctions *fpl*

to **fund** financer

funded from cashflow autofinancé

funding financement *m*

funding from cashflow autofinancement *m*

funding method méthode de financement *f*

funding plan plan de financement *m*
futures actions à terme *fpl*
futures market marché à terme *m*

futures order ordre à terme *m*
futures trading négociations à
terme *fpl*

gain boni *m*
galloping inflation inflation
galopante *f*
**GATT (=General Agreement on
Tariffs and Trade)** GATT *m*,
AGETAC *m*
GDP (=gross domestic product)
PIB *m*
gearing taux d'endettement *m*
general administration costs frais
d'administration générale *mpl*
**General Agreement on Tariffs and
Trade** Accord général sur les tarifs
douaniers et le commerce *m*
general manager directeur à
responsabilités générales *m*;
**General Manager, European
Operations** Directeur des
Opérations européennes *m*
general overheads frais
d'administration générale *mpl*
general strike grève générale *f*
to **give a discount** accorder un
escompte
to **give one's word** engager sa
parole

given in [*quoted*] libellé en
GNP (=gross national product)
PNB *m*
goal objectif *m*
going-concern status continuité
d'exploitation *f*
gold standard étalon-or *m*
golden handshake indemnité de
départ *f*
golden hello pont d'or *m*
good investment placement
avantageux *m*
good will fonds de commerce *m*,
fonds commercial *m*
goods marchandise *f*
goods and services biens et
services *mpl*
go-slow grève du zèle *f*
governing body instances
dirigeantes *fpl*
government bond obligation du
gouvernement *f*
government decree ordonnance *f*
government funds fonds publics *mpl*
government grant subvention
d'état *f*

government organization
collectivité publique *f*

government revenue recettes
publiques *fpl*

government stocks rentes de
l'Etat *fpl*

grace: period of grace jours de
grâce *mpl*

to **grade jobs** hiérarchiser les
emplois

grading of jobs hiérarchisation des
fonctions *f*

graduated progressif

graduated income tax impôt
progressif *m*

graduation [*of tax*] progressivité *f*

grand total total général *m*

grant allocation *f*; [*to company*]
subvention *f*, subside *m*

to **grant** accorder; [*patent*] concéder;
[*issue*] délivrer

granting octroi *m*

granting of a loan ouverture de
crédit *f*

graph graphe *m*

gratuity gratification *f*

gross brut

gross (amount) montant brut *m*

gross dividend dividende brut *m*

gross domestic product produit
intérieur brut *m*

gross earnings [*of company*] recette
brute *f*

gross income [*on accounts*] produit

brut *m*; [*of individual*] revenu
brut *m*

gross loss perte brute *f*

gross margin marge brute *f*

gross national product produit
national brut *m*

gross proceeds produit brut *m*

gross profit bénéfice brut *m*

gross profit margin marge
commerciale brute *f*

gross salary salaire brut *m*

gross value valeur brute *f*

gross wage salaire brut *m*

group groupe *m*

group leader chef de groupe *m*

group manager chef de groupe *m*

group of accounts classe de
comptes *f*

growing croissant

growth rate taux de croissance *m*

guarantee [*financial deposit*]
caution *f*, cautionnement *m*; [*for
product*] garantie *f*; ***under
guarantee*** sous garantie

guarantee fund fonds de garantie *m*

guaranteed bond obligation
garantie *f*

guaranteed by [*on financial
document*] pour aval, bon pour
aval

guarantor garant *m*; [*of bill*]
donneur d'aval *m*

guesstimate calcul au pifomètre *m*

guidelines directives *fpl*

H

half year semestre *m*

to **hand in one's resignation** remettre sa démission

to **handle a matter** gérer une affaire

to **handle money** manier de l'argent

handling fee frais d'administration *mpl*

hard core [*of trade union etc*] noyau dur *m*

head [*of department*] chef *m*

head hunter chasseur de têtes *m*

head of department chef de service *m*

head office siège principal *m*, siège social *m*

heading [*of account*] intitulé *m*

health and safety committee comité d'hygiène et de sécurité *m*

health insurance assurance maladie *f*

health insurance scheme caisse de maladie *f*

hierarchical hiérarchique

hierarchy hiérarchie *f*

high finance haute finance *f*

high value added à haute valeur ajoutée

to **hire** [*labour*] embaucher

hire purchase location-vente *f*, achat à crédit *m*

histogram histogramme *m*

hive-off of assets scission d'actifs *f*

to **hoard** thésauriser

hoarding thésaurisation *f*

to **hold a job** occuper un emploi

to **hold a lease on** tenir à bail

to **hold a meeting** tenir une réunion, se réunir

to **hold as security** détenir en garantie

to **hold up** [*stock exchange prices*] se maintenir

holder [*of shares*] détenteur *m*; [*of account*] titulaire *mf*

holder in due course tiers porteur *m*

holder of a power of attorney porteur d'une procuration *m*

holder of a proxy porteur d'une procuration *m*

holding [*in company*] participation *f*

holding a meeting tenue d'une réunion *f*

holding company société de gestion *f*, holding *m*

holiday congé *m*

home sales ventes sur le marché intérieur *fpl*

honorary honoraire

honorary member membre honoraire *m*

to **honour** honorer

hot money capitaux fébriles *mpl*

hourly rate tarif horaire *m*

human ressources ressources humaines *fpl*

I

idle capital capital improductif *m*
illegal illégal
illegality illégalité *f*
ILO (= International Labour
    Organization) OIT *f*
IMF (=International Monetary
    Fund) FMI *m*
implied implicite
to import goods importer des
    marchandises
import-export import-export *m*
importer importateur *m*
importing *adj* importateur
imports importations *fpl*
to impose a ban on sth frapper qch
    d'interdit
to impose a fine on sth frapper qch
    d'une amende
to impose a price freeze imposer un
    blocage des prix
to impose tax on sth frapper qch
    d'un impôt
incidental acquisition expenses frais
    accessoires d'achat *mpl*
incidental costs frais accessoires *mpl*
incidental expenses frais
    accessoires *mpl*, faux frais *mpl*,
    menus frais *mpl*
incidental income revenus
    accessoires *mpl*, produits
    annexes *mpl*
incidental selling expenses frais
    accessoires de vente *mpl*
inclusive inclusivement

inclusive of tax toutes taxes
    comprises, TTC
income revenu *m*
income account compte de
    produits *m*
income from operations produits de
    gestion courante *mpl*, produits
    d'exploitation *mpl*
income statement *Am* compte de
    résultat *m*
income tax impôt sur le revenu *m*,
    taxe sur le revenu *f*
income tax return déclaration de
    revenus *f*
incorrectly [*improperly*] indûment
increase augmentation *f*,
    accroissement *m*
to increase augmenter, accroître;
    [*wages*] majorer
to increase the value of valoriser
increase in bank lending
    gonflement du volume du crédit *m*
increase in capital augmentation de
    capital *f*
increase in prices hausse des prix *f*
increase in the price of sth
    augmentation du prix de qch *f*
increasing croissant
increasing demand demande
    croissante *f*
increasing payments paiement
    progressif *m*
increasing rate tarif progressif *m*
to incur debts contracter des dettes

to **incur expenses** encourir des frais
indebtedness endettement *m*
to **index-link a pension to the cost of living** indexer une retraite sur le coût de la vie
index-linked indexé
index-linked bond obligation indexée *f*
index-linking indexation *f*
index-linking of salaries indexation des salaires *f*
indexation clause clause d'indexation *f*
indexed loan emprunt indexé *m*
indirect cost coût indirect *m*
indirect labour costs coûts de main-d'œuvre indirecte *mpl*
indirect tax impôt indirect *m*
industrial industriel
industrial accident accident du travail *m*
industrial accident insurance assurance contre les accidents du travail *f*
industrial arbitrator prud'homme *m*
industrial concern exploitation industrielle *f*
industrial dispute conflit du travail *m*
industrial espionage espionnage industriel *m*
industrial expansion expansion industrielle *f*
industrial group groupe industriel *m*
industrial monopoly trust industriel *m*
industrial plant équipement industriel *m*
industrial property propriété industrielle *f*
industrial redeployment reconversion industrielle *f*
industrial tribunal conseil de

prud'hommes *m*
industrialist industriel *m*
industrialization industrialisation *f*
to **industrialize** industrialiser
industry industrie *f*
inflation inflation *f*
inflation rate taux d'inflation *m*
inflationary inflationniste
inflationary spiral spirale inflationniste *f*
inflow of capital afflux de capitaux *m*
inflow of money rentrée d'argent *f*
influx of capital afflux des capitaux *m*
to **inform** aviser
to **inform sb of sth** informer qn de qch
in-house interne
initial initial
to **initial** parapher
initials paraphe *m*
to **inject capital into a business** injecter des capitaux dans une entreprise
injection of capital injection de capital *f*, injection de capitaux *f*
Inland Revenue fisc *m*
to **innovate** innover
innovation innovation *f*
input tax TVA récupérée *f*
insolvency insolvabilité *f*
insolvent insolvable
insolvent debtor débiteur insolvable *m*
inspector of taxes contrôleur des contributions *m*
instalment versement *m*, acompte *m*, tranche de paiement *f*; *to buy by instalments* acheter à tempérament
installment plan *Am* location-vente *f*, achat à crédit *m*
institution établissement *m*

institutional investor investisseur institutionnel *m*

instruction instruction *f*, directive *f*

insufficient funds provision insuffisante *f*, insuffisance de provision *f*

insurance assurance *f*; *to take out insurance* s'assurer

insurance broker courtier d'assurances *m*

insurance certificate certificat d'assurance *m*

insurance claim déclaration de dommages *f*

insurance company compagnie d'assurances *f*

insurance contract contrat d'assurance *m*

insurance document document d'assurance *m*

insurance policy police d'assurance *f*; *to take out an insurance policy* souscrire une police d'assurance

insurance portfolio portefeuille d'assurances *m*

insurance premium prime d'assurance *f*

insurance proposal proposition d'assurance *f*

insurances assurances *fpl*

to **insure** assurer

insured *adj* assuré

insured (party) assuré *m*

insured value valeur assurée *f*

insurer assureur *m*

intangible [*asset*] incorporel

intangible fixed assets immobilisations incorporelles *fpl*

interbank [*rate*] interbancaire

interest intérêt *m*

interest accrued fraction d'intérêt *f*

interest and dividend

income produits financiers *mpl*

interest-bearing productif d'intérêts, rémunérateur

interest-bearing note bon de caisse *m*

interest charges frais financiers *mpl*

interest days jours d'intérêt *mpl*

interest due intérêts dus *mpl*

interest due and payable intérêts exigibles *mpl*

interest-free loan prêt sans intérêt *m*

interest on arrears intérêt de retard *m*

interest on capital rémunération de capital *f*

interest payable intérêt exigible *m*

interest rate taux d'intérêt *m*

interest receivable intérêt à percevoir *m*

interim intérimaire

interim dividend acompte sur dividende *m*

interim manager directeur intérimaire *m*

interim statement bilan intérimaire *m*

intermediate rate taux intermédiaire *m*

internal interne

internal auditor vérificateur interne *m*

internal company document document interne à l'entreprise *m*

internal promotion [*of employee*] promotion interne *f*

Internal Revenue *Am* fisc *m*

International Chamber of Commerce Chambre de commerce internationale *f*

International Labour Organization Organisation internationale du travail *f*

international liquid assets liquidités

internationales *fpl*
International Monetary Fund
Fonds monétaire international *m*
international organization
organisme international *m*
international payments paiements
internationaux *mpl*
international trade échanges
internationaux *mpl*
international trading corporation
société de commerce
international *f*, SCI *f*
interpretation of a contract
interprétation d'un contrat *f*
inter-union intersyndical
interview entretien *m*, entrevue *f*
intra-Community VAT TVA
intracommunautaire *f*
to **introduce on the Stock Exchange**
introduire en Bourse
invalidity of a contract nullité d'un
contrat *f*
inventory inventaire *m*
to **inventory** inventorier, mettre en
inventaire
to **inventory goods** recenser des
marchandises
inventory account compte de
stock *m*
inventory balance balance
d'inventaire *f*
inventory management gestion des
stocks *f*
inventory method système
d'inventaire *m*
inventory of fixtures état des
lieux *m*
inventory of goods inventaire des
marchandises *m*
inventory turnover rate vitesse de
rotation des stocks *f*
inversion of figures inversion de
chiffres *f*

to **invest** investir, placer
to **invest capital** engager des
capitaux, investir des capitaux
investigation enquête *f*
investment investissement *m*,
placement *m*, mise de fonds *f*; *to*
make an investment at interest
placer à intérêts
investment of capital investissement
de capitaux *m*
investment trust fonds commun de
placement *m*
investor investisseur *m*
invoice facture *f*; *within 30 days of*
invoice dans les 30 jours après la
facturation; *payable against*
invoice à payer à réception de la
facture
to **invoice for** facturer
to **invoice monthly** établir les
factures mensuellement
to **invoice sb for sth** facturer qch à
qn
invoice clerk facturier *m*
invoice date date de facturation *f*
invoice price prix facturé *m*
invoicing facturation *f*
invoicing address adresse de
facturation *f*
to **invoke a guarantee** faire jouer
une garantie
IOU reconnaissance de dette *f*
irredeemable [*bond*] irrachetable,
irremboursable
irregularities irrégularités *fpl*
irrevocable letter of credit lettre de
crédit irrévocable *f*
issue [*of bonds, shares*] émission *f*;
[*of notes*] mise en circulation *f*; [*of*
certificate] délivrance *f*
to **issue** [*bonds, shares*] émettre;
[*notes*] mettre en circulation;
[*certificate*] délivrer

to **issue a bond** lancer un emprunt

to **issue loan stock** émettre un emprunt

issued securities titres émis *mpl*

issuer of a draft émetteur d'une traite *m*

item article *m*; [*on balance sheet*] poste *m*, écriture *f*

to **itemize** détailler

itemized détaillé

J

job emploi *m*, travail *m*

Jobcentre® Agence nationale pour l'emploi *f*, ANPE *f*

job description profil de poste *m*, description de poste *f*

job offer offre d'emploi *f*

job seeker demandeur d'emploi *m*

job wanted advertisement demande d'emploi *f*

joint account compte joint *m*

joint and several debtor débiteur solidaire *m*

joint and several guarantor garant solidaire *m*

joint and several liability responsabilité solidaire et indivise *f*

joint committee commission paritaire *f*

joint debtor codébiteur *m*

joint holder codétenteur *m*

joint management cogestion *f*

joint owner copropriétaire *mf*

joint ownership copropriété *f*; *to have joint ownership of* coposséder

joint purchaser coacquéreur *m*

joint representations démarche collective *f*

joint venture entreprise en participation *f*, entreprise commune *f*, société commune *f*

joint venture agreement accord de partenariat *m*

jointly conjointement; *to own jointly* coposséder

jointly and severally conjointement et solidairement

journal [*for accounts*] livre de comptes *m*

journal entry contre-passation *f*, passation d'écriture *f*

judgement jugement *m*

junior subalterne *mf*

junior *adj* subalterne

K

to **keep in order** [*accounts*]
entretenir

to **keep the books up to date** tenir
les livres à jour

to **keep up a correspondence**
entretenir une correspondance

know-how savoir-faire *m*

L

labor code *Am* code du travail *m*

labor laws *Am* code du travail *m*

labour main-d'œuvre *f*

labour force [*of company*] main-
d'œuvre *f*

labour-intensive qui demande une
main-d'œuvre importante

labour laws droit du travail *m*

labour legislation législation du
travail *f*

labour market marché du travail *m*

labour relations relations de
travail *fpl*

labour saving économie de main-
d'œuvre *f*

labour shortage pénurie de main-
d'œuvre *f*

lack of funds manque de fonds *m*;
for lack of funds faute de
provision

land terrains *mpl*

land charge dette foncière *f*

landlord [*of property*] bailleur *m*

to **lapse** tomber en déchéance

large profit gros bénéfice *m*

large sum of money forte somme *f*

last financial year exercice
écoulé *m*

late payment penalty indemnité de
retard *f*

latest: at the latest ... au plus tard ...

launch lancement *m*

to **launch** [*product*] lancer, introduire sur le marché

to **launch a new company** lancer une nouvelle entreprise

law firm cabinet juridique *m*

law of supply and demand loi de l'offre et de la demande *f*

lawsuit action *f*

lawyer avocat *m*

to **lay off** débaucher

to **lay off staff** dégraisser les effectifs

laying off débauchage *m*

layoff licenciement *m*

layout aménagement *m*

LBO (=leveraged buy-out) OPA à crédit *f*

L/C (=letter of credit) l/c *f*

lead manager [*of syndicated loan*] chef de file *m*

lead time délai de production *m*; [*for delivery*] délai de livraison *m*

lease bail *m*; [*of equipment*] location *f*

to **lease** louer

lease charges charges locatives *fpl*

lease contract [*for property*] contrat de bail *m*; [*for equipment*] contrat en location *m*

leasehold droit au bail *m*

leasehold acquisition costs [*item on balance sheet*] droit au bail *m*

lease-purchase crédit-bail *m*

lease-purchase contract contrat de crédit-bail *m*

leasing [*of equipment*] location *f*; [*on lease-purchase*] location-bail *f*; [*system*] crédit-bail *m*

leave congé *m*; *to be on leave* être en congé

ledger journal *m*, grand livre *m*

legal juridique; [*permissible*] légal

legal action action (en justice) *f*; *to take legal action against sb* poursuivre qn en justice, attaquer

qn en justice

legal adviser conseil juridique *m*, conseiller juridique *m*

legal department contentieux *m*

legal dispute litige *m*

legal document document légal *m*

legal entity personne morale *f*

legal fees frais juridiques *mpl*

legal proceedings: to start legal proceedings engager une action en justice

legal recourse recours contentieux *m*

legal reserve réserve légale *f*

legal status statut légal *m*, statut juridique *m*

legislation législation *f*

to **lend against securities** prêter sur titres

to **lend at interest** prêter à intérêt

to **lend money** prêter de l'argent

lender prêteur *m*

less moins

lessee preneur *m*

lessor bailleur *m*

to **let by the month** louer au mois

letter of confirmation lettre de confirmation *f*

letter of credit lettre de crédit *f*

letter of dismissal lettre de licenciement *f*

letter of guarantee lettre de garantie *f*

letter threatening legal action lettre menaçant de poursuite judiciaire *f*

to **level down** niveler par le bas

to **level off** plafonner

to **level out** plafonner

leverage effet de levier *m*

leveraged buy-out OPA à crédit *f*

levying of taxes levée des impôts *f*

liabilities passif *m*

liability dette *f*; [*responsibility*] responsabilité *f*

liable to tax passible de taxe, passible d'impôts; *person liable for tax* assujetti *m*

LIBOR (=London Inter-Bank Offer Rate) *equivalent to* TIOP *m*

licence licence *f*

licensee concessionnaire *mf*

life assurance *Br* assurance-vie *f*

life interest usufruit *m*

to **lift a mortgage from** déshypothéquer

to **lift an encumbrance from** déshypothéquer

lifting [*of mortgage, ban*] mainlevée *f*

lightning strike grève surprise *f*

to **limit production** limiter la production

limited liability responsabilité limitée *f*

limited liability company société à responsabilité limitée *f*

limited market marché étroit *m*

line [*on graph*] droite *f*

line of business genre d'affaires *m*, branche *f*

line of credit ligne de crédit *f*

liquid disponible; [*asset*] liquide

liquid assets disponibilités *fpl*, liquidités *fpl*

liquid resources moyens liquides *mpl*

liquidation liquidation *f*; *to go into liquidation* entrer en liquidation

liquidation of assets liquidation des biens *f*

liquidator liquidateur *m*

liquidity liquidité *f*

liquidity ratio ratio de liquidité *m*

to **list** répertorier

to **list on the Stock Exchange** introduire en Bourse

list of bills for discount bordereau d'escompte *m*

list of shareholders liste des actionnaires *f*

listed on the Stock Exchange coté en Bourse

litigation contentieux *m*, recours contentieux *m*

loan prêt *m*, emprunt *m*

loan against securities prêt sur titres *m*

loan agreement contrat de prêt *m*

loan application demande d'ouverture de crédit *f*

loan at interest prêt à intérêts *m*

loan capital capital sur prêt *m*

loan insurance assurance crédit *f*

loan maturity échéance emprunt *f*

loan note titre d'obligation *m*, titre de créance *m*

loan risk cover couverture du risque de crédit *f*

loan stock emprunt obligataire *m*

loans and advances to customers créances clients *fpl*

loans outstanding encours *m*

local tax taxe locale *f*

location emplacement *m*

lock-out lock-out *m*

to **lodge security** déposer une caution

to **log** enregistrer

log book journal de bord *m*

logging enregistrement *m*

logging of an order enregistrement d'une commande *m*

logistic logistique

logistics logistique *f*

logo sigle *m*

long [*bill*] effet à longue échéance *m*

long-dated bill effet à longue échéance *m*, traite à longue échéance *f*

long lease bail emphytéotique *m*

long service award prime
d'ancienneté f
long-term à long terme
long-term asset actif stable m
long-term borrowings emprunts à
long terme mpl
long-term capital capitaux
permanents mpl
long-term credit crédit (à) long
terme m
long-term financing financement à
long terme m
long-term investment placement à
long terme m; *to make a long-term
investment* investir à long terme
long-term investments [*on balance
sheet*] immobilisations
financières fpl
long-term loan prêt à long terme m
long-term planning planification à

long terme f
to lose money on perdre sur
loss perte f
loss adjuster expert-répartiteur m
loss of earnings manque à gagner m
loss of interest perte d'intérêts f
loss of no-claims bonus malus m
loss suffered préjudice subi m
low income faible revenu m
to lower baisser, rabaisser
lowering baisse f, rabaissement m
lowest bidder moins-disant m
Ltd (=limited) SARL
lump sum forfait m; *in a lump sum*
forfaitairement
lump sum adj forfaitaire
luncheon voucher ticket
restaurant m
luxury tax taxe de luxe f

M

machine-hour heure-machine f
made out in libellé en
mailshot publipostage m, mailing m
mail transfer virement par
courrier m
main cost centre centre principal des
coûts m
main line of business activité
principale exercée f, APE f

main occupation occupation
principale f
to maintain relations entretenir des
relations
maintenance costs frais
d'entretien mpl
majority holding participation
majoritaire f
to make a business viable viabiliser

une entreprise

to **make a cheque payable to** établir un chèque à l'ordre de

to **make a down payment** verser un acompte

to **make a payment** effectuer un paiement, effectuer un versement

to **make a profit** réaliser un profit

to **make a transfer** opérer un virement

to **make good** [*deficit, loss*] combler

to **make large profits** gagner gros

to **make out** rédiger

to **make out a cheque** libeller un chèque, établir un chèque

to **make out a statement of account** établir un relevé de compte

to **make out an invoice** libeller une facture

to **make out to the order of** libeller à l'ordre de

to **make up for lost time** combler un retard

to **manage** [*business*] diriger, gérer

to **manage an account** gérer un compte

to **manage assets** régir des biens

to **manage jointly** cogérer

management gestion *f*, direction *f*; [*of an account*] gestion *f*; [*managers*] direction *f*

management *adj* directorial

management accounts comptes de gestion *mpl*

management buyout rachat de société par la direction *m*

management by objectives gestion selon objectifs *f*

management committee comité de direction *m*

management consultant conseiller en gestion (d'entreprise) *m*

management function fonction

d'encadrement *f*

management report rapport de gestion *m*; [*accounts statistics*] tableau de bord *m*

management team équipe dirigeante *f*

management tool outil de gestion *m*

manager directeur *m*; [*of department*] chef *m*; *as a manager, he ...* en tant que gestionnaire, il ...

managerial level échelon directorial *m*

managerial staff staff de direction *m*

managing director directeur général *m*; [*board member*] administrateur délégué *m*

mandate mandat *m*

man-hour heure-travail *f*

manpower main-d'œuvre *f*

manpower crisis crise de main-d'œuvre *f*

manual [*accounts*] manuel

manual worker ouvrier *m*, travailleur manuel *m*

manufacture fabrication *f*

to **manufacture** fabriquer

manufacturer fabricant *m*

manufacturer's liability responsabilité du fabricant *f*

manufacturing company entreprise industrielle *f*

manufacturing concern entreprise industrielle *f*

manufacturing costs frais de fabrication *mpl*

manufacturing manager chef de fabrication *m*

manufacturing plan planning de fabrication *m*

man-year année-personne *f*

margin marge *f*

marginal marginal

market marché *m*

market *adj* marchand
to **market** commercialiser
market place marché *m*
market rate cours du marché *m*,
taux privé *m*
market research étude de marché *f*
market research studies études de
marché *fpl*
market share part de marché *f*
market study étude de marché *f*
market value valeur marchande *f*
marketable securities valeurs
réalisables *fpl*, valeurs
négociables *fpl*
marketing [*of product*]
commercialisation *f*; [*discipline*]
mercatique *f*, marketing *m*
marketing department direction
mercatique *f*
marketing director directeur de
marketing *m*
marketing manager directeur de
marketing *m*
marketing mix plan de marchéage *m*
marketing network circuit de
commercialisation *m*
marketing subsidiary filiale de
distribution *f*
marketing team équipe
commerciale *f*
markup majoration *f*
to **mark up** majorer
markup ratio taux de marge *m*
mass production fabrication en
série *f*
material defect vice rédhibitoire *m*
maternity allowance allocation de
maternité *f*
mathematical formula formule de
calcul *f*
matter affaire *f*
to **mature** [*loan*] arriver à échéance,
arriver à maturité

maturity échéance *f*, maturité *f*
maturity date terme d'échéance *m*,
date d'échéance *f*
maturity of a policy échéance d'une
police *f*
maturity value valeur à l'échéance *f*
maximum maximum
maximum amount montant
maximum *m*
maximum salary salaire plafond *m*
MBO (=management buyout)
rachat de société par la direction *m*
MBO (=management by objectives)
gestion selon objectifs *f*
MD (=managing director) directeur
général *m*
mean moyenne *f*
means of payment moyens de
paiement *mpl*
mediation médiation *f*
mediator médiateur *m*
medium-term credit crédit (à)
moyen terme *m*
medium-term financing
financement à moyen terme *m*
**medium-term investment: to make
a medium-term investment**
investir à moyen terme
to **meet** [*the board*] se réunir;
[*shareholders*] s'assembler
to **meet demand** faire face à la
demande
meeting réunion *f*; [*larger*]
assemblée *f*, conférence *f*
meetings secretary secrétaire de
séance *mf*
member of the board membre du
conseil d'administration *m*
memo note de service *f*,
mémorandum *m*
**memorandum and articles of
association** statuts de société *mpl*
merchandizing marchandisage *m*

merchant négociant *m*,
  commerçant *m*
merchant bank banque d'affaires *f*
to **merge** fusionner
merger fusion *f*
method of payment mode de
  règlement *m*, mode de paiement *m*
methods of payment modalités de
  paiement *fpl*
middle management cadres
  moyens *mpl*
middle manager cadre moyen *m*
minimum minimum
minimum amount montant
  minimum *m*
minimum charge charge minimum *f*
minimum wage salaire minimum *m*
minority interests intérêts des
  minoritaires *mpl*
minus moins
minutes compte rendu *m*, procès-
  verbal *m*
minutes book registre des procès-
  verbaux *m*
**misappropriation of corporate
  funds** délit d'abus de biens
  sociaux *m*, abus de droits
  sociaux *m*
miscalculation erreur de calcul *f*
mobility mobilité *f*
modus operandi mode opératoire *m*
monetary monétaire
monetary compensation montants
  compensatoires monétaires *mpl*
monetary flow flux monétaire *m*
monetary fluctuations mouvements
  monétaires *mpl*
monetary parity parité des
  monnaies *f*
monetary policy politique
  monétaire *f*
monetary standard étalon
  monétaire *m*

monetary unit unité monétaire *f*
money argent *m*
money market place monétaire *f*,
  marché monétaire *m*
money of account monnaie de
  compte *f*
money supply masse monétaire *f*
monies deniers *mpl*
to **monitor** contrôler
monthly mensuel
monthly *adv* mensuellement; *to*
  make sth payable monthly
  mensualiser qch
monthly average moyenne
  mensuelle *f*
monthly instalment acompte
  mensuel *m*
monthly instalments mensualités *fpl*
monthly payment mensualisation *f*,
  paiement mensuel *m*
monthly report rapport mensuel *m*
monthly transfer virement
  mensuel *m*
moratorium moratoire *m*
moratorium on payment suspension
  de paiements *m*
mortgage crédit immobilier *m*
to **mortgage an asset** hypothéquer un
  bien
mortgage bond obligation
  hypothécaire *f*
mortgage debt dette foncière *f*
mortgage over assets gage
  mobilier *m*
mortgage over property gage
  immobilier *m*
mortgageable hypothécable
mortgagee créancier hypothécaire *m*
to **move into** [*diversify into*] se
  reconvertir dans
movement of capital mouvement
  des capitaux *m*
multilateral multilatéral

multinational multinationale *f*
to **multiply** multiplier
multisector multisectoriel
mutual mutuel; *by mutual agreement* de gré à gré

mutual fund fonds commun de placement *m*
mutual insurance company mutuelle *f*

national insurance contributions cotisations à la Sécurité sociale *fpl*
nationalization nationalisation *f*
to **nationalize** nationaliser
nationalized nationalisé
nationalized company société nationalisée *f*
needs study étude des besoins *f*
negotiability of an instrument négociabilité d'un titre *f*
negotiable négociable
negotiable paper effet négociable *m*
to **negotiate** négocier
negotiation négociation *f*
net net
net (amount) somme nette *f*
net assets actif net *m*
net book value valeur comptable nette *f*
net costs charges nettes *fpl*
net current assets actif circulant net *m*
net dividend dividende net *m*
net income [*in accounts*] produit

net *m*; [*of individual*] revenu net *m*
net interest income net financier *m*
net loss perte nette *f*
net margin marge nette *f*
net of tax [*goods*] hors taxe, HT; [*revenue*] net d'impôt; *the invoice value net of tax* le montant HT de la facture
net of VAT hors TVA, H. TVA
net payable net à payer *m*
net present value rate taux d'actualisation *m*
net proceeds produit net *m*
net profit bénéfice net *m*
net receipts recette nette *f*
net return retour net *m*, montant du retour net *m*
net (total) montant net *m*
net variance écart net *m*
net worth actif net *m*, situation nette *f*
new borrowings nouveaux emprunts *mpl*
new issue [*of shares*] nouvelle

numbered, dated and signed

émission *f*

NIC (=national insurance contributions) cotisations à la Sécurité sociale *fpl*

niche créneau *m*

nominal capital capital nominal *m*

nominal ledger grand livre général *m*

nominal rent loyer nominal *m*

nominal value valeur nominale *f*

nominee company prête-nom *m*

non-competition clause clause de non-concurrence *f*

non-convertible inconvertible

non-EC country pays hors communauté *m*

non-fulfilment non-exécution *f*

non-negotiable cheque chèque non endossable *m*

non-payment non-paiement *m*, refus de paiement *m*; *for non-payment* faute de paiement

non-performance non-exécution *f*, inexécution *f*

non-performance of a contract inexécution d'un contrat *f*

non-productive [*capital*] improductif

non-profit-making sans but lucratif

non-returnable sans réserve de retour

non-transferability incessibilité *f*

non-transferable incessible

non-union worker non-syndiqué *m*

non-wasting [*asset*] indéfectible

no-return sans réserve de retour

notarized contract contrat notarié *m*

notarized deed acte notarié *m*

not due inexigible

note note *f*; [*bank note*] billet *m*

to **note** constater

notes to the accounts annexes *fpl*

notice avis *m*; [*of leaving, dismissal*] préavis *m*

notice of a/the meeting convocation *f*

notice of claim déclaration de sinistre *f*

notice of meeting lettre de convocation *f*

notification avis *m*

to **notify sb of sth** notifier qn de qch, informer qn de qch

NPV (=net present value) rate taux d'actualisation *m*

null and void nul et non avenu

number chiffre *m*; [*of account, order etc*] numéro *m*; [*of company*] matricule *m*

number of employees effectif *m*

numbered, dated and signed coté, daté et paraphé

O

object of a contract objet d'un
contrat *m*
obtaining of a loan obtention d'un
prêt *f*
occupation [*on form*] qualité *f*
OECD (=Organization for
Economic Co-operation and
Development) OCDE *f*
off-balance sheet hors bilan
offer offre *f*
offer of employment offre
d'emploi *f*
offer price cours vendeur *m*
office bureau *m*
office expenses frais de bureau *mpl*
office hours heures de bureau *fpl*
office manager chef de bureau *m*
office staff personnel de bureau *m*
office worker employé de bureau *m*
official [*civil servant*]
fonctionnaire *mf*
official brokerage courtage
officiel *m*
official channels: through official
channels par la voie hiérarchique
official market marché officiel *m*
official rate taux officiel *m*
official receiver syndic de faillite *m*,
administrateur judiciaire *m*
official receivership liquidation
judiciaire *f*
offset agreement accord de
compensation *m*
O&M (=organization and methods)

department bureau des
méthodes *m*
ombudsman médiateur entre
individus et instances
gouvernementales *m*
oncosts frais généraux *mpl*
one-man business entreprise
unipersonnelle *f*
one price prix unique *m*
to open an account ouvrir un compte
to open negotiations entamer des
négociations
opening an account ouverture d'un
compte *f*
opening balance sheet bilan
d'ouverture *m*
opening hours heures d'ouverture *fpl*
opening price cours d'ouverture *m*
opening speech discours
d'ouverture *m*
opening stock stock initial *m*
opening time heure d'ouverture *f*
to operate [*a business*] exploiter
operating activities: income from
operating activites produits
d'exploitation *mpl*
operating cost charge
opérationnelle *f*
operating costs coûts
d'exploitation *mpl*, frais
d'exploitation *mpl*
operating cycle cycle
d'exploitation *m*
operating expenses frais

d'exploitation *mpl*
operating income produits
d'exploitation *mpl*
operating loss perte d'exploitation *f*
operating margin marge
d'exploitation *f*
operating profit bénéfice
d'exploitation *m*
operating profit or loss résultat
d'exploitation *m*
operating ratio coefficient
d'exploitation *m*
operation [*of a business*]
exploitation *f*
operational cost accounting
comptes analytiques
d'exploitation *mpl*
operational cost centre centre
d'analyse opérationnel *m*
operational headquarters siège
d'exploitation *m*
operations management direction
de l'exploitation *f*
operations manager directeur des
exploitations *m*
operator [*of a business*] exploitant *m*
opposite number homologue *mf*
option option *f*
option spread écart de prime *m*
option to buy option d'achat *f*
option to sell option de vente *f*
optional reserve réserve facultative *f*
options trading négociations à
prime *fpl*
order [*for goods, services*]
commande *f*; [*of government*]
ordonnance *f*; **to order:** [*on
financial document*] clause à ordre:
to **order** commander
to **order a payment** ordonnancer un
paiement
order book livre de commandes *m*,
carnet de commandes *m*

order form bulletin de commande *m*
order number numéro de
commande *m*, numéro d'ordre *m*
order to pay ordonnance de
paiement *f*
order to sell ordre de vente *m*
ordinary activities activités
ordinaires *fpl*; [*balance sheet item*]
opérations courantes *fpl*
ordinary creditor créancier
ordinaire *m*
ordinary share action ordinaire *f*
organization organisation *f*
organization chart
organigramme *m*, schéma
d'entreprise *m*
**Organization for Economic Co-
operation and Development**
Organisation de coopération et de
développement économique *f*
to **organize** organiser
original original *m*
original invoice facture originale *f*
original value valeur d'origine *f*
other debtors [*item on balance
sheet*] créances diverses *fpl*
to **oust a competitor** évincer un
concurrent
out of court settlement arrangement
à l'amiable *m*
outflow sortie *f*
outgoing [*chairman etc*] sortant
outgoings sorties de fonds *fpl*
outline agreement protocole
d'accord *m*
outlook for recovery perspectives de
reprise *fpl*
output [*of factory*] production *f*,
rendement *m*
output tax TVA encaissée *f*
outside externe
outstanding [*invoice, amount*] en
souffrance

outstanding account compte en
souffrance *m*
over-accumulation of capital
suraccumulation de capital *f*
overbid surenchère *f*
overcapitalization surcapitalisation *f*
to **overcapitalize** surcapitaliser
overdraft découvert *m*
overdraft facility facilités de
caisse *fpl*
to **overdraw** tirer à découvert
overdrawn: to be overdrawn
[*company, individual*] avoir un
découvert
overdrawn account compte à
découvert *m*
overdue en souffrance, en retard
overdue account compte en
souffrance *m*
overestimate surestimation *f*
to **overestimate** surestimer

overgearing surendettement *m*
overhead charge opérationnelle *f*
overhead budget budget des
charges *m*
overheads frais généraux *mpl*
over-indebtedness surendettement *m*
overmanning sureffectif *m*
overseas outre-mer
overstock excédent de stock *m*
overtime heures supplémentaires *fpl*
to **overtrade** avoir une marge
d'exploitation trop étroite
over-valuation surévaluation *f*
to **over-value** surévaluer
to **owe** devoir
to **owe money** devoir de l'argent
owing dû
owner propriétaire *mf*
owner's capital account compte de
l'exploitant *m*

P

paid payé
paid leave congés payés *mpl*,
absence rémunérée *f*
paid-up share capital capital appelé
et libéré *m*
paper money monnaie de papier *f*,
papier-monnaie *m*
par: at par au pair

parent company compagnie mère *f*,
maison mère *f*, société mère *f*
parity parité *f*
part payment paiement partiel *m*
partial loss perte partielle *f*
partial payment paiement partiel *m*
participant participant *m*
partner associé *m*

partnership [*company*] société de personnes *f*; [*co-operation*] partenariat *m*; *to enter into partnership with* s'associer avec/à

partnership agreement accord de partenariat *m*

partnership deed acte d'association *m*

part-time à mi-temps, à temps partiel

part-time contract contrat à temps partiel *m*

part-time work travail à mi-temps *m*, travail à temps partiel *m*

par value nominal *m*, valeur nominale *f*

pass book livret de dépôts *m*

patent brevet (d'invention) *m*

to **patent** breveter

patented breveté

patentee concessionnaire *mf*

pay paie *f*, rémunération *f*

to **pay** payer; [*employee*] payer, rémunérer; [*invoice*] régler; [*taxes*] acquitter

to **pay a dividend** distribuer un dividende

to **pay at sight** payer à vue

to **pay back** rembourser

to **pay by cheque** payer par chèque

to **pay by instalments** payer à tempérament

to **pay cash** payer (au) comptant

to **pay for** payer

to **pay in** [*into an account*] verser

to **pay in advance** payer à l'avance

to **pay in cash** [*by means of cash*] régler au comptant, payer en espèces; [*pay into an account*] encaisser de l'argent

to **pay money into an account** alimenter un compte, approvisionner un compte

to **pay off a debt** liquider une dette, amortir une dette, éteindre une dette

to **pay out** décaisser

payday jour de paie *m*

pay dispute conflit salarial *m*

pay ledger livre de paie *m*

pay rise augmentation de salaire *f*

payroll feuille de paie *f*

payroll ledger journal de paie *m*, livre de paie *m*

pay slip feuille de paie *f*, fiche de paie *f*, bulletin de paie *m*

pay to bearer payez au porteur

pay to bearer clause clause au porteur *f*

payable payable, exigible; *to make sth payable by the month* mensualiser qch

payable at maturity payable à l'échéance

payable at the bank payable à la banque

payable at thirty days exigible : trente jours

payable in arrears payable à l'échéance

payable in cash payable comptant

payable to the order of à l'ordre de

PAYE (=pay as you earn) impôt sur le revenu *m*

PAYE and NIC return déclaration sociale *f*

payee accrédité *m*, bénéficiaire *mf*

payee of a bill of exchange preneur de lettre de change *m*

payer payeur *m*

paying agent domiciliataire *m*

paying bank domiciliataire *m*, établissement payeur *m*, domiciliation bancaire *f*

paying in encaissement *m*

paying-in slip bordereau de versement *m*, feuille de versement *f*, bordereau de remise *m*

paying off [*of debt*] amortissement *m*

paying up of a share libération d'une action *f*

payment paiement *m*; [*of employee*] rétribution *f*; [*of invoice*] règlement *m*; [*of taxes*] acquittement *m*; [*into account*] versement *m*; *to present a cheque for payment* présenter un chèque à l'encaissement

payment advice avis de paiement *m*

payment at maturity paiement à échéance *m*

payment at sight paiement à vue *m*

payment by cheque paiement par chèque *m*, règlement par chèque *m*

payment by electronic transfer paiement électronique *m*

payment by instalments paiement par acomptes *m*

payment card carte de paiement *f*

payment day jour fixé comme échéance de paiement *m*

payment facilities facilités de paiement *fpl*

payment in advance paiement anticipé *m*, paiement par anticipation *m*, paiement d'avance *m*

payment in arrears paiement arriéré *m*

payment in cash paiement comptant *m*, règlement au comptant *m*

payment in full paiement intégral *m*

payment in kind paiement en nature *m*

payment instrument instrument de paiement *m*

payment of a dividend passation d'un dividende *f*, distribution d'un dividende *f*

payment of the balance paiement du solde *m*

payment on account acompte *m*; *to make a payment on account* donner un acompte

payment order ordre de paiement *m*

payment received [*stamped on invoice*] pour acquit

payment term délai de paiement *m*

payments coding clerk chiffreur *m*

p/e ratio taux de capitalisation *m*

pecuniary pécuniaire

penal rate taux d'usure *m*

penalty pénalité *f*

penalty clause clause pénale *f*

penalty interest pénalité de retard *f*, intérêts moratoires *mpl*

pension contribution cotisation vieillesse *f*

pension fund caisse de retraite *f*

pension plan régime de retraite *m*

pension scheme système de retraite *m*

per cent pour cent

percentage pourcentage *m*

to **perform a contract** exécuter un contrat

performance performance *f*; [*of employee*] rendement *m*, performance *f*; [*of shares*] rendement *m*

performance bond garantie de bonne exécution *f*, garantie de bonne fin *f*

performance bonus prime de rendement *f*

performance ratio coefficient d'exploitation *m*

period période *f*; *within a period of seven days* dans un délai de sept

jours
period of grace délai de grâce *m*
period of notice délai-congé *m*
period of validity délai de
  validité *m*, durée de validité *f*
periodic payments paiements
  périodiques *mpl*
periodical périodique
permanent full-time contract
  contrat à durée indéterminée à
  temps plein *m*
permanent inventory stock de
  sécurité *m*, stock stratégique *m*,
  inventaire permanent *m*
person in charge responsable *mf*
person liable for tax redevable *mf*
person on short time travailleur à
  temps réduit *m*
personal data données
  nominatives *fpl*
personal financial statement état de
  fortune *m*
personal loan prêt personnalisé *m*
personal organizer agenda *m*
personal wealth statement état de
  fortune *m*
personnel personnel *m*
personnel consultant conseiller du
  travail *m*
personnel (department) service du
  personnel *m*
personnel director directeur du
  personnel *m*
personnel management direction du
  personnel *f*, administration du
  personnel *f*
personnel manager directeur du
  personnel *m*
personnel representative délégué du
  personnel *m*
petition in bankruptcy dépôt de
  bilan *m*
petty cash petite caisse *f*

petty cash management tenue de
  caisse *f*
petty expenses menus frais *mpl*
physical inventory inventaire
  effectif *m*
picket [*strike*] piquet de grève *m*
pie chart graphique à secteurs *m*,
  camembert *m*
pilot plant usine pilote *f*
to **place** [*securities*] placer
to **place an order** passer une
  commande
to **place an order for sth** passer
  commande de qch
to **place an order with sb** passer
  commande à qn
place of issue lieu d'émission *m*
place of payment lieu de paiement *m*
placing of an order passation de
  commande *f*
plan [*timetable*] planning *m*; [*for the
  future*] projet *m*
to **plan** planifier
planner chronogramme *m*
planning planification *f*
plant [*factory*] usine *f*; [*equipment*]
  installations techniques *fpl*
plc (=public limited company) SA *f*
pledge nantissement *m*, caution *f*
to **pledge sth as security** gager qch
pledge over property gage
  immobilier *m*
pledged gagé
pledgee gagiste *mf*
pledgor gageur *m*
plus plus
policy [*of company*] politique *f*;
  [*insurance*] police *f*
policy meeting séance de
  concertation *f*
poor performance contre-
  performance *f*
portfolio [*of shares*] portefeuille *m*

portfolio management gestion de portefeuille *f*

position on an account état de compte *m*

possessions avoir *m*

to **post an amount** passer un montant

post office account compte postal *m*

post office cheque chèque postal *m*

post office cheque account compte chèque postal *m*

post office transfer virement postal *m*

posted price prix affiché *m*

to **postpone** renvoyer, ajourner; [*deadline*] reporter

postponement renvoi *m*, ajournement *m*; [*of deadline*] report *m*

power of attorney procuration *f*

PR (=Public Relations) manager responsable des relations publiques *mf*

prebilling préfacturation *f*

precedent précédent *m*

pre-contract conditions préalables d'un accord *mpl*

pre-contractual negotiations négociations précontractuelles *fpl*

preference share action privilégiée *f*

preferential préférentiel

preferential rate tarif préférentiel *m*

preferred creditor créancier privilégié *m*

preferred debt dette privilégiée *f*, créance privilégiée *f*

preferred share *Am* action privilégiée *f*

pre-financing préfinancement *m*

pre-inventory balance balance avant inventaire *f*

premises locaux *mpl*

premium prime *f*

prepaid payé d'avance, constaté d'avance

prepaid income produit constaté d'avance *m*

preparation of accounting entries précomptabilisation *f*, pré-imputation *f*

prepayment paiement préalable *m*; [*accounting*] charge constatée d'avance *f*

prepayment and accrued income compte de régularisation *m*

to **present for collection** présenter à l'encaissement

to **present invoices** présenter des factures

present value valeur actualisée *f*

presentation présentation *f*

presentation for acceptance présentation à l'acceptation *f*

presentation for payment présentation au paiement *f*

presentation of accounts for audit reddition de comptes *f*

president président *m*

press: the press la presse

press conference conférence de presse *f*

pressure group groupe de pression *m*

presumption of liability présomption de responsablité *f*

pre-tax avant impôt

price prix *m*; [*on Stock Exchange*] cours *m*

price before tax prix hors taxe *m*

price/earnings ratio taux de capitalisation *m*

price fluctuation fluctuation des prix *f*, mouvement des prix *m*; [*Stock Exchange*] mouvement des cours *m*

price inclusive of tax prix taxe comprise *m*

price increase augmentation de prix *f*
price index indice des prix *m*
price inflation inflation des prix *f*
price levels niveau des prix *m*
price list tarif *m*, liste de prix *f*
price markup majoration de prix *f*
price policy politique des prix *f*
price range fourchette de prix *f*, gamme de prix *f*
price reduction réduction de prix *f*
price rise hausse de prix *f*
price scale barème des prix *m*
price structure structure des prix *f*
price war guerre des prix *f*, guerre des tarifs *f*
pricing policy politique des prix *f*
primary debtor débiteur principal *m*
prime rate taux préférentiel *m*
principal [*of order etc*] mandant *m*, commettant *m*; [*sum of money*] principal *m*
principal and interest principal et intérêts *m*
principal debt créance principale *f*
principal debtor débiteur principal *m*
printed statement état imprimé *m*
prior antérieur
prior engagement engagement antérieur *m*
private privé
private company entreprise privée *f*
private investments investissements privés *mpl*
private investor investisseur privé *m*
private sector secteur privé *m*
privatization privatisation *f*
to **privatize** privatiser
procurement (department) service des achats *m*
to **produce** produire

producer producteur *m*
product produit *m*
product category catégorie de produit *f*
product manager directeur de produit *m*, responsable produit *mf*
product range gamme de produits *f*
production production *f*
production budget budget de production *m*
production control direction de la production *f*
production cost coût de production *m*
production director directeur de production *m*
production factors facteurs de production *mpl*
production flowchart organigramme de production *m*
production line chaîne de fabrication *f*
production management [*activity*] gestion de la production *f*; [*department*] direction de la production *f*
production manager directeur de production *m*
production plan plan de production *m*
productivity productivité *f*
profession profession *f*
professional association syndicat professionnel *m*
professional body organisme professionnel *m*
professional category catégorie professionnelle *f*
professional indemnity insurance assurance d'indemnisation professionnelle *f*
professional misconduct faute professionnelle *f*

profit bénéfice *m*, profit *m*; *to make a profit* réaliser un bénéfice

profit and loss pertes et profits *mpl*

profit and loss account compte de pertes et profits *m*, compte de résultat *m*

profit before tax and extraordinary items résultat courant *m*

profit centre centre de profit *m*

profit margin marge bénéficiaire *f*

profit or loss résultat *m*

profit or loss for the financial year résultat de l'exercice *m*

profit sharing participation aux bénéfices *f*

profit-sharing scheme système de participation aux bénéfices *m*

profit-taking prise de bénéfices *f*

profitability rentabilité *f*, profitabilité *f*

profitability ratio ratio de rentabilité *m*

profitable rentable; *to be profitable* rapporter des bénéfices

pro forma pro forma

pro forma bill traite pro forma *f*

pro forma invoice facture pro forma *f*

progress report état de situation *m*

project projet *m*

promissory note reconnaissance de dette *f*, billet à ordre *m*

to promote [*products, employee*] promouvoir

promoter promoteur *m*

promotion promotion *f*

promotion from within the company promotion interne *f*

promotional promotionnel

promotional campaign campagne de promotion *f*

proof of debt affirmation de créance *f*

proof of payment justificatif de paiement *m*

property immobilier *m*; [*financial assets*] patrimoine *m*; *a property* une propriété immobilière

property development promotion immobilière *f*

property improvement cost impense *f*

property tax impôt foncier *m*

proportion proportion *f*

proposal proposition *f*

to propose a dividend proposer un dividende

pro rata proportionnel

pro rata *adv* proportionnellement

pro rata payment paiement proportionnel *m*

prospective client futur client *m*

prospects perspectives d'avenir *fpl*

prospectus prospectus *m*

protest strike grève de protestation *f*

protestable protestable

to provide funds fournir des fonds

to provide security fournir une caution

provision provision *f*; [*term, condition*] disposition *f*; *to make a provision* doter une provision

provision for charges provision pour frais *f*

provision for depreciation provision pour dépréciation *f*

provision for liabilities provision pour sommes exigibles *f*

provision for the future prévoyance *f*

provision of capital prestation de capitaux *f*

provision of services prestation de services *f*

provisional provisoire

proxy [*authority*] fondé de

pouvoir *m*; [*document*]
procuration *f*; [*person*]
mandataire *mf*; **by proxy** par
procuration
proxy vote vote par procuration *m*
public authorities pouvoirs
publics *mpl*
public body corporation de droit
public *f*
public company entreprise
publique *f*
public company law loi sur les
sociétés anonymes *f*
public corporation corporation de
droit public *f*
public funds deniers publics *mpl*
public liability responsabilité civile *f*
public liability insurance assurance
responsabilité civile *f*
public limited company société
anonyme *f*
public money deniers publics *mpl*
public relations relations
publiques *fpl*
public sector secteur public *m*
public utility association d'utilité
publique *f*
publicity publicité *f*
publicity document document
publicitaire *m*
punitive damages dommages
punitifs *mpl*

purchase achat *m*
to **purchase** acheter
to **purchase a debt** racheter une
créance
purchase budget budget des
approvisionnements *m*
purchase contract contrat d'achat *m*
purchase cost coût d'achat *m*
purchase entry écriture d'achats *f*
purchase invoice facture d'achat *f*
purchase invoice ledger journal
factures-fournisseurs *m*
purchase ledger grand livre des
achats *m*, journal des achats *m*
purchase ledger clerk facturier
d'entrée *m*
purchase of debts rachat des
créances *m*
purchase on credit achat à crédit *m*
purchase order bon de commande *m*
purchase price prix d'achat *m*
purchase value valeur d'achat *f*
purchaser acheteur *m*
purchasing co-operative
groupement d'achat *m*
purchasing (department) service
des achats *m*
purchasing power pouvoir
d'achat *m*, capacité d'achat *f*
to **put a company back on its feet**
redresser une entreprise
putting up for sale mise en vente *f*

Q

qty (=quantity) quantité *f*
qualified diplômé
qualified personnel personnel
   qualifié *m*
quality control contrôle qualité *m*
quality control (department)
   service contrôle qualité *m*
quality management gestion
   qualité *f*
to quantify chiffrer
quantity quantité *f*
quarter trimestre *m*
quarterly trimestriel; *to pay*
   quarterly payer par trimestre
quick ratio ratio de liquidité

immédiate *m*
quorum quorum *m*, quorum des
   votes *m*
quotation [*on Stock Exchange*]
   cotation *f*
quote devis *m*
to quote [*on Stock Exchange*] coter
to quote a price faire un prix,
   indiquer un prix
quoted in libellé en
quoted on the Stock Exchange coté
   en Bourse
quoted securities valeurs de
   bourse *fpl*, valeurs cotées *fpl*
quotient quotient *m*

R

raise *Am* augmentation de salaire *f*
to raise [*increase*] augmenter,
   hausser; [*funds*] réunir
to raise a credit limit déplafonner un
   crédit

to raise a loan obtenir un prêt
to raise money mobiliser des fonds
raising of funds mobilisation de
   fonds *f*
rampant inflation inflation

rampante *f*

range étendue *f*

range of products éventail de produits *m*

rate taux *m*; [*price*] tarif *m*

rate of depreciation taux d'amortissement *m*

rate of exchange taux d'échange *m*, cours du change *m*

rate of growth taux d'accroissement *m*, taux de croissance *m*

rate of increase taux d'accroissement *m*

rate of inflation taux d'inflation *m*

rate of interest taux d'intérêt *m*

rate of return rendement *m*

rate of VAT taux de TVA *m*

to ratify entériner

rating [*for credit*] notation *f*

ratio ratio *m*

rationalization rationalisation *f*

to rationalize rationaliser

raw materials matières premières *fpl*

R&D (=research and development) department bureau d'études *m*

real profit profit réel *m*

real salary salaire réel *m*

realizable securities valeurs réalisables *fpl*

to realize [*asset etc*] réaliser

to reallocate réaffecter

to reassign réaffecter

rebate remise *f*, rabais *m*

receipt [*document*] reçu *m*, acquit *m*, quittance *f*; [*receiving*] réception *f*

to receipt acquitter, quittancer

receipt of a dividend perception de dividende *f*

receipt stamp timbre-quittance *m*

receipts recettes *fpl*

receivable à recevoir

receivables créances *fpl*

to receive a commission percevoir une commission

to receive interest toucher un intérêt

to receive money encaisser de l'argent

to receive unemployment benefit percevoir l'allocation chômage

received with thanks pour acquit

receiver syndic de faillite *m*, administrateur judiciaire *m*

receivership liquidation judiciaire *f*; *to go into receivership* entrer en liquidation judiciaire

receptionist réceptionniste *mf*; [*at trade fair*] hôtesse d'accueil *f*

recipient [*of benefits*] allocataire *mf*

recognized agréé

to reconcile [*figures, bank statement*] rapprocher

reconciliation statement état de rapprochement *m*

to record enregistrer

record form bordereau de saisie *m*

recording enregistrement *m*

recording of an order enregistrement d'une commande *m*

to recoup one's expenditure récupérer ses débours

to recoup one's investment rentrer dans ses fonds

recourse recours *m*

to recover [*loan*] récupérer

to recover one's expenses rentrer dans ses frais

recoverable recouvrable

recoverable debt créance recouvrable *f*

recovery [*economic, of business*] reprise *f*; [*of debt*] recouvrement *m*

to recruit [*staff*] recruter, embaucher

recruitment [*of staff*] recrutement *m*, embauche *f*

red: in the red dans le rouge

red clause credit crédit "red clause" *m*

to **redeem** [*debt, policy*] rembourser, racheter

to **redeem a bond** racheter une obligation

to **redeem a loan** racheter une dette

to **redeem a mortgage** purger une hypothèque

redeemable rachetable

redemption rachat *m*

redeployment [*of assets*] redistribution *f*

rediscount réescompte *m*

to **rediscount** réescompter

to **redistribute** redistribuer

to **reduce** réduire, rabattre

to **reduce capital** diminuer le capital

to **reduce stocks** déstocker des marchandises

to **reduce taxes** minorer des impôts

reduced réduit

reduced rate taux réduit *m*; [*price*] tarif réduit *m*

reduced rate loan prêt à taux réduit *m*

reduction réduction *f*, rabais *m*

reduction in borrowings désendettement *m*

reduction in salaries diminution des salaires *f*

reduction in staff compression de personnel *f*

reduction in stocks déstockage *m*

reduction of capital réduction de capital *f*

reduction of expenditure réduction de dépenses *f*

reduction of taxes allègement des impôts *m*

ref (=reference) réf.

refer: hereinafter referred to as ci-après dénommé

reference référence *f*; [*from employer*] lettre de recommandation *f*, certificat de travail *m*

reference number numéro de référence *m*

to **refinance** refinancer

refinancing refinancement *m*

refund remboursement *m*

to **refund** rembourser

refundable remboursable

regional director directeur régional *m*

regional manager directeur régional *m*

to **register** inscrire; [*trade mark*] déposer

register of shareholders livre des actionnaires *m*

registered bond obligation nominative *f*

registered office siège social *m*

registered security titre nominatif *m*, valeur nominative *f*

registered share action nominative *f*

registered trademark marque déposée *f*, marque protégée *f*

registration inscription *f*

registration fees droits d'enregistrement *mpl*

registration in the trade register inscription sur le registre du commerce *f*

registration of a mortgage inscription hypothécaire *f*

registration of a trademark dépôt d'une marque *m*

to **regrade** [*salaries*] reclasser

regular customer rebate ristourne de fidélité *f*

regulation règlement *m*

regulations réglementation *f*

to **rehire** [*staff*] réembaucher,

rengager
reinsurance réassurance *f*
to **reinsure** réassurer
reinsurer réassureur *m*
to **reinvest** réinvestir
related annexe
related activity activité annexe *f*
relative majority majorité relative *f*
release [*of mortgage*] mainlevée *f*
to **release a debtor** libérer un
débiteur
to **release funds** dégager des fonds,
débloquer des fonds
release of funds dégagement de
fonds *m*
to **relieve sb of his/her duties** relever
qn de ses fonctions
relocation allowance allocation de
déménagement *f*
remainder restant *m*
reminder rappel *m*
reminder of account outstanding
rappel de compte *m*
to **remit** remettre
to **remit for collection** remettre à
l'encaissement
to **remit for discount** remettre à
l'escompte
remittance [*payment*] paiement *m*,
règlement *m*
remittance advice avis de remise *m*
remittance of bills remise
d'effets *f*
remittance of funds remise de
fonds *f*, envoi de fonds *m*
to **remove sb from his/her post**
démettre qn de ses fonctions
remuneration rémunération *f*
to **renegotiate** renégocier
renegotiation renégociation *f*
to **renew a bill of exchange**
renouveler une traite
to **renew a lease** reconduire un bail

renewable [*lease, contrat*]
reconductible, renouvelable
renewal reconduction *f*,
renouvellement *m*
renewal premium prime de
renouvellement *f*
rent loyer *m*
to **rent** louer
to **rent by the month** louer au mois
rent arrears loyer arriéré *m*
rental location *f*
rental charges charges locatives *fpl*
rental expenses charges locatives *fpl*
re-opening réouverture *f*
to **reorganize** réorganiser
to **repay** rembourser
repayable remboursable
repayment remboursement *m*
to **replace sb** [*temporarily take the
place of*] suppléer qn
replacement [*temporary*]
suppléant *m*
replacement cost coût de
remplacement *m*
report compte rendu *m*, rapport *m*
report of the board of directors [*in
annual account*] rapport de
gestion *m*
to **re-present a cheque** représenter
un chèque à l'acceptation
to **represent a company** représenter
une société
representation représentation *f*
representative représentant *m*
repurchase rachat *m*; *with a
repurchase option* pignoratif
repurchase right droit de rachat *m*
request: at the request of à la
demande de; *on request* sur
demande
to **request** demander
request for information demande de
renseignements *f*

request for payment demande de règlement *f*

resale value valeur de revente *f*

to **reschedule a debt** rééchelonner une dette

rescheduling [*of debt*] rééchelonnement *m*

research and development recherche et développement *f*

research manager chef des études *m*

reserve [*of money*] réserve *f*

reserve account compte de réserve *m*

reserve capital capital de réserve *m*

reserve currency monnaie de réserve *f*

reserve funds fonds de réserve *m*

reserves réserves *fpl*

residual value valeur résiduelle *f*

to **resign** démissionner

resignation démission *f*; *to hand in one's resignation* remettre sa démission

resolution [*of meeting*] délibération *f*

resolutions passed by a meeting résolutions d'une assemblée *fpl*

resource ressource *f*

responsibilities [*of employee*] fonctions *fpl*

to **resource** [*project*] encadrer financièrement, humainement et matériellement

to **restock** réapprovisionner, reconstituer des stocks

restocking réapprovisionnement des stocks *m*

to **restore** restituer

restrictive restrictif, limitatif

to **restructure** restructurer

restructuring [*of company*] restructuration *f*

resumé *Am* curriculum vitae *m*

retail price prix de détail *m*

retail price index indice des prix de détail *m*

retained earnings revenu non distribué *m*

retained profit bénéfices non distribués *mpl*

retained revenue revenu non distribué *m*

retaxation réimposition *f*

retention of title clause clause de réserve de propriété *f*

to **retire a bond** racheter une obligation

retirement retraite *f*

retirement pension pension de retraite *f*

retirement savings plan plan d'épargne retraite *m*, PER *m*

retroactive rétroactif; *making a rise retroactive* rétroaction d'une augmentation de salaire *f*

retroactive cancellation annulation rétroactive *f*

retroactive effect effet rétroactif *m*

return retour *m*; [*piece of merchandise returned*] rendu *m*; [*document for VAT etc*] déclaration *f*; *by return (of mail)* par retour du courrier

to **return a bill** retourner un effet

to **return to work** reprendre le travail

return on capital retour sur capital *m*

return on capital employed rendement sur capital immobilisé *m*

return on investment retour sur investissement *m*

return on sales retour sur ventes *m*

returned cheque chèque retourné *m*

returns ledger journal des rendus *m*

revaluation réévaluation *f*

to **revalue** réévaluer

revenue account compte de
    produits *m*
revenue and expenditure recettes et
    dépenses *fpl*
reversionary bonus prime
    d'intéressement *f*
reversionary owner nu-
    propriétaire *m*
reversionary ownership nue-
    propriété *f*
review rétrospective *f*
to **revise** réviser
to **revive an industry** relever une
    industrie
revocable révocable
revolving credit crédit revolving *m*
rider avenant *m*
right droit *m*
right of access droit d'accès *m*
right of use droit d'usage *m*
rights issue émission de droits *f*
to **rise** [*shares, rates*] s'inscrire en
    hausse
rise in the price of a product
    élévation du prix d'un produit *f*
rising [*stock market*] orienté à la
    hausse
risk risque *m*; *to take a risk* prendre
    un risque, assumer un risque

risk asset ratio coefficient de
    solvabilité *m*
risk-taker preneur de risque *m*
room for negotiation marge de
    négociation *f*
rotation rotation *f*
rough book brouillard *m*
rough estimate estimation
    approximative *f*
to **round down** arrondir
to **round off** arrondir
to **round up** arrondir
round table [*meeting*] table ronde *f*
royalties royalties *fpl*
RPI (=retail price index) indice des
    prix de détail *m*
rubber cheque chèque en bois *m*,
    chèque sans provision *m*
to **run** [*business*] diriger, exploiter
to **run risks** encourir des risques
to **run up expenses** faire des frais
running [*of department*]
    fonctionnement *m*; ***her running of
    the department*** la façon dont elle
    dirige le service
running cost [*of equipment*] coût de
    fonctionnement *m*
running costs charges
    d'exploitation *fpl*

S

saddled with debts grevé de dettes

safe custody garde en dépôt de titres *f*

safe custody fees droits de garde *mpl*

safeguard clause clause de sauvegarde *f*

safety margin marge de sécurité *f*

salaried employee salarié *m*

salaried worker travailleur salarié *m*

salary salaire *m*, traitement *m*, appointements *mpl*

salary *adj* salarial

salary level niveau des salaires *m*

salary scale barème des salaires *m*, grille des salaires *f*, échelle des salaires *f*

sale vente *f*

sale agreement compromis de vente *m*

sale by private agreement vente à l'amiable *f*

saleability facilité d'écoulement *f*

sales ventes *fpl*; [*turnover*] chiffre d'affaires *m*, CA *m*

sales analysis analyse des ventes *f*

sales and marketing vente-marketing *f*

sales and marketing manager responsable du service commercial *mf*

sales budget budget des ventes *m*

sales campaign campagne de vente *f*

sales department service des ventes *m*

sales director directeur des ventes *m*

sales engineer ingénieur technico-commercial *m*, ingénieur des ventes *m*

sales entry écriture de ventes *f*

sales figures chiffre de vente *m*

sales force équipe de vente *f*, force de vente *f*

sales forecast prévision des ventes *f*

sales invoice facture de vente *f*

sales invoice ledger journal factures-clients *m*

sales ledger grand livre des ventes *m*, journal des ventes *m*

sales ledger clerk facturier de sortie *m*

sales management [*activity*] gestion commerciale *f*; [*department*] direction commerciale *f*

sales manager chef des ventes *m*, responsable des ventes *mf*

sales promotion animation des ventes *f*

sales representative agent commercial *m*

sales subsidiary filiale de vente *f*

sales target objectif de vente *m*

sales tax taxe sur le chiffre d'affaires *f*, TCA *f*

sales team équipe de vente *f*

sales technician agent technico-commercial *m*

sales volume volume des ventes *m*

to **save** [*time, money*] économiser, épargner

saving épargne *f*

savings économies *fpl*

schedule planning *m*

scheduling ordonnancement *m*

scheduling and planning department bureau d'ordonnancement *m*

to **scrap** enterrer

seal cachet *m*

seasonal saisonnier

seasonal variation variation saisonnière *f*

seasonally adjusted corrigé en fonction des variations saisonnières

seat: to have a seat on the board siéger au conseil d'administration

secondary cost centre centre auxiliaire des coûts *m*

secret ballot vote au scrutin secret *m*

secretary secrétaire *mf*

to **secure a loan** garantir un emprunt, nantir un prêt

secured bond obligation cautionnée *f*

secured creditor créancier nanti *m*

secured debt créance garantie *f*

secured loan emprunt garanti *m*

securities papiers valeurs *mpl*, valeurs mobilières *fpl*, titres *mpl*

securities issued valeurs émises *fpl*

securities market marché des titres *m*

securities portfolio portefeuille de titres *m*

security [*for loan*] nantissement *m*, caution *f*; [*share etc*] titre *m*; [*of premises*] sécurité *f*

security guard [*for transport of money*] convoyeur de fonds *m*

to **seize** [*property*] saisir

selection procedure démarche de sélection *f*

self-employed [*worker*] indépendant

self-employed person travailleur indépendant *m*

to **sell at a loss** vendre à perte

to **sell for cash** vendre au comptant

to **sell forward** vendre à terme

to **sell on credit** vendre à crédit

to **sell out** retirer sa participation d'une société

to **sell privately** vendre de gré à gré

seller vendeur *m*

selling price prix de vente *m*

semi-skilled [*worker*] spécialisé

senior supérieur

senior clerk chef de bureau *m*, commis principal *m*

senior executive cadre supérieur *m*

senior management cadres supérieurs *mpl*, haute direction *f*, direction générale *f*

senior official haut fonctionnaire *m*

seniority ancienneté *f*

service company entreprise prestataire de services *f*

service provider prestataire de services *m*

services prestations *fpl*

servicing a loan service d'un emprunt *m*

session séance *f*

to **set a ceiling** fixer un plafond

to **set the rate of** tarifer

to **set up** [*business*] fonder, monter, créer; [*account*] ouvrir

to **set up overseas** s'implanter à l'étranger

set-up fee [*for an account*] frais de constitution *mpl*

setting of rates tarification *f*

setting up an account ouverture d'un compte *f*

setting up of a business création d'une entreprise *f*, fondation d'une entreprise *f*

to **settle** régler

settlement règlement *m*; [*of debt*] liquidation *f*

settlement day jour de liquidation *m*

settlement discount remise pour règlement rapide *f*

settlement note feuille de liquidation *f*

settlement period délai de règlement *m*, terme de liquidation *m*

settlement value valeur transactionnelle *f*

severance pay indemnité de licenciement *f*, indemnité de rupture *f*

share action *f*; *to own 51% of the shares* détenir 51% du capital; *to have shares in a company* détenir des actions d'une société; *to have a share in the profits* participer aux bénéfices

to **share the costs** répartir les frais

to **share the profits** partager le bénéfice

to **share the risks** répartir les risques

share account compte-titres *m*

share capital capital social *m*

share certificate titre d'action *m*, certificat de titres *m*

share dividend dividende d'action *m*

shareholder actionnaire *mf*

shareholders' equity capitaux propres *mpl*

shareholders' funds capitaux propres *mpl*, haut de bilan *m*

shareholders' meeting réunion d'actionnaires *f*, assemblée des actionnaires *f*

shareholding participation *f*; *to have*

a shareholding in avoir des actions dans

share index indice boursier *m*

share issue émission d'actions *f*

share market marché des valeurs mobilières *m*

share movements mouvement des valeurs *m*

share of capital part sociale *f*

share of profits part aux bénéfices *f*

share owner détenteur d'actions *m*

share ownership actionnariat *m*

share premium [*from a merger*] prime de fusion *f*

share price index indice des cours d'actions *m*

share subscription form bulletin de souscription d'actions *m*

shares actions *fpl*

sharp rise forte hausse *f*

to **shed jobs** supprimer des emplois

shedding of jobs suppression d'emplois *f*

sheet [*of bank statement etc*] feuillet *m*

shipping (department) service expédition *m*

shop steward délégué syndical *m*

short-dated bill effet à courte échéance *m*, traite à courte échéance *f*

shortfall [*in figures*] déficit *m*

short payment moins-perçu *m*

short-term à court terme

short-term borrowings emprunts à court terme *mpl*

short-term credit crédit (à) court terme *m*

short-term deposits dépôts à court terme *mpl*

short-term financing financement à court terme *m*

short-term investment placement

(à) court terme *m*, investissement à court terme *m*; ***to make a short-term investment*** investir à court terme, placer à court terme

short-term loan prêt à court terme *m*, emprunt à court terme *m*

short-term objective objectif à court terme *m*

short-term undertaking engagement à court terme *m*

short time (working) chômage partiel *m*

shortage of capital pénurie de capitaux *f*

to **show a profit** dégager un bénéfice

showing a deficit déficitaire

sickness benefit indemnité de maladie *f*

sight: at sight à vue

sight bill effet à vue *m*

sight clause disposition à vue *f*

sight deposit dépôt à vue *m*

sight draft traite à vue *f*

sight maturity échéance à vue *f*

sight paper papier à vue *m*

to **sign** signer; ***a manager with signing authority*** un fondé de pouvoir

to **sign a bill** signer un effet

to **sign a contract** signer un contrat, passer un contrat

to **sign a deal** passer un marché

to **sign by proxy** signer par procuration

signatory signataire *mf*

signature: to put one's signature to apposer sa signature à

signature by proxy signature par procuration *f*

signing of a contract signature d'un contrat *f*

simple average moyenne simple *f*

simple interest intérêt simple *m*

Single Market Marché unique *m*

single price prix unique *m*

sinking fund caisse d'amortissement *f*

site [*location*] emplacement *m*

six-monthly [*dividend*] semestriel

six months semestre *m*

size of a loan importance d'un crédit *f*

skilled [*worker*] qualifié

slack inactif

sliding scale échelle mobile *f*

slip [*piece of paper*] bon *m*

slowdown ralentissement *m*

sluggish inanimé

small business PME *f*

to **soar** monter en flèche

social accounting bilan social *m*

social security sécurité sociale *f*

social security charges charges sociales *fpl*

social security contributions cotisations de sécurité sociale *fpl*

social security provisions prévoyance sociale *f*

society association *f*

soft loan prêt bonifié *m*

sole agent agent exclusif *m*

sole trader entreprise unipersonnelle *f*

solvency solvabilité *f*

solvent solvable

soon: as soon as possible dans les plus brefs délais

sort code code banque *m*

to **source** [*project*] encadrer financièrement, humainement et matériellement

source of funds source de fonds *f*

source of revenue source de revenus *f*

special account compte spécial *m*

specialized spécialisé

specification spécification *f*

to **speculate** [*on the Stock Exchange*] spéculer

speculation [*on the Stock Exchange*] spéculation *f*

speculator spéculateur *m*

speech allocution *f*, discours *m*

to **spend** dépenser

to **split a company** scinder une société

to **split shares** fractionner des actions

to **sponsor** parrainer

sponsorship parrainage *m*

spot trading négociations au comptant *fpl*

to **spread (out) over several financial years** étaler sur plusieurs exercices

to **spread out payments** échelonner des paiements

spreadsheet feuille de calcul *f*; [*software*] tableur *m*

to **squander funds** dilapider des fonds

stable stable

staff effectif *m*, personnel *m*

staff costs [*wages, NIC*] masse salariale *f*

staff cutback réduction de personnel *f*

staff increase augmentation des effectifs *f*, hausse des effectifs *f*

staff layoffs compression de personnel *f*

staff redundancies compression de personnel *f*

staff reshuffle remaniement du personnel *m*

staff spokesperson porte-parole du personnel *m*

staff turnover roulement du personnel *m*

staged payments paiements échelonnés *mpl*

to **stagger payments** échelonner des paiements

stagnant stagnant

stagnation stagnation *f*

to **stamp a bill** viser un effet

to **stand guarantor for** se porter garant envers

to **stand surety for** se porter garant envers, cautionner

standard cost coût standard *m*, coût préétabli *m*

standard deviation écart type *m*

standard rate taux normal *m*

standing charges charges locatives *fpl*

standing committee commission permanente *f*

standing order ordre de prélèvement permanent *m*

to **start a job** démarrer un travail

to **start legal proceedings** engager une action en justice

start-up démarrage *m*

start-up capital capital initial *m*, capital de départ *m*

start-up costs [*of company*] frais d'établissement *mpl*

starting salary traitement initial *m*, traitement de départ *m*

to **state** affirmer

state-of-play report état de situation *m*

state of the market état du marché *m*

statement affirmation *f*; [*document*] relevé *m*

statement of account relevé de compte *m*, extrait de compte *m*

statement of changes in working capital tableau de roulement *m*

statement of claim for an unpaid debt déclaration de créance impayée *f*

statement of sources and applications of funds tableau de financement *m*

statement of sources and uses of funds tableau de financement *m*

statistical report rapport statistique *m*, état statistique *m*

statistician statisticien *m*

statistics statistiques *fpl*

status enquiry [*about creditworthiness*] prise de renseignements sur la solvabilité *f*

status report état de situation *m*

statutory statutaire

statutory reserves réserves statutaires *fpl*

steadiness of prices fermeté des prix *f*

steadiness of the market fermeté du marché *f*

to **stipulate** stipuler

stipulation stipulation *f*

stock stock *m*

stock [*Am: shares*] actions *fpl*, titres *mpl*

to **stock goods** stocker des marchandises

stock book livre des inventaires *m*

stockbroker agent de change *m*

stock control gestion de stocks *f*

Stock Exchange Bourse *f*

Stock Exchange commitments engagements à la Bourse *mpl*

Stock Exchange transactions transactions boursières *fpl*

stockholder *Am* actionnaire *mf*

stock keeping tenue des stocks *f*

Stock Market Bourse *f*

stock market *adj* boursier

stock market crash krach boursier *m*

stock market gamble spéculation boursière *f*

stock market movement mouvement boursier *m*

stock market panic panique boursière *f*

stock market rise hausse des cours *f*

stock market transaction opération boursière *f*

stock market trend orientation de la Bourse *f*

stock market value valeur en Bourse *f*

stock outage rupture de stock *f*

to **stockpile** accumuler

stockpiling accumulation *f*

stock sheet fiche de stock *f*

stock take inventaire *m*, recensement de stocks *m*

stock taking inventaire *m*, recensement de stocks *m*

stock turnaround rotation des stocks *f*

stock turnover rotation des stocks *f*

stock turnover ratio coefficient de rotation *m*

to **stop a cheque** faire opposition à un chèque

to **stop payments** suspendre les paiements

stoppage [*strike*] arrêt de travail *m*; [*from salary*] retenue *f*

stoppage of payment(s) [*definitive*] arrêt de paiement *m*, cessation de paiement *f*

straightline depreciation amortissement linéaire *m*

straightline rate taux linéaire *m*

strain: to put a strain on a budget grever un budget

strategic stratégique

strict deadline délai de rigueur *m*

strike grève *f*; *to go on strike* faire (la) grève

to **strike a deal** conclure un marché

strike breaker briseur de grève *m*

strike notice préavis de grève *m*

strike price [*for share*] prix d'exercice *m*

striker gréviste *mf*

striking out [*of item*] radiation *f*

study étude *f*

sub-account sous-compte *m*

to subcontract sous-traiter

subcontractor sous-traitant *m*

to subdivide subdiviser

subdivision subdivision *f*

to subject to tax soumettre à l'impôt

subject to payment moyennant paiement

to submit a report soumettre un rapport

subordinate subordonné *m*

subscribed capital capital souscrit *m*, souscription *f*

subscriber [*of loan, shares*] souscripteur *m*

subscription fee [*for share purchase*] droit de souscription *m*

subsidiary filiale *f*

subsidiary account sous-compte *m*

to subsidize a company subventionner une entreprise

subsidy subside *m*, subvention *f*

subtotal sous-total *m*

to subtract soustraire

success fee prime de rendement *f*

sudden rise hausse subite *f*

to sue sb poursuivre qn en justice

to suffer losses subir des pertes

sum somme *f*

sum payable somme à payer *f*

to summarize récapituler

summary récapitulation *f*, résumé *m*; [*in tabular form*] tableau synoptique *m*

summary balance sheet bilan condensé *m*

summons to a meeting convocation à une réunion *f*

sums due from customers créances clients *fpl*

sundries divers

sundry expenses dépenses diverses *fpl*

superior supérieur *m*

to supervise a company superviser une entreprise

supervision supervision *f*

supervisor surveillant *m*

supervisory board conseil de surveillance *m*

supplementary pension retraite complémentaire *f*

supplier fournisseur *m*

supplier credit crédit-fournisseur *m*, avoir-fournisseur *m*

supplies fournitures *fpl*

to supply fournir; [*sb*] approvisionner

to supply information fournir des renseignements

to supply sb with sth approvisionner qn en qch

supply and demand l'offre et la demande *f*

supply price prix d'offre *m*

supply(ing) fourniture *f*

surcharge surcharge *f*

surety caution *f*

surety for a loan sûreté en garantie d'un crédit *f*

surplus excédent *m*, surplus *m*

surplus *adj* excédentaire, en surplus; [*staff*] en sureffectif

surrender value valeur de rachat *f*

survey enquête *f*

to suspend payment suspendre les paiements

suspense account compte d'attente *m*

suspension of payments suspension

de paiements *f*
SWIFT transfer virement SWIFT *m*
sympathy strike grève de solidarité *f*

symposium colloque *m*
synopsis synopsis *f*; [*in tabular form*] tableau synoptique *m*

T

table tableau *m*
table of account codes grille d'imputation *f*
to **take a profit** tirer un bénéfice
to **take legal proceedings** entamer des poursuites
to **take on** [*employee*] engager
to **take out insurance** contracter une assurance
to **take part in** participer à
to **take steps** effectuer des démarches
to **take stock** faire le point
to **take up one's duties** entrer en fonction
takeover rachat *m*
takeover bid offre publique d'achat *f*, OPA *f*
takings recettes *fpl*
tangible assets actif corporel *m*
tangible fixed assets immobilisations corporelles *fpl*
tapering rate tarif dégressif *m*
target cible *f*
target *adj* cible
to **target a market** cibler un marché
target sales figures chiffre de ventes

ciblé *m*
target setting arrêt des objectifs *m*
tariff tarif *m*
tariff *adj* tarifaire
tax impôt *m*, taxe *f*
to **tax** imposer, taxer
tax allowance déduction fiscale *f*, abattement fiscal *m*
tax assessment avis d'imposition *m*, fixation de l'impôt *f*
tax authorities administration fiscale *f*
tax benefit avantage fiscal *m*
tax bracket tranche d'imposition *f*
tax burden pression fiscale *f*, poids de la fiscalité *m*
tax centre centre des impôts *m*, CDI *m*
tax clearance quitus fiscal *m*
tax code code taxe *m*
tax collection recouvrement d'impôts *m*, perception d'impôts *f*
tax collector percepteur *m*, receveur des impôts *m*
tax consultant conseiller fiscal *m*, fiscaliste *mf*

161

tax credit avoir fiscal *m*

tax cut réduction des impôts *f*

tax deductible déductible des impôts

tax deduction prélèvement fiscal *m*

tax deduction at source perception à la source *f*

tax domicile foyer fiscal *m*, domicile fiscal *m*

tax evasion évasion fiscale *f*, fraude fiscale *f*

tax exempt exempt d'impôts

tax exemption exonération d'impôts *f*, exonération fiscale *f*, exemption d'impôts *f*

tax expert expert fiscal *m*

tax haven paradis fiscal *m*

tax impact incidence fiscale *f*

tax incentive incitation fiscale *f*

tax inspector inspecteur des contributions *m*

tax law droit fiscal *m*

tax loophole échappatoire fiscale *f*

tax man fisc *m*

tax on wages and salaries impôt sur les traitements et salaires *m*

taxpayer contribuable *mf*

tax point date de facturation *f*

tax provision disposition fiscale *f*

tax rebate dégrèvement fiscal *m*

tax reduction abattement fiscal *m*

tax refund remise fiscale *f*; [*on goods*] détaxe *f*

tax relief dégrèvement fiscal *m*, dégrèvement *m*

tax return déclaration fiscale *f*, feuille d'impôts *f*

tax revenue recettes fiscales *fpl*

tax stamp timbre fiscal *m*

tax system système fiscal *m*, fiscalité *f*, régime d'imposition *m*

tax year exercice fiscal *m*

taxable imposable, taxable

taxable income revenu imposable *m*, assiette d'impôt *f*

taxable profit bénéfice imposable *m*

taxable transaction opération imposable *f*

taxation imposition *f*, taxation *f*, ponction fiscale *f*

team of workers équipe de collaborateurs *f*

teamwork travail d'équipe *m*

technical director directeur technique *m*

technical manager directeur technique *m*

telex (message) télex *m*, message télex *m*

telex transfer virement par télex *m*

temporary temporaire; [*employee*] intérimaire

temporary contract [*for temporary employment*] contrat de mission d'intérim *m*

tenant locataire *mf*

tender soumission *f*

term [*duration*] durée *f*; [*condition*] condition *f*

term deposit dépôt à terme *m*

term insurance cover couverture à terme *f*

term loan crédit à terme *m*

term of lease terme de bail *m*

to **terminate a contract** résilier un contrat

termination clause clause de résiliation *f*

terms and conditions of a contract conditions d'un contrat *fpl*

terms of payment conditions de paiement *fpl*, termes de paiement *mpl*

test essai *m*

third party holder tiers détenteur *m*

third party owner tiers possesseur *m*

thirty: to pay at 30 days payer dans

les 30 jours

thousand francs kilofranc *m*

to **tie up one's money** immobiliser son argent

time and motion studies organisation scientifique du travail *f*, OST *f*

time bill traite à terme *f*

time off in lieu repos compensateur *m*

time saving économie de temps *f*

time scale échelle de temps *f*

title [*of account*] intitulé *m*

title deed acte de propriété *m*, titre de propriété *m*

today: from today à dater de ce jour

total total *m*

to **total** [*amount to*] se chiffrer à; [*add up*] totaliser

total amount montant total *m*

total annual expenses consommations de l'exercice *fpl*

total asset value valeur de bilan *f*

total fixed cost coût fixe total *m*

total guarantee garantie totale *f*

total payable total à payer *m*

total receipts total des recettes *m*

total sales chiffre d'affaires global *m*

total unit cost coût complet unitaire *m*

totalling chiffrage *m*

trade commerce *m*, échanges commerciaux *mpl*

trade *adj* commercial

to **trade** faire du commerce, commercer

trade agreement accord commercial *m*

trade association groupement professionnel *m*, corps de métier *m*, syndicat professionnel *m*

trade debtor compte client *m*, créance client *f*

trade discount escompte commercial *m*

trademark marque *f*, marque de commerce *f*

trade name nom commercial *m*, dénomination commerciale *f*

trade policy politique commerciale *f*

trade register Registre du Commerce *m*

trade tribunal tribunal de commerce *m*

trade union syndicat *m*

trade union council conseil syndical *m*

trade union member syndiqué *m*

trade unionist syndicaliste *mf*

trading account compte d'exploitation générale *m*

trading and profit and loss account compte de résultat *m*

trading company société de négoce *f*

trading day jour de Bourse *m*

trading partners partenaires commerciaux *mpl*

training programme programme de formation *m*

transaction transaction *f*, opération *f*

to **transcribe** transcrire

to **transcribe entries** transcrire des écritures

transfer transfert *m*; [*financial*] virement *m*; [*disposal: of assets, shares etc*] cession *f*

to **transfer** transférer; [*money*] virer; [*dispose of: assets, shares etc*] céder

transfer by endorsement transmission par endossement *f*

transfer cheque chèque de virement *m*

transfer of capital transfert de capitaux *m*

163

transfer of funds transfert de fonds *m*

transfer of shares transfert d'actions *m*

transfer of title cession de titre *f*

transfer order ordre de virement *m*

transferable transférable; [*assets, shares etc*] cessible

transferable by endorsement transmissible par endossement

transferable document document transmissible *m*

transferable letter of credit crédit transférable *m*

transferee cessionnaire *mf*

transport allowance prime de transport *f*

to **travel on business** voyager pour affaires

travel allowance indemnité de déplacement *f*

travel expenses frais de déplacement *mpl*

treasurer trésorier *m*

Treasury ministère de l'Economie et des Finances *m*

trend tendance *f*

trial essai *m*

trial balance balance de vérification *f*

trial period période d'essai *f*

triplicate: in triplicate en triple exemplaire

true and fair view image fidèle *f*

trust company société fiduciaire *f*

trustworthy digne de confiance

turnover chiffre d'affaires *m*, CA *m*

turnover of capital roulement de capitaux *m*

turnover tax impôt sur le chiffre d'affaires *m*

twinning of companies jumelage d'entreprises *m*

U

unaffordable inabordable
unaudited non vérifié
unavailable indisponible
uncalled capital capital non
appelé *m*
unconditional guarantee garantie
inconditionnelle *f*
under-capitalized sous-capitalisé
under-employment sous-emploi *m*
underpriced bradé
to underwrite garantir, souscrire
undiscountable inescomptable
unemployment benefit allocations
de chômage *fpl*, indemnité de
chômage *f*
unemployment contribution
cotisation chômage *f*
unemployment fund fonds de
chômage *m*
unemployment insurance assurance
chômage *f*
unfair competition concurrence
déloyale *f*
unfavourable défavorable
to unfreeze credits dégeler des
crédits
unfreezing of prices déblocage des
prix *m*
uniform rate taux uniforme *m*
union branch section syndicale
d'entreprise *f*
union demands revendications
syndicales *fpl*
union leader responsable

syndical *m*, dirigeant syndical *m*
union movement mouvement
syndical *m*
union representative délégué
syndical *m*, représentant
syndical *m*
to unionize [*trade*] syndiquer
unit cost coût unitaire *m*
unit labour costs coût unitaire de
travail *m*
unit of account unité de compte *f*
unit price prix unitaire *m*
unit trust société d'investissement à
capital variable *f*, SICAV *f*
unlimited illimité; [*cover*] sans
limitation de somme
unlisted [*share*] incoté
unlisted market bourse coulisse *f*
unpaid impayé
unpaid bill impayé *m*
unpaid debt créance impayée *f*
unpaid leave absence non
rémunérée *f*
unproductive capital capital
improductif *m*
unquoted [*share*] incoté
unrealized gain gain latent *m*
unrealized loss perte latente *f*
unrecoverable irrécouvrable
unrecovered debt créance impayée *f*
unsalaried non-salarié
unsecured creditor créancier
ordinaire *m*
unsecured loan prêt non garanti *m*

unsettled [*stock market*] instable
unsteadiness of prices instabilité des cours *f*
unsteady [*stock market*] irrégulier
untapped [*resources*] inexploité
UP (=unit price) PU *m*
up: up 22% on last year en augmentation de 22% par rapport à l'an dernier
up to 500 jusqu'à 500
up to date [*file etc*] à jour
update mise à jour *f*, actualisation *f*
to **update** mettre à jour, actualiser
updating mise à jour *f*

upsurge in poussée de *f*
upward movement mouvement ascensionnel *m*
upward trend tendance ascensionnelle *f*
to **use** employer
to **use up** épuiser
use of funds affectation des fonds *f*
useful life vie utile *f*
USM (=unlisted securities market) marché hors cote *m*, bourse coulisse *f*
usual habituel
usufruct usufruit *m*

vacancy emploi vacant *m*, poste à pourvoir *m*
vacancy on the board siège à pourvoir au conseil d'administration *m*
vacation *Am* congé *m*
valid valable
validity validité *f*; [*of claim*] bien-fondé *m*
valuation évaluation *f*; [*by expert*] expertise *f*, rapport d'expertise *m*
value valeur *f*
to **value** expertiser
value added tax taxe sur la valeur ajoutée *f*

value date date de valeur *f*, jour de valeur *m*
value for collection valeur à l'encaissement *f*
variable variable *f*
variable costs frais variables *mpl*, coûts variables *mpl*, charges variables *fpl*
variable-rate interest intérêt variable *m*
VAT (=value added tax) TVA *f*
VAT credit crédit de TVA *m*
VAT exempt exonéré de TVA
VAT exemption franchise de TVA *f*
VAT rate taux de TVA *m*

VAT rebate décote de TVA *f*
VAT reference number code assujetti TVA *m*
VAT-registered person déclarant de TVA *m*
VAT registration number code assujetti TVA *m*
VAT return déclaration de TVA *f*, état (de) TVA *m*
venture capital capital-risque *m*
venture capitalist pourvoyeur de capital-risque *m*
viability viabilité *f*
viable viable
vice-chairman vice-président *m*

vice-presidency vice-présidence *f*
vice-president vice-président *m*
violation of infraction à *f*
violation of rights abus de droits *m*
volume of business volume des affaires *m*
voluntary redundancy départ volontaire *m*
vote délibération *f*
to **vote in favour of a proposal** voter une proposition
vote by a show of hands vote à main levée *m*
voucher bon *m*; [*accounting*] pièce justificative *f*

wage salaire *m*
wage and price spiral spirale des prix et des salaires *f*
wage ceiling salaire plafonné *m*
wage cut réduction des salaires *f*
wage deductions retenues salariales *fpl*, retenues sur salaire *fpl*
wage earner salarié *m*
wage inflation inflation des salaires *f*
wages ledger grand livre de paie *m*, journal de paie *m*, journal des salaires *m*

wages policy politique des salaires *f*
wages sheet bordereau de salaires *m*
waiting period délai de carence *m*
waiver renonciation *f*
warehousing costs frais d'entreposage *mpl*
warranty garantie *f*; *under warranty* sous garantie
waste of money gaspillage d'argent *m*
waybill connaissement *m*
to **weaken** faiblir
wear and tear usure *f*
weekly hebdomadaire

to **weight an average** pondérer une moyenne

weighted pondéré

weighted average moyenne pondérée *f*

weighted average unit cost coût unitaire moyen pondéré *m*

weighting pondération *f*

welfare *Am* sécurité sociale *f*

white-collar workers cols blancs *mpl*

white knight chevalier blanc *m*

wholesale price prix de gros *m*

wholesale price index indice des prix de gros *m*

wholesaling vente en gros *f*

wholly-owned subsidiary filiale à 100% *f*

wildcat strike grève sauvage *f*

to **wind up** [*company*] dissoudre, liquider

winding up of a company dissolution d'une société *f*

to **window-dress accounts** camoufler un bilan, habiller un bilan

window-dressing camouflage *m*

window-dressing of a balance sheet habillage de bilan *m*, camouflage de bilan *m*

to **withdraw** retirer

withdrawal retrait *m*; *cash withdrawal* décaissement *m*

to **withhold** prélever

to **withhold taxes** prélever des taxes

withholding prélèvement *m*, retenue *f*

within dans un délai de

wording of a clause énoncé d'une clause *m*

work travail *m*

work force main-d'œuvre *f*, force de travail *f*

work group groupe de travail *m*

work in progress produits en cours *mpl*

work method méthode de travail *f*

work permit permis de travail *m*

work standard norme de travail *f*

work to rule grève du zèle *f*

worker travailleur *m*

workers and management partenaires sociaux *mpl*

working capital fonds de roulement *m*, capital de roulement *m*, capital roulant *m*

working capital requirements besoins en fonds de roulement *mpl*

working conditions conditions de travail *fpl*

working day jour ouvrable *m*

working hours heures de travail *fpl*

working lunch déjeuner de travail *m*

working party groupe de travail *m*

worst-case scenario scénario catastrophe *m*

worth valeur *f*; *to be worth* valoir

to **write a cheque** créer un chèque, établir un chèque, libeller un chèque

to **write down** déprécier

to **write off** amortir

to **write off a debt** amortir une dette

write-back of provisions reprises sur provisions *fpl*

write-down dépréciation *f*

write-off of expenditure amortissement de dépenses *m*

writing: in writing par écrit

writing off [*of debt*] amortissement *m*

written document écrit *m*

written undertaking engagement écrit *m*

wrongful abusif

year an *m*, année *f*; *per year* par an
year-end de fin d'exercice
year-end accounts compte de
    résultats *m*
year-end closing of accounts clôture
    annuelle des livres *f*

yearly average moyenne annuelle *f*
yield rendement *m*
to **yield annually** rapporter par an
to **yield 5%** [*investment*] rendre 5%
to **yield interest** rapporter des
    intérêts, porter intérêt

Z

zero growth croissance zéro *f*
zero-rated exonéré de TVA

zero-rating franchise de TVA *f*, taux
    zéro *m*, taux nul *m*

Annexes
Appendices

Facture

Entreprise VERMEIL
11 rue d'Espagne
25000 BESANÇON

                        DOIT   Société GOMEZ
                                        Place des Anglaises
                                        25000 BESANÇON
Facture n° 458
Commande n° 6790   Date 21-3-93

Code produit	Désignation	Prix unitaire H.T.	Quantité	Montant
2396	Rame papier	32,90	10	329,00
		Total H.T.		329,00
		Remise 5%		16,45
		Net commercial		312,55
		TVA 18,60%		58,13
		Net à payer		370,68

Hartfield Building Co
267 River Road
London
SW56 5RT

Bank Account Details

Thameside Bank PLC
23 Palace Drive
McAdams Greengrocers   London
45 Surrey Place   SW19 3CR
London
SW45 4RY   Sort Code: 92-07-32
                         Account No.: 9281102

INVOICE No. 93/0157 Tax Point 28.3.93 VAT registration 5207-193-92

DETAILS	AMOUNTS	VAT 171/2%	TOTAL
Shelves fitted (ref.4597) 23 July 1993	141.00	28.68	165.68
TOTAL	141.00	28.68	165.68

PAYMENT 30 DAYS

Maison MERCIER
18 rue de Ligny
30000 NIMES

Avoir

Société GOFFIN
67 rue des Pins
30000 NIMES

Avoir n°   4567Y
Date   23 avril 1993
Code client   30076

Réf.	Désignation	Quantité	P.U.H.T.	Montant
34	Serviettes	30	50,00	1 500,00
		Total hors TVA		1 500,00
		TVA 18,60%		279,00
		A VOTRE CREDIT T.T.C.		1 779,00

Lakeland Construction
13 Birmingham Road
Glasgow
G56 8DF

CREDIT NOTE
1

Hunter's Pharmacy
37 Sutton Tce.
Glasgow
G6 5FR

24 July 1993

REF	DETAILS	NETT	VAT
GRA213	CREDIT DUE	40.00	7.00
		TOTAL NETT	40.00
		TOTAL VAT	7.00
		CREDIT TOTAL	47.00

BILAN

ACTIF

Société VARLET

	Montant brut	Exercice Amort. ou Prov.	Montant net	Exercice précédent au : 31/12/92
Capital souscrit non appelé				
ACTIF IMMOBILISÉ				
<u>**Immobilisations Incorporelles**</u>				
Frais d'établissement				
Frais de recherche et développement				
Concessions, brevets et droits similaires	123 789	10 034	113 755	
Fonds commercial	115 509	4 507	111 002	
Autres immobilisations incorporelles				
Avances et acomptes				
Total	**239 298**	**14 541**	**224 757**	
<u>**Immobilisations Corporelles**</u>				
Terrains				
Constructions	152 000	2 000	150 000	
Installations techniques, matériel et outillage industriels	413 355	1 156	412 199	
Autres immobilisations corporelles	104 509	1 214	103 295	
Immobilisations en cours				
Avances et acomptes				
Total	**669 864**	**4 370**	**665 494**	
<u>**Immobilisations Financières**</u>				
Participations	104 333		104 333	
Créances rattachées à des participations	10 130		10 130	
Autres titres immobilisés				
Prêts				
Autres immobilisations financières	41 000		41 000	41 000
Total	**155 463**		**155 463**	**41 000**
Total de l'Actif immobilisé	**1 064 625**	**18 911**	**1 045 714**	**41 000**
ACTIF CIRCULANT				
<u>**Stocks**</u>				
Matières premières, approvisionnements	34 075		34 075	
Encours de production de biens	54 230	4 599	49 631	
Encours de production de services				
Produits intermédiaires et finis	9 780	3 495	6 285	
Marchandises				
Total	**98 085**	**8 094**	**89 991**	
Avances et acomptes versés sur commandes	3 447		3 447	
<u>**Créances**</u>				
Clients et comptes rattachés	288 045		288 045	
Autres créances	107 789		107 789	34 306
Capital souscrit et appelé, non versé				
Total	**395 834**		**395 834**	**343**
<u>**Divers**</u>				
Valeurs mobilières de placement	54 167	2 389	51 778	
Disponibilités	144 548		144 548	41 289
Total	**198 715**	**2 389**	**196 326**	**41 289**
Charges constatées d'avance	7 782		7 782	
Total de l'actif circulant et des charges constatées d'avance	703 863	10 483	693 380	75 595
Charges à répartir sur plusieurs exercices				
Primes de remboursement des obligations				
Ecarts de conversion Actif				
TOTAL DE L'ACTIF	**1 768 488**	**29 394**	**1 739 094**	**116 595**

PASSIF

		Exercice	Exercice précédent
CAPITAUX PROPRES			
Capital (dont versé:	459038	460000	94856
Primes d'émission, de fusion, d'apport			
Ecarts de réévaluation			
Réserves			
Réserve légale			
Réserves statutaires			
ou contractuelles			
Réserves réglementées			
Autres réserves			
Report à nouveau		7011-	4930-
Résultats antérieurs en instance d'affectation			2940-
Résultat de la période (bénéfice ou perte)		831909	29310
Situation nette avant répartition		1284898	87484
Subventions d'investissement		49056	
Provisions réglementées			
Total		**1333954**	**87484**
AUTRES FONDS PROPRES			
Titres participatifs			
Avances conditionnées		98856	
Total		**98856**	
PROVISIONS			
Provisions pour risques		30057	
Provisions pour charges			
Total		**30057**	
DETTES			
Emprunts et dettes assimilées			
Emprunts obligataires convertibles			
Autres emprunts obligataires			
Emprunts et dettes auprès des établissements de crédit		20593	
Emprunts et dettes financières divers		105939	
Total		**126532**	
Avances et acomptes reçus sur commandes		2049	
Dettes fournisseurs et comptes rattachés		103945	
Dettes fiscales et sociales		30549	
Dettes sur immobilisations et comptes rattachés		11103	
Autres dettes		2049	299
Total		**147646**	**299**
Produits constatés d'avance			
Total des dettes et des produits constatés d'avance		276227	299
Ecarts de conversion Passif			
TOTAL DU PASSIF		**1739094**	**116595**

BALANCE SHEET AS AT 31 DECEMBER 1992

	1992		1991	
	£	£	£	£
FIXED ASSETS				
Tangible assets (Note 7)		3,118,214		4,124,201
CURRENT ASSETS				
Stocks (Note 8)	3,377,968		4,216,941	
Debtors (Note 9)	2,945,887		2,392,976	
Cash at bank and in hand	2,874,654		782,321	
	9,198,509		7,392,238	
CREDITORS (amounts falling due within one year) (Note 10)	2,534,603		1,992,756	
NET CURRENT ASSETS		6,663,906		5,399,482
TOTAL ASSETS LESS CURRENT LIABILITIES		9,782,120		9,523,683
CREDITORS (amounts falling due after more than one year) (Note 11)		(450,317)		(432,572)
PROVISIONS FOR LIABILITIES AND CHARGES (Note 12)		(509,510)		(579,510)
		8,822,293		8,511,601
CAPITAL AND RESERVES				
called up share capital (Note 13)		140,000		140,000
Profit and loss account		8,682,293		8,371,601
		8,822,293		8,511,601

PROFIT AND LOSS ACCOUNT
FOR THE YEAR ENDED 31 DECEMBER 1992

	1992 £	1991 £
TURNOVER (Note 2)	11,925,402	12,324,925
Cost of sales	(8,235,542)	(9,273,210)
GROSS PROFIT	3,689,860	3,051,715
Distribution costs	(992,759)	(1,120,325)
Administrative expenses	(985,237)	(827,920)
Other operating expenses	(428,351)	(292,321)
OPERATING PROFIT	1,283,513	811,149
Other interest receivable and similar income	124,392	132,442
Interest payable and similar charges - term loans and overdrafts wholly repayable within five years	(9,205)	(10,471)
PROFIT ON ORDINARY ACTIVITIES BEFORE TAXATION (Note 3)	1,398,700	9,331,20
TAX ON PROFIT ON ORDINARY ACTIVITIES (Note 6)	(588,008)	(392,280)
PROFIT ON ORDINARY ACTIVITIES AFTER TAXATION	810,692	540,840
Dividends	(500,000)	(500,000)
AMOUNTS TRANSFERRED (FROM)/ TO RESERVES	310,692	40,840
PROFIT AND LOSS ACCOUNT BROUGHT FORWARD	8,371,601	8,330,761
PROFIT AND LOSS ACCOUNT CARRIED FORWARD	8,682,293	8,371,601

COMPTE DE RESULTAT   *Ets BEAUCARNE*

Période
DU 01/01/91 AU 31/12/91
DU 01/01/92 AU 31/3/93

	France	Exportation	Total	Exercice précédent
PRODUITS D'EXPLOITATION				
Ventes de marchandises				
Production vendue { biens	600 987	4 597	605 584	
{ services	34 980		34 980	
Chiffre d'affaires net	635 967	4 597	640 564	
Production stockée			56 943	
Production immobilisée				
Subventions d'exploitation			12 765	
Reprises sur amortissements et provisions, transferts de charges				
Autres produits			14 590	
Total			724 862	
CHARGES D'EXPLOITATION				
Achats de marchandises				
Variation de stock				
Matières premières et autres { Achats			9 078	
approvisionnements : { Variation de stocks			34 075 -	
Autres achats et charges externes			19 670	4 590
Impôts, taxes et versements assimilés			6 097	1 002
Salaires et traitements			3 284	
Charges sociales			1 102	
Dotations d'exploitation: sur immobilisations { amortissements { provisions				
{ sur actif circulant			6 340	
{ pour risques et charges			670	
Autres charges			5 693	
Total			17 859	5 592
Résultat d'exploitation (A)			707 003	5 592-
OPERATIONS EN COMMUN				
Bénéfice attribué ou perte transférée (B)				
Perte supportée ou bénéfice transféré (C)				

PRODUITS FINANCIERS

Produits financiers de participations		6 790	
Produits financiers d'autres valeurs mobilières et créances de l'actif immobilisé			34 902
Autres intérêts et produits assimilés		50 976	
Reprises sur provisions et transferts de charges			
Différences positives de change		450	
Produits nets sur cessions de valeurs mobilières de placement		34 901	
	Total	**93 117**	**34 902**

CHARGES FINANCIERES

Dotations financières aux amortissements et provisions		34 002	
Intérêts et charges assimilées		5 602	
Différences négatives de change		1 205	
Charges nettes sur cessions de valeurs mobilières de placement		12 004	
	Total	**52 813**	

RESULTAT FINANCIER	(D)	40 304	34 902

RESULTAT COURANT AVANT IMPOTS (± A + B - C ± D)	(E)	747 307	29 310

PRODUITS EXCEPTIONNELS

Produits exceptionnels sur opérations de gestion		34 356	
Produits exceptionnels sur opérations en capital		92 018	
Reprises sur provisions et transferts de charges			
	Total	**126 374**	

CHARGES EXCEPTIONNELLES

Charges exceptionnelles sur opérations de gestion		4 590	
Charges exceptionnelles sur opérations en capital		12 903	
Dotations exceptionnelles aux amortissements et provisions		11 679	
	Total	**29 172**	

RESULTAT EXCEPTIONNEL	(F)	97 202	

Participation des salariés	(G)		
Impôt sur les bénéfices	(H)	12 600	

BENEFICE OU PERTE (± E ± F - G - H)		831 909	29 310

LETTRE DE RELANCE DES IMPAYES

Lille, le 30 juin 1993

Société DUMAS
34 rue d'Angleterre
59800 LILLE

<u>Réf.</u> : <u>facture n° 21136</u>

Messieurs,

Nous tenons à vous rappeler que, malgré notre précédente lettre du 30 mai 1993, notre facture n° 13426 en date du 30 mars 1993 se rapportant au montant de FF 11 630 demeure toujours impayée.

Etant donné que c'est la première fois que nous sommes confrontés à un incident de cette nature, nous vous informons que nous vous accordons un délai de sept jours, avant d'entamer une procédure de recouvrement.

Veuillez agréer, Messieurs, nos salutations distinguées.

Sébastien JOURDAIN
Contrôleur crédit

DEBT CHASING LETTER

30 June 1993

Thompson Bros.
34 Waterloo Place
Manchester
M23 7ED

re: overdue account on our invoice No. 21136

Dear Sirs,

We would like to remind you that, in spite of our previous letter of 30th May 1993, our invoice No. 21136 dated 30 March 1993 for the sum of £1,940 is still outstanding.

Since we have received no indication of any dissatisfaction on your part, we would like to advise you that, if we do not receive your remittance within the next seven days, we will regrettably be obliged to initiate recovery proceedings.

Yours faithfully,

Seline McAdams
(Credit Controller)

COMMANDE			Page: 1/1			

Nom/adresse du Fournisseur

Contact PAPYRUS: Mathieu Druart
Code Affectation: F2036

Ets. Watrin et fils
rue du Bocage 34
4800 VERVIERS
BELGIQUE

Date	Commande No	Total H.T.	Devise
3/8/93	84091120	15.20	GBP

Lieu de livraison

S.A. PAPYRUS 2000
18 avenue Chantecler
74000 ANNECY
FRANCE

Adresse de facturation

S.A. PAPYRUS 200
18 avenue Chantecler
74000 ANNECY
FRANCE

Livraison		Paiement : 30 FDM LE 25 Règlement chèque : à 0 jour le 25				

Poste	Désignation	Quantité	P.U.	Remise	Délai	Total
1	FOURNITURES SCOLAIRES	1 000	15,20	0,00	31/8/93	15 200,00

Cette commande est soumise aux conditions indiquées au verso (sauf dispositions particulières indiquées ci-dessous).

Total de la page   15 200,00
Total depuis le poste 1 :   15 200,00

VISA
ACHAT......................

Tél. : (43) 95.25.40.40 Fax : (43) 95.25.41.42

Purchase order

Clyde Accounts Bureau	Purchase Order No. 5298507
52 Marlborough Cres.	Page 1
Glasgow	Supplier No. 5DL902
G13 9HI	Issuing Dept. DEX
	Requisition ref. 29057
	Date 02-07-93

CONTACT/DELIVERY POINT:

ABC Ltd
125 New Road
Glasgow
G52 3TN

Clyde Accounts Bureau
52 Marlborough Cres.
Glasgow
G13 9HI

Please supply the goods/services specified subject to our general conditions and any special conditions/instructions set out below unless otherwise indicated. The relevant goods/services should be delivered to the person at the above address to whom any queries should be directed.

ITEM	QTY	DESCRIPTION	PRICE(exc.VAT)	REQUIRED DATE
1	2 boxes	9.5x241 mm 2 part nct plain list paper	20.00	02.3.93

Special conditions/instructions

Please deliver these goods to the above address

Authorised by............

GENERAL CONDITIONS FOR SUPPLY OF GOODS AND SERVICES

1. The Purchase Order No. must be quoted on all correspondence, advice notes and invoices.

2. All invoices must be sent to the Finance Dept. at the above address to ensure payment. Goods and/or services must be supplied by the required date indicated above.